Nils Jönsson-Rose

Lawns and Gardens

How to plant and beautify the Home lot, the Pleasure Ground and Garden

Nils Jönsson-Rose

Lawns and Gardens
How to plant and beautify the Home lot, the Pleasure Ground and Garden

ISBN/EAN: 9783337080839

Printed in Europe, USA, Canada, Australia, Japan

Cover: Foto ©Andreas Hilbeck / pixelio.de

More available books at **www.hansebooks.com**

" HAWTHORN ON OUTSKIRTS OF A WOOD "

HOW TO PLANT AND BEAUTIFY THE HOME LOT
THE PLEASURE GROUND AND GARDEN

BY

N. JÖNSSON-ROSE

———

WITH NUMEROUS PLANS AND ILLUSTRATIONS
BY THE AUTHOR

———

G. P. PUTNAM'S SONS

NEW YORK   LONDON
27 WEST TWENTY-THIRD STREET   24 BEDFORD STREET, STRAND

The Knickerbocker Press

1897

The Knickerbocker Press, New York

CONTENTS.

Contents

Contents

ILLUSTRATIONS.

vii

Illustrations

x

Illustrations

PART I.

PRINCIPLES AND PRACTICE OF LANDSCAPE ART.

I.

ON THE STUDY OF NATURAL SCENERY.

N the practice of the art of landscape gardening, which chiefly aims to create natural scenery by natural means and methods, or to restore the original beauty in places where it has been destroyed through some cause or other, a thorough study of nature is imperative. The landscape gardener, in the higher realms of his art, should attempt no artificial effects: all the products of his thoughts and labor must appear to have sprung from the bosom of nature itself without effort or external interference. The plants used should be of sufficiently sturdy kinds to root and spread under natural conditions without constant aid and culture, and all the elements introduced must be of so harmonious a character as not to interfere with individual development, or to cause disturbance in the whole, through such development. Naturally, this requires an intimate knowledge, not only of every herb and tree used, but also an insight into the secret methods of nature, which cannot be taught by books,—the artist must sit down humbly at the knees of Mother Nature and learn. It is not so much grandeur as beauty that comes within the province of his work, not so much creation as adaptation that is essential in his design. Nature in every instance must furnish the canvas which he is to paint upon, and only in a superficial way can that canvas be prepared to receive the colors—grass, flowers, and ligneous vegetation.

In studying nature, it is well to remember that everything natural is not necessarily beautiful. In the untrodden paths of the primitive forest, death, desolation, monotony, and a depressing gloom are often the more characteristic features.

FIG. 1.—MOUNTAIN RIVULET.

It is not always the extremely picturesque and rural that is desirable in landscape art—this is generally the result of accident or interference of some kind. The beautiful scenes spread about in the wilderness, the little effusions wherein the heart of nature touches that of man, the luxury of form and color on the sides of a ravine, the world of flowers in the crevices of cliffs and rocks, the tiny mountain rill gurgling over a pebbly bottom—these are a few of the models with which the landscape gardener can afford to be content.

It is evident that nowhere in the world a wholly natural

scenery exists; even in the high Alps the mountaineer builds his dingy cottage and surrounds it with degrading associations; there are hardly any primitive forests left, and if there were they would not be wholly "natural." In the Northern hemisphere, at least, everything has changed, century after century. Forests have been destroyed and regenerated; culture has reclaimed vast tracts of land only to be conquered by nature in its turn. But the world is not the less beautiful because of this struggle. Even man in his most destructive work has done much to create diversity in the scenery, when tempted by gain or forced by circumstances to destroy the existing vegetation and to open endless forests for fields of grain or patches of garden land. The result of this destruction is by no means an unmixed evil, as many would have us to believe. The beautiful reaches of open land; wide prospects of grassy fields, dotted over with scattered trees and bordered by copse and wood, forming the smiling landscapes of many northern countries, are essentially the result of man's interference. His axe opened the murky woods and let air into the lungs of nature; some of the most beautiful plants that at best led a precarious existence in the forest darkness spread and developed in the opened woodlands. The weaker and more tender vegetation got a chance, not only to exist, but to increase rapidly, painting hill and dale in glorious colors. Nature quickly rehabilitated herself after such destruction when left alone; a new beauty sprang up over the perishing world of giant trees, youthful and vigorous forms took the place of the old gloomy hosts of the forest.

But the beautiful variety brought about by the cultivation of the soil is on the other hand easily lost, especially
in fertile countries where every trace of original nature
is destroyed, as witness many parts of continental Europe.
Dreary hedgerows, closely divided fields with a few straight
rows of trees here and there, is all the variety to be
seen. Such a monotony lacks the dignity in which the
monotony of nature is always clothed. Pity a country
where this has become a reality; where there are no sunny
meadows stretching far away to the horizon, no woods
except those planted in squares and rows and cultivated like
a field of grain; where there is no wilderness with woodland flowers, where there are no streams, no springs, no
woodland rivulets gushing forth from the bosom of the
earth.

Knowing how the natural beauty of so many countries has been hopelessly destroyed, all thinking people
ought to work for the preservation of as much natural
scenery as possible; for a country that has lost all this, has
lost more than the value of miles on miles of fertile acres,
more than any riches can ever redeem.

In other places man has changed the face of the earth in
a better and opposite way by means of building and
planting. The prairies of this country will some day be
quite different from what they are now; they are different
to-day from what they were some years ago. Now, woods
and groves and orchards lend variety and beauty to the vast
plains in many parts of the West.

Planting of this kind, as has been amply demonstrated,
will also tend to regulate the climatic conditions, making

rains more frequent and the violence of storms and cyclones less severe.

But leaving these meditations, let us make a hasty survey of the great panorama of nature, as it unfolds before us, scene after scene in ever-changing succession. Let us take a walk through fields and woods, along the winding rivers, up to the alpine world where the mossy rock-plants are even greater in their beauty than the towering and frowning cliffs in their immensity. We will observe how the little seedling roots in the fissure of a rock and gradually forms a leafy mat covered with flowers; how the various kinds of trees and herbs seek different positions and there make their homes; how the rivulets are born and grow; the natural positions of lakes, and cliffs, and many other things that will help us to make the garden beautiful.

We know the primary causes of the diversity of the surface of the earth: how hills and mountains have been lifted up through volcanic forces, how the broken sides of the rocks were afterwards rounded and polished by the action of glaciers and, more slowly but in a no less marked manner, through constant changes of temperature and moisture. We know how the alluvial soil along streams and rivers has been formed, by means of successive sedimentary deposits, and how even now the ground is slowly changing, as if the great landscape-gardener, Nature, took pleasure in constantly creating new and startling effects.

It will not be necessary to attempt explanations of subjects so foreign to this work, but merely to observe what actually exists as beautiful objects and nothing more.

Commencing by the seaside, we find even there many

things available for our purpose.   We note the form of the
shore; here extending into low promontories; there forming
sheltered coves and bays.   The shore is sometimes rocky and
precipitous, with bowlders scattered along the base of the
cliffs, but more often even and gradually sloping, covered
with dazzling white sand.   The masses of seaweeds washed
ashore form little furrows and beds bordering the high-water
mark, and give nutriment to many curious forms of vegetable life.   The sea rocket forms dense masses of glisten-
ing, fleshy leaves, almost covered with delicate pink flowers,
sea holly grows in the pure sand, the spiny-edged, milky
white leaves form quite effective foliage, well in harmony
with the surroundings.   Coarse grasses of a glaucous color
border the higher parts of the shore.   As a rule the vegetation is of a peculiar silvery gray color, generally dwarf
and tufted, often forming mats of leaves and bright flowers.
A common plant on sandy, level shores is the sea pink, one
of the neatest of all flowering plants; its tufted masses of
narrow, bright green leaves and rosy-red flowers cover the
ground as far as the eye can see.   In other places we find
bright patches of wild thyme with purple flowers, and
golden immortelle weaves over the sand a carpet of silvery
foliage and yellow flowers.   Among the woody plants
peculiar to sea-shores, stunted and gnarled pines are common and characteristic, as are also, in some parts of Europe,
tamarix, and sea buckthorn.   When the shore is rocky,
many kinds of rock roses, crowberries, and other plants
form a scant covering to the weather-beaten cliffs.

Sometimes dunes of ever-shifting sand extend far inland;
almost destitute of vegetation they bury trees and shrubs

and even buildings under their masses. The sea-shore has no vegetation on the margin of the water, as have most lakes, owing to the changing tides and the salty nature of the water. When low and watery ground extends far inland from the sea, it gives rise to salt marshes—desolate wastes of coarse grass, rushes and reeds, enlivened here and there by isolated and scattered clumps of sea lavender and marshmallows with showy flowers.

Many really beautiful plants may be naturalized on sandy shores, and very delightful natural gardens can be made in such places by these means. Bulbous plants such as narcissi, squills, and some lilies will do well on the higher parts of the sandy beach. On sloping banks, sand clover, furze and broom and other kinds of cytisus may be used to form dense masses of leaves and flowers. Many maritime plants are insignificant as individuals, but when they appear in great numbers they form an important feature of the seaside landscape.

Fens and marshes are rich and varied in many ways. Zig-zag channels of transparent water make bewildering mazes among the tall grass. Clumps of birch and willow are common on the higher ground, accompanied by low bushes of sweet gale, and other shrubs. To the casual observer these watery tracts of land are void of interest and beauty, but in the interior they are rich in animal and vegetable life and have a charm of their own. Gayly-colored birds build their nests on the slender reeds, and fill the mornings with their carols; butterflies hover from flower to flower; water trefoil, marsh marigold, and golden senecio line the winding, sharp-edged channels, and on the grassy banks masses of blue violets and other flowers appear in spring.

The meadow is still more interesting, and there we may learn how many of our most beautiful ornamental plants should be grown. Meadows are low grassy lands on the shores of rivers and lakes; they form the bottom-lands of many, both lowland and alpine, valleys, and are very rich in soft grasses and flowering plants. The lowland meadow, especially in southern countries, is simply a form of a marsh on somewhat higher ground, with almost as coarse and robust a vegetation. In the far North and in high altitudes, the meadow takes on a more and more refined and pleasing appearance, the grass becomes softer and more dense as we ascend above the level of the sea, the flowers become smaller, more numerous, and of exquisite forms and colors, until close to the everlasting snow we meet a scene beautiful beyond description, where the flowers are intensely colored and much larger, and the plants smaller than those of the lowland meadow. Some of the most attractive flowers cultivated in gardens were originally meadow plants. Globe flowers, daffodils, gentians, lilies shining like fires in the distance, purple orchis, wide stretches of meadow cress, and saxifrage lend interest and color to the scenery. Many grow in almost dry positions, others in places where the soil is steeped in water. The level surface is broken and relieved by light groves of birch and alder, forming little islands in this sea of grass and flowers, or lining the shores of the winding streams. In alpine regions, these meadow landscapes are often closed in by steep cliffs, the sides of which are clothed with rock plants, or, if less steep, covered by woods of spruce or pine. Farther down, the meadow gradually rises into undulating fields, or disappears among deciduous woods.

The meadow, as seen in alpine regions, is the best model for a lawn on moderately rich ground, and by proper means it can be reproduced in the garden. The lawn, void of all vegetation except grass, when well cared for, is beautiful; still it is desirable to make it as natural as possible in many places. Meadow saffron and crocus, harebells, primroses, daisies, daffodils, and lilies are a few among the numerous plants that may be used for this purpose.

Far inland, formed by the growth of mosses and the decay of vegetable matter in marshy ground, the peat bogs, peculiar to some countries, in many respects resemble a marsh or meadow. The soil here is black and watery, and the flora is wholly different. The vegetation is scanty, consisting of sharp, grayish grasses, cottongrass, sweet gale, hagberry, alder, and birch. The trees are few, and scattered on the higher knolls that formed the islands long ago, when the bog was a lake. In many places there are still black pools of water with the innumerable flowers of the water anemone and the wild calla growing in the shallow water near the margin. Here is also found the large spearwort, some senecios with bright golden-yellow flowers, and the marsh marigold, which grows in all moist ground. On higher, but moist ground, the sundews (*Drosera*) are numerous, and the bird's-eye primrose forms tufts of small, mealy leaves among the grass and, in summer, paints the whole expanse with bright rosy-red flowers. Scattered in irregular and loose masses, the blue windflower or gentian, is seen later in summer among the grass. The Grass of Parnassus, with chaste and beautiful flowers of a snowy whiteness, and numerous other things, make this dreary waste as beautiful and interesting as life and only life can make it.

Dwarf shrubs of the heath family are here common, in fact, they make one of the redeeming features of the often desolate scene. The blueberries and cranberries, and, sometimes, purple heather and cross-leaved heath, are found in large patches on the higher ground among the bog-plants. In America the white alder (*Clethra*), various vacciniums, and sheep laurel partake of the nature of bog-plants, as do also, among the herbaceous vegetation, veratrum, some lilies, orchids, and pitcher-plants.

In parks and gardens such plants can be successfully grown in places where the land is naturally low, or in moist places in rockeries. Bog-plants are very numerous and beautiful; few weeds thrive in a peaty soil. Mosses abound, and the greatest attraction in bogs with arborescent vegetation are the rich masses and great variety of ferns, some small and only remarkable because of their great number; others tall and stately with the most exquisitely divided foliage.

Open, grassy fields on high ground are chiefly a result of cultivation, although in the course of time they may have been reclaimed by nature. If surrounded by woods and left uncultivated they soon become a part of the wood. Grassy fields and pastures give an impression of peace and quiet. Like the meadow, they are rich in flowers throughout the season. On open hillsides, blue asters, purple gerardias, and golden rods are plentiful in summer and autumn. Cone flowers and coreopsis are more addicted to level ground. Bluets, germander speedwell, bird-grass and milkwort, lilies, harebells, field scabious, and larkspur are common plants of dry, grassy fields. Open to the sun, with broad prospects to all points of the compass, and perhaps a few groves here and there, the fields wear a cheerful expression, exhilarating to the mind of the beholder. Here everything combines to make a pleasing impression; the purity of air and sky, the fragrance and color of the flowers, the wind moving the grass in long shining billows, and the effects of light and shade, as the clouds come and go.

The prairies of the West are, on the other hand, too extensive and monotonous; one feels exceedingly small and lonely in those grassy deserts, and the scanty clumps of cottonwood and willows along a distant, winding river, is a welcome sight indeed. Much of the charm of open fields is due to the presence of birds and animals, browsing sheep and cattle, or other signs of animal life.

The fields of southern latitudes generally become infested with coarse and weed-like plants, such as the large and showy sun-flowers, the giant cow parsnips, large milkweeds, pokeberries, and thorn apples—and in dry steppes and prairies the ground is covered with grayish wormwood, prickly pears, and similar plants.

The fields of the extreme North, with their fine, tufted grasses and delicate flowers, are by far the most beautiful. Here the white and yellow daisies are found in thousands. Scarlet poppies, blue cornflowers, and white chamomiles crowd together as if conscious of the beautiful combination they make, where they cluster along the side of the little

rivulet and weave their masses of color into the most exquisite patterns along the roadside.

This reminds me that the roadside itself is one of the
most charming natural gardens that can be found anywhere.
When a road is old and the sods along its sides become
solid, the coarser weeds disappear, and such neat flowers as
the mouse ear, wild thyme, field stone crop, golden bedstraw, St. John's-wort, harebells, blue buttons, meadow
saxifrage, broad-leaved plantain, and dropwort take their
place. Here we may learn how to plant the borders of
drives and walks in a pleasing manner. But, unfortunately,
every roadside is by no means a proper subject for this
study.

The heath is a form of an open, generally barren field;
when overgrown in parts with juniper and pine it is a
moorland. Ling and cross-leaved heath, many species of
vaccinium and dwarf junipers cover the surface with a
low and dense growth, relieved in places by patches of
furze, golden-yellow in summer. When the heather blooms
late in summer, the heath is one mass of purple blossoms.
At other seasons it is of a dull brownish green or brighter
during times of rain. Many delicate herbaceous plants
find a shelter here, such as the exceedingly beautiful pasque-
flower, hieracium, mountain tobacco or arnica, and a number of ferns, especially large masses of bracken. Graceful
groups and single specimens of weeping birch are generally
scattered here and there, and the tree-like juniper often
encroaches upon the territory of the heath. Scenery of this
kind can be introduced with good effects on barren hillsides
and in places where the soil is too thin for a close growth

of grass, but, at the same time, it may be made much more
varied in a garden, than it is in nature, where the endless
length of the heath tends to monotony.

The scenery of the open field has by no means any sharp
boundaries. There is a place where woodlands and fields
meet and mingle. The meadows stretch far into the heart
of the forest; groves, copses, masses of trees and shrubs

FIG. 2.—IVIED TREES ON THE OUTSKIRTS OF A WOOD.

lend more or less variety to the open field, and even the
most desolate marshes are not absolutely void of arborescent vegetation.

In southern latitudes, marshes are transformed into
impenetrable swamps by means of a dense growth of trees
such as bald cypress, magnolias and gum trees. These
swamps are beautiful and interesting in their own mysteri-
ous way, but they are gloomy and depressing to the mind.
Trunk by trunk in unbroken numbers the giants of the
swamps tower a hundred feet high, or more, their roots forming curious pillars all around making progress exceedingly
difficult. Ferns are common in the deep shades below, and
graceful climbers weave the mass into impenetrable barriers,
putting forth their blossoms high up among the giant

crowns of the trees, and forming beautiful drapery of foliage. The silence is depressing, even the birds are silent, and only the hammering of the woodpecker is heard now and again. In this wilderness, so utterly beyond reproduction by artificial means, and, withal, so undesirable, we can only observe the beautiful association of trees and climbers which may be of some use, but in our northern woodlands this association is much more beautiful and applicable to gardening.

When low, watery places in the North are overgrown by a woody vegetation some of the most charming natural scenery is the result. The deciduous trees are more merciful to the vegetation below. Here we find a wealth of form and color; masses of delicate-leaved ferns, swamp honeysuckle with showy blossoms, andromedas with white, bell-like flowers, white alder, stemless lady's-slipper, dwarf cornel, and purple violets in more open and sunny positions; here jack-in-the-pulpit speaks to his congregation of meadow beauties and purple phlox. Meadow-sweets, farkleberry, virgin's bower and like plants are very numerous on the border of swampy woods.

The beauty of deciduous woods on higher ground is enhanced by many familiar flowers. Under the spreading branches of the oak a great variety of tender and delicate plants find a home, and, in spring and early summer, clothe the surface of the ground with a carpet of flowers. If the woods are open and rocky, brambles and arrow wood are found in abundance. The maiden-hair fern grows in clumps at the base of rocks, or finds a snug place of refuge between the roots of some tall forest tree. Eagle ferns form larger and bolder masses, the leaf stalks rising singly from the ground, supporting a blade a couple of feet wide and about twice as long. In springtime, under birch and shad bush, before the snow departs, the trailing arbutus peeps shyly out among the masses of fallen leaves. Later,

FIG. 3.—UNDERGROWTH IN OAK-WOOD.

come anemone and dwarf meadow rue, wake robins and dog-tooth violets. In stony ravines, Solomon's seal, bane-berry and ferns make the most charming effect in this beautiful natural garden. Wherever a little stream trickles down a stony hillside in open woods, there the diadem flower (*Tiarella*) makes a border of delicate leaves and holds up little spires of white blossoms. In the West shooting-stars are common in rich woods, and farther North, twin-flowers, babes-in-the-wood (*Polygala pauciflora*) yellow wood-violets, and others too numerous to mention, make a beautiful display in early summer. Above all in many respects, lilies and moccasin-flowers and numerous kinds of terrestrial orchids, form admirable groups of flowers with which no formal groups in our gardens can compare. European woods are not less rich: the blue anemone, the yellow anemone, lily-of-the-valley, fumitory, woodruff, Turk's cap lily, oxlips and cowslips, spotted orchid, night violet and bellflowers, are only a few of the treasures found there. The flowering shrubs of deciduous woods, especially in mountain regions, are very numerous; mock orange, the various kinds of viburnum and meadow-sweets, are perhaps not less attractive than the herbaceous plants among which they grow. The glory of American woods, mountain laurel, azaleas and rhododendrons, make the wilderness of our mountainous and rocky woods richer and more beautiful than any garden or park has ever been up to the present time. Farther south a new and peculiar feature is introduced in the form of evergreen trees and shrubs, such as hollies of many species, with shining green foliage and brightly colored fruits in winter. As a rule, the flowering shrubs and trees prefer the outskirts of woods and thickets. Not so the evergreens; they thrive best in a moderate shade where they are somewhat sheltered from the rays of the sun in winter. Climbers are plentiful in most woods, and, generally, they grow in half-open positions, twining about the branches of shrubs and trees in copses and thickets, of which they form a striking feature. In Europe, the ivy is found in all countries and in every imaginable position, growing over stones and rocks in sunny places, on trunks of elm and other trees in mixed woods, or covering the ground farther north, a beautiful symbol of enduring faith. With us the Virginian creeper, grape-vines, green briar, and various forms of clematis are most common and noteworthy. Growing everywhere over dead trees, on the face of rocks, climbing to the crowns of the tallest trees and falling in graceful drapery from the branches, they add a beauty and a luxury to the scenery which it would be well to imitate in many a garden.

As to the trees themselves, they are almost as varied in form and character as the lesser vegetation. In most deciduous woods they mingle in a familiar manner: birch and maple, beech and chestnut, lindens and hickories, many species of oak and numerous flowering trees, such as halesias, cherries, and flowering dogwood, are familiar objects in American woods. In many parts of Europe, one species very often forms the main body of deciduous woods, as birch or beech. Beautiful in spring, when the tender leaves unfold, and still more so in the fall, when the autumn colors dazzle the eye with the most vivid shades of gold and scarlet; imposing in summer or winter, with massive trunks or widely branching crowns, the deciduous trees form a most important part of the natural scenery in temperate countries.

Now and then the hemlock and the white cedar become familiar objects in mixed, deciduous woods, and add a charm of their own to the scenery. But there is a line where the coniferous evergreen trees take hold in earnest and the deciduous trees become more and more rare. Hemlock, spruce and pine are mixed for a time, but at last endless forests, in which one kind predominates, stretch their awful silence far and wide. Here in the holy of holies of nature the surface is clean, as if trimmed by a careful hand, and sprinkled over with fallen cones and needles, forming a deep and even covering. Herbaceous plants are scarce except where a fallen tree has made an opening, or where a ravine or a river with grassy banks admits sufficient light for shrubs and flowers. Among the flowers common in somewhat open pine woods, the hepatica is perhaps the most familiar. Twinflowers (*Linnea borealis*), a minute trailing plant, rattlesnake plantain and the fragrant night violet are not uncommon, and shade-loving ferns are plentiful in rocky places.

Some species of pine form vast forests on low and watery ground, such as our own white pine. Pine-forests are most common in northern latitudes, where they cover whole provinces; mountain, plain and valley alike, for miles and miles; but they form special features of mountainous regions.

Extensive pine-barrens form a peculiar feature of many southern States—wide sandy plains covered with a more or less dense growth of yellow pine, black and willow-leaved oak, sometimes intermixed with hummocks of deciduous woods of hickory, oak and maple. Delicate herbaceous plants abound in the light sandy soil among tufted masses of heath-like shrubs, sand myrtles and vacciniums. Here the lupine, with its fingered leaves and long racemes of blue

flowers, is seen in perfect beauty. The birds-foot violet
covers the ground, not closely, but as if thinly sown over
the surface. Where the ground is low and watery, abounding in pools of brownish water, bladderworts cover the surface with their clusters of uniquely formed flowers, and on
water margins broad bushes of andromeda are the most
common plants.

Besides pine, most coniferous trees—spruces, firs, and larch
—form extensive forests of one species alone. Cedars and

FIG. 4.—A WOODLAND SCENE.

arbor-vitæ grow on undulated and rocky ground; aggre-
gating in smaller and larger, picturesque groups, divided by
open sunny glades, they seldom form a close and continuous growth, as do pines and firs. In the open and sunny
evergreen woods formed by juniper and cedar, a rich
herbaceous growth covers the ground, and among rocks in
deep gullies and ravines, rare and beautiful rock-plants grow

and flower under the most favorable conditions; columbine, four-leaved silkweed, stonecrop, and saxifrage are among the most common of these. Annual climbers, Virginian creeper and green smilax, are often found in the company of red cedar and arbor-vitæ, forming garlands of bright green leaves in the dark crowns of the evergreens.

The woodland is perhaps the most interesting of all landscapes, as it embraces all other scenery ; open glades and vistas, broad meadows and bogs, winding streams and lakes mirroring the beauty of leaf and flower.

A body of water, whether it be a river, a spring, or lake, has an infinite charm ; it lends beauty to nature in a thousand ways ; as sparkling pearls of dew on the grass, as rhime-crystals on the frozen boughs—wonderful embroidery, coming and going like a dream,—or as a mist rising over the still valley of early summer mornings.

Springs are clear, transparent bodies of water, the main sources of brooks and rivers ; they are found in low valleys as well as in high mountain regions, but more often in hilly and undulated countries, as on grassy hillsides, where the overflow forms small streams and rivulets bordered by forget-me-not and similar flowers. If a spring happens to be on a high mountain side, it may be the source of a considerable water system. In its higher course the infant stream forms innumerable cascades, creeping in and out among bowlders and rocks, welling forth through every little opening and precipitating itself over cliffs and ledges, or leaping gently from terrace to terrace, forming smooth sheets of water here and there bordered by velvety alpine meadows. Along its course, the mountain

flowers grow rarer and larger than higher up among the hillsides; ferns grow out of the moist crevices of the mossy
rocks.   As the stream grows in strength it forms sand and
gravel, erodes rocks and tumbles the remains about in con-
fused masses—rockeries in which most alpine flowers delight
to grow.   As the river descends, cascades and rapids grow
larger through the increased mass of water gathered from
other mountain rivulets that join here and there, perhaps
merely formed by a fall of rain, or by melting snow during
the approach of spring and summer.   Soon the alpine
meadows become larger, the river widens into clear lakes;
birch and willow and mountain ash are more common than
higher up, where there are only spruce and larch.   Below
these mountain lakes a fall or rapid is inevitable.   It may
be an immense ledge of rock that has dammed up the river
and thus formed the lake, or a series of rocks and ledges
cemented together with sediment.

More often the water undermines the rocks, carries away
the sand and gravel, and forms deep winding ravines, where
a rich and varied vegetation takes root on the steep sides.
In such ravines, through which the never silent mountain
river flows slowly and meditatingly, an innumerable host
of the choicest of flowers grows in the light shade of birch,
aspen and mountain ash.   The trees lean over, here almost
horizontally, there rising on bent and picturesque trunks
into a more upright position.   Here a bridge of foliage
and flowers has been formed across the stream as a climber
has grown to the utmost limb of a leaning tree, and twining its stem among the trees on the other side, forms garland after garland.   If you want to study the loveliest

scenery of nature, here it is, in these sequestered valleys among the mountains, with rocks, water, and vegetation woven into a harmonious whole.

But the river cannot stay ; an irresistible force is drawing it along ; it grows larger and larger, forms mighty cataracts, and at last reaches the deep valleys and plains but little above the sea.   Now it flows slowly and majestically, a picture of strength and peace, winding in and out in a hundred ways, rounding a low promontory, bending along a steep bank, watering fertile meadows and islands rich in

FIG. 5.—LOWLAND RIVER ; MEADOW AND WOODS.

vegetable and animal life.   It is difficult to decide which is the more beautiful, the little purling stream with its grassy and stony bed, or the mighty river on the shores of which groves and meadows mingle together ; the cascade of the rivulet near its source, or the irresistible cataract throwing itself with a deafening roar into the deep ; the mountain spring or the lake in the valley, for each is beautiful in its own way.

The vegetation of the riverside is generally exceptionally beautiful and interesting, perhaps because there the conditions of growth and development are so generous. On the river shore the iris—the Flor de Luce of old—is found in its highest beauty. Here the vermilion cardinal-flower luxuriates among the grass; forget-me-nots, butter-cups and ox-eye daisies grow in harmony among meadow-sweets and other familiar flowers; many forms of marsh plants are generally found in moist places on the shores of lakes and rivers. Where the water forms deep, shallow bays we find the water lily, and nearer the shore, water violet, arrowhead, and water anemone; the first two

FIG. 6.--BROOK.

growing singly, the last one forming carpets of floating leaves and pretty, white, yellow-eyed flowers. Alders, birch, and willows are the most familiar trees on the shores of lowland rivers and lakes. When a river has reached the level of the sea, it becomes subject to tidal changes, and unless the shores are covered with pebbles and sand, they are often slimy and unsightly. Here again the woody vegetation becomes scarcer and assumes the grayish tint peculiar to maritime plants; but very often the shores and deltas of the river form moist, velvety meadows, which

abound in a beautiful herbaceous flora, devoid of the
coarseness common to so many marsh-plants.

Cliffs and rocks form part of some of the most impressive
natural scenery. As we know, they are not confined to
high mountain regions, but occur even on plains and sea-
shores; lifting bold, bare masses above the surface of the
ground; jutting forth from broken and steep hillsides, or
forming the sides of gullies and ravines on the shores of
running water. They often assume strange and grotesque
shapes, or a vivid coloring, as the sandstone formations of
the Rocky Mountains. Even on level plains, beautiful
rock scenery is not uncommon along streams and rivers.
In our northern woods rocks are very common; they form
the main body of the soil, and protruding here and there
show a grooved and polished surface, on which mighty
isolated blocks and bowlders still remain, adding greatly to
the picturesque beauty of the undulating ground, so rich in
vegetation and so varied in the character of its surface. In
higher mountain ranges, rocks become more and more evident, full of crevices, mossgrown and rounded by time and
supporting the rarest and most beautiful flowers. Where
running water slowly and steadily undermines a rocky
shore, bowlder after bowlder piles, one above the other;
sediment of all kinds collects among the stones, creepers
and vines and small flowering shrubs take root in the
moist, rich soil collected in the cavities; tender herbaceous
plants spring up in the crevices, where they find nutriment
enough for subsistence, but where no coarser weeds can
exist; and so we have a natural rockery on the river shore
still washed by the water or left high and dry on a sandy

beach, with the perpendicular cliffs for a background, and
no longer in danger of destruction. Often these cliffs are
covered with ivy and other climbers, and in every fissure
stonecrops, saxifrage, and other rock plants find a place
sooner or later. When this phenomenon takes place in
higher altitudes, the flora is of a different and less robust
type. True alpine plants are confined to high mountain
regions, but many delicate and truly beautiful rock plants
are common in most countries. Sandstone rocks support a

FIG. 7.—ERODED ROCKS, FORMING A SMALL ROCKERY ON THE SHORES OF A RIVER.

greater and more varied vegetation than any other kind.
They are also seen in a great diversity of forms, as they are
easily acted upon by heat and moisture, or turned and
polished by heavy sandstorms. Limestone is also liable to
erosion in a greater or less degree; the surface becomes more
polished, and undermined rocks are seldom ground to gravel,
but remain as stones and bowlders in the streams and rivers
by which they are undermined. Here also we find numerous
rock plants, often of a different type. But nearly all rocks,
even the solid granite and trap, form cracks and fissures in

which plants lodge, and grow, and blossom. High up, just below the everlasting snow, we find the sunny slopes gayly decked with innumerable, brightly colored, or sometimes pure white flowers.

Isolated blocks in rocky woods often afford shelter and protection for a very diverse flora of vines, creepers, and herbaceous plants, under whose masses they jut forth gray, mossy corners. They are often split and broken by the action of frost on water collecting in the fissures. In the wide openings the bramble plants its little seed, and soon grows up to cover the whole mass with its wealth of leaves and flowers; or a grapevine may have been introduced in some way or other, and in that case the effect is very picturesque and beautiful.

Here and there, these erratic blocks are so numerous as to completely cover the surface, and if the ground is low they soon become imbedded in a tufted growth of ling and grass. Rocks and water in combination form the most picturesque and beautiful scenery, not only in the manner already pointed out, but in many other ways; here, tremendous precipices, there, grottos and caves in which a peculiar flora of mosses and filmy ferns finds an ideal home, growing in tufted masses in deep shady crevices and continually covered with dew.

So everywhere, from the deep dungeons of the cavern to the bright cliffs bathing in light and sunshine, the rocks support an innumerable host of flowers of delicate forms and colors, and beautiful enough to interest the most indifferent.

No landscape of one character is separated abruptly and

distinctly from that of another; the transformation is gradual, we go from one scene to another without knowing until the difference suddenly strikes us. Meadow and woodland, field and forest, are all woven into one pattern without any strong boundaries, except where man comes in; but even there, the waving fields of corn and the blue smoke from the farmer's chimney have their beauty, and fit into the natural setting as perfectly as the gossamers' airy castles, or the weaver-bird's nest. The stone bridge over the creek, mossy and ivied, bordered by graceful birches and bushy willows, fits admirably into the scenery; the tall, distant church spire, rising above a mass of foliage, adds decidedly to the beauty of the landscape.

It would be of no use to go into further details. I have simply endeavored to show how and where to study the natural landscape. In every imaginable place there is something to learn; even in the most desolate and monotonous wilderness there are scattered scenes of rare and perfect beauty. In the open woodland, in the mountain valley, by lake and river, the landscape-gardener, whether amateur or professional, must learn the greatest secret of his art; and he should always remember that no copying of the outward form alone will give the living impression of nature. Although this is considered the humblest of the beautiful arts, it is the one that speaks the most natural language to the heart and imagination; it is capable of the most useful and universal influence upon the moral development of a country; it is conducive to health and happiness and purity of mind and body.

To make the garden what it ought to be the designer must have a perfect knowledge of the different things that go to form a landscape. The nature, habit, and habitat of every species used, must be well understood in order to ensure success in planting. In the natural part of a park or garden, the plant should be able to develop without culture or attention, and the attention given should be for the sake of regulating the growth in certain cases only. Knowing the materials used, it will be comparatively easy to arrange everything correctly, to give every species the natural position, where it will thrive best, and plant it in the right proportion.

The details of the constructive work are of no less importance. Roads and lawns and natural scenery, to be lasting and satisfactory, must be made in the best possible manner. The natural scenery especially, in order not to become a mere collection of plants, without character and expression, must be formed by an artist's hand and under the scrutiny of an artist's eye, yet with the careful detail of the experienced, practical gardener to ensure life and health and permanency.

The care of already existing natural scenery is of no less importance, and the gardener intrusted with its care should have a keen perception of the beautiful in nature, in addition to his ability in formal gardening. The thinning of crowded shrubberies, the removal of trees that may have become too large for the place they occupy, and work of a like nature, should be promptly attended to. As a rule, it is best to plant trees and shrubs at a considerable distance from one another so as to prevent all crowding;

the outlines of a plantation will be so much more graceful
and much work and expense will be saved. Even the
herbaceous vegetation, or shrubs used as an undergrowth
in woods and thickets, are apt to spread beyond their
proper limit.

Of late years wild gardening has been much recommended, and it has been claimed that anybody, by sowing a
mixture of flower seeds in the garden, would obtain the
most charming results. So far from this being the case, most
people who attempt it without any adequate knowledge
succeed only in making a desert of weeds; going to work
blindly as they do without knowing the nature or character of the plants introduced in this manner. Woodland
scenery is not difficult to produce, but the plants should
be comparatively few in number and of a similar nature.
Wind-flowers, anemone-flowered rue, purple phlox, oxlips
cowslips, and orchids, as well as many species of bulbous
plants, are especially adapted for this purpose, and with
these the effect will be beautiful. But if a number of
plants are used without discrimination, especially those
easily propagated by seeds, we only succeed in making the
weediest of weedy spots—in fact, an anarchy in nature
without law and order. Although the scenery as represented in nature is the foundation of the modern park and
garden, it must be remembered that there are artificial
additions which add greatly to its variety and beauty.
The roads and walks are necessary for communications
between the different parts, shelters are convenient for
protection from rain and sunshine, and bridges are needed
to carry us across streams and rivulets. By contrast also,

a temple on the top of a knoll, or a rural cottage in the outskirts of a wood or shrubbery, relieves and heightens the beauty of the landscape.

The surrounding country should always be taken into consideration when planning a garden, and, as much as

FIG. 8.—TEMPLE.

possible, garden and surroundings should be in harmony with each other, but at the same time all unsightly objects must be hidden from within by means of plantations. It would be a mistake to hem in a seaside cottage on a bare coast by too luxurious a vegetation, unless the whole coast could be changed into more or less rich scenery. So also in the mountains and on the plains, there is a special class of vegetation in harmony with each.

In suburban towns, laid out on a uniform plan, in one continuous stretch of lawn with groups of trees and shrubs, garden walls and hedges here and there are out of place. But where it is desirable to ensure privacy or protection, the plan of enclosing a garden by screens of some kind is not a bad one, as it admits of the culture of rarer flowers, and the grounds within can be made one harmonious whole without the necessity of outside help, except by an opening here and there in the shrubbery for some particularly interesting view. Hedges and garden walls are therefore not to be wholly despised, and it will be shown in a subsequent chapter how they may be used without obstructing or interfering with the scenery in any way. In cold and windy countries, open to every blast, they are not only desirable but necessary for the protection of the plants within, from the killing effect of sandstorms and high, frosty winds.

In small lots around suburban cottages much cannot be done in the way of natural effects, but there is always some corner where rare and beautiful woodland plants may be allowed to run wild among the shrubs and grass. The choicest of flowering shrubs and herbaceous plants, the smallest and most ornamental species of shade trees, and the most velvety grass should be chosen for these little home grounds. Creepers and vines can be employed in many ways to brighten the cottages, and unsightly objects should be hidden by means of evergreen trees. In very small gardens large trees are out of place, and buildings, with the possible exception of a rustic pavilion or shelter, should be excluded. There are, however, grounds hardly large enough for one good-sized oak to live on, yet capable of being converted into the most charming garden spots. There is a special class of flowers adapted for just such gardens, a class of plants that has developed with gardening since the earliest days of horticulture, and which are nowhere to be found in nature. Among these are the many varieties of the rose, the hollyhock, peonies, poppies, phlox, dahlias, and the double forms of annual and biennial plants—the border and cottage plants of old. They are floriferous and effective from an ornamental point of view, and should be employed where vivid and striking colors are desirable.

By observing and analyzing what is really beautiful in

3

nature, the gardener, besides cultivating his taste, will lay
up a store of knowledge which it is difficult to find in any
other way. And this knowledge will be needed by the
future landscape gardener. Already now, such costly display as the gorgeous, and in its way effective, carpet
bedding, is passing away, and it must be admitted, that it
never excited any true and enthusiastic admiration. Observe, on the other hand, with what genuine pleasure
everybody, rich and poor, rambles among the wild flowers
of field and wood, and it is easily seen what gardening
must become before it will be sincerely appreciated. It is
the simple and unaffected that is admired in art as in
nature. But aside from this study of natural scenery,
there is much to be learned from the gardens and gardening
of the present time. The parks of the larger American
cities are fine models in many respects, but as to the smaller
gardens we must necessarily learn of other countries, for it
is a well-known fact—and a cause for regret—that America
with all its wealth has no villa or cottage gardens worth
mentioning.

May we not hope that this will be different some day,
and that our suburbs will not always have so many
uncared for, weed-grown lots littered with empty tin cans,
badly kept " yards," and impassable roads.

II.

IMPLEMENTS.

HE instruments used in surveying and levelling ordinary places are few and simple, such as tape-line, compass, and water-level.

The tape-line is made in lengths of fifty or a hundred feet and can be wound up in a circular leather case when not in use. It is made of steel or linen with steel wires to prevent stretching, and divided into feet, tenths of feet, or inches and quarter inches. The tape-line can be used for measuring plots of ground when no other instrument is convenient, the angles being taken in a simple manner by setting off given lengths on the line, thus 3, 4, and 5 feet will give an angle of 45°. If we desire to find out the distance between a given base-line and some interesting object, such as a tree, a flower-bed, or shrubbery, the tape-line must be held at right angles to the base-line, or, in other words, the shortest distance between two parallel lines should always be measured. It is also important to hold the line horizontally above the surface when measuring distances on broken or undulating ground. Curves of walks and drives, outlines of shrubberies and other plantations may be located by this simple means as correctly as if a compass or transit were used.

The compass is used for measuring angles. It consists of a horizontal plate with two vertical arms provided with

hairsights, and a circular box with a graduated edge and a magnetic needle hanging on a fine point in the centre. The blue end of the needle always turns due north, or as nearly so as necessary for all practical purposes. By means of a capstan screw the varia-

FIG. 9.—COMPASS. tion of the needle can be set off. The

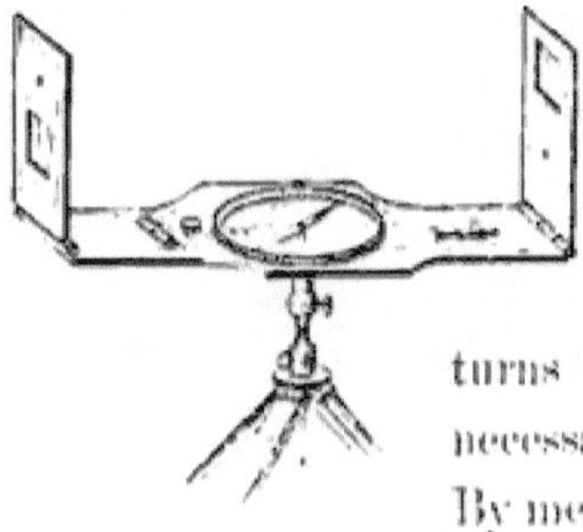

instrument is attached to a ball-joint and socket for a simple stake or "Jacob's staff." It can also be used with a tripod for more exact measurements. When in use it is placed above a given station, as A in Fig. 10; the joint upon which the needle is hung should be precisely above that station. Adjusting the instrument in a level and vertical position, we point the arms in the direction of B, where a flagstaff has been placed previously, and bring the hairsights to bear on the staff. Now it is easy to count the number of degrees between the blue point of the needle and the line indicated by the direction of the two arms of the compass. The angle is noted in the fieldbook, we measure the distance from A to B with a tape-line, and shift the instrument to B and proceed in the same manner there. More often the instrument is placed only on every other station, and the length and degree of the two lines are taken from that point, as B and E in Fig. 10. A whole plot of land may also be measured from one central point in the manner shown in Fig. 11, the length of the diagonal lines being measured with a tape-line and the angles noted on a rough outline drawing in the field-book, afterwards to be drawn to a scale with the help of compass and protractor.

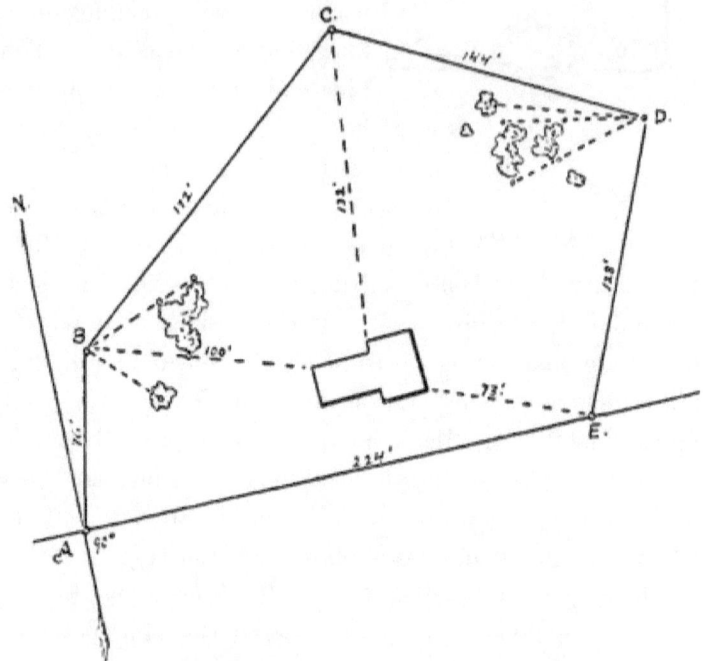

FIG. 10.—HOW TO MEASURE A SMALL PLOT OF LAND BY MEANS OF COMPASS.

The compass is also used in fixing curved stakes for walks and drives as seen in Fig. 11. In this case the angles and the length of the diagonal lines must be plainly marked on the working drawing, and some central point should be properly located, as the station A in the diagram which is

ten feet from the corner of the building. The compass
being adjusted the needle points as usual due north, we
fix the needle with the capstan pinion and set the arms of
the compass to 60°, stake out the line, and measure the
distance, 18′ 6″ to *a*, where a stake is driven in, and so on
until the curve is fully marked. Any object may be located
in the same manner, such as shrubs and trees, flower-beds,
the outlines of hills and rockeries, and so forth.

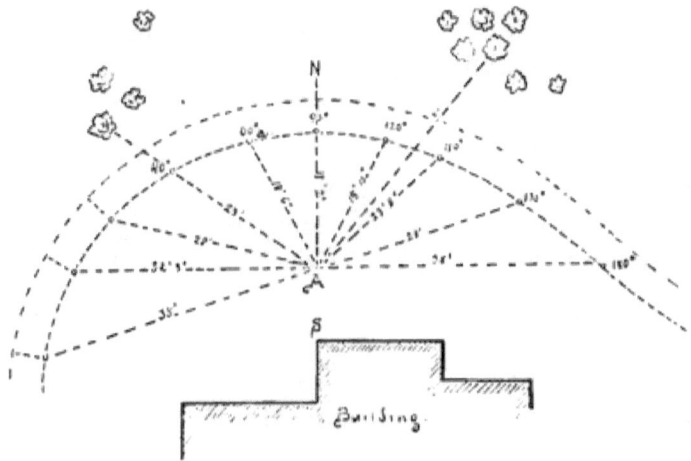

FIG. 11.—HOW TO STAKE OUT A WALK BY MEANS OF COMPASS.

A staff-head is an octagonal prism of brass with a
socket for the Jacob's staff. Each side has a narrow longitudinal opening by means of which angles of 45° and 90°
can be staked out on the ground; the staff with the instrument being placed vertically on the spot where the lines are
to cross, stakes are placed exactly in the same manner as
by means of the compass. The flagstaffs are simply square
or octagonal strips of wood, six or eight feet long and

about an inch in diameter, pointed at one end to admit of
insertion in the ground. If they are used to locate long
straight lines or at a great distance, a piece of white or red
cloth is put on the top; they will be best seen if painted
red and white alternately. It is clear that when a line has
to be staked out on the ground the operator needs an
assistant to place the staff in the right position; he is
directed to the right or left as the case may be by motions
of the hand.

The water-level is a handy instrument for placing grade
stakes and for levelling small
plots of land. It consists of a
simple tube of brass or zinc with
two vertical arms in which glass
tubes have been placed. In filling the
instrument the water rises to the same
level in the two glass tubes and it needs
therefore no adjustment. Now supposing
we desire to measure the grade and alti-
FIG. 12.—WATER-LEVEL.
tude of the knoll represented in Figure 13, we first stake
out the line A–B, putting stakes in the places indicated by
the figures. Placing the instrument at A, the assistant
holds a levelling rod in the first station (1), we now sight
along the surface of the water in the two tubes and
read the height in feet and inches on the levelling rod.
This done the assistant goes to the second station, the
height of which is read and noted in the same manner.
The instrument is then shifted to B, and after reading the
height of the two stations 2 and 3, the instrument is again
shifted to C, and so on. The field-notes are taken in the

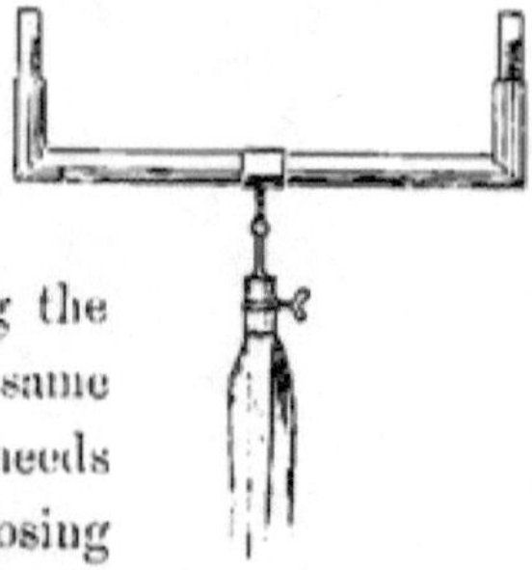

following manner. In the first column the number of each
station is noted; in the second, the distance between the
stations in feet and inches; in the third under foresights,
the heights in feet and tenths of feet in the direction of B
(see Figure 13): in the fourth, the height of the instru-

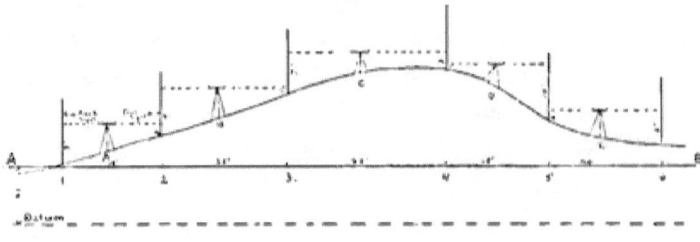

FIG. 13.—LEVELLING.

ment above the "datum-line," a line that can be fixed at
random, 10 or 100 feet below the surface; in the fifth, the
actual height above the datum-line; in the sixth under backsights the height of the stations in the direction of A.

Stations	Distance	Foresights	Height of instr. above datum line.	Actual height above datum line.	Backsights.	Remarks.
1			17 00	10 00	7 00	
2	18	2 00	23 00	15 00	8 00	
3	22	1 00	29 00	22 00	7 00	
4	28	3 00	27 00	26 00	1 00	
5	15	10 00	19 00	17 00	2 00	
6	20	6 00		13 00		
	133 00	22 00		—3 00	25 00	

It is necessary to note the "foresights" and "backsights"
only, in the field-notes, the rest is calculated afterwards as
follows. Supposing the datum-line to be fixed at 10 and
the backsight to station 1, is 7 feet, these sums added together give the height of the instrument at A, or 17 feet.

The foresight to station 2 is 2 feet, that is 2 feet less than 17, or 15 feet, which is the actual height of station 2. The instrument having been shifted to B, the backsight to station 2 is 8 feet, namely 8 feet higher than the actual height of that station, or 23 feet, which is the height of the instrument in the new position. The foresight to station 3 is 1 foot, that is 1 foot less than the height of the instrument; the actual height of station 3 is therefore 22 feet. All the rest is calculated in the same manner. Finally, foresights and backsights are summed up; if the sum of the foresights is larger than that of the backsights, the last station is so much below the first one, and

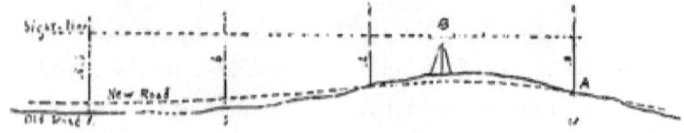

FIG. 14. — HOW TO PLACE GRADE STAKES BY MEANS OF WATER-LEVEL.

vice versa. In the present example, station 6 is 3 feet higher than station 1. All the readings are here supposed to be in even feet, something never occurring in actual practice, but it makes the example easier to comprehend. Very often the whole line can be levelled from one point, and this greatly simplifies the matter.

The water-level is also used in fixing grade stakes. Supposing the continuous line in Figure 14 to represent the rugged surface of an ill-made road, and the dotted line the suggested improvement. A is a plane of reference or "bench mark," and all stakes are placed so much higher or lower than this mark as the dotted line indicates. Placing

the level at B and the levelling rod at A we take the readings of that point: 8 feet. Stake 1, when driven in to a
sufficient depth, should be 1 foot 3 tenths lower; the readings at that point will therefore be: 1´ 7´´ + 8´ = 9´ 7´´.
Stake 2, 18 feet distant, is 7 tenths higher; the readings
will be 9 feet, and so on in proportion.

The levelling rod is simply a square stake, about ten feet
high, divided into feet, each foot being subdivided into
tenths and hundreds. The main divisions are painted red
and white alternately. While the levelling is being done,
the rodman is directed to hold a lead pencil in a horizontal
position across the rod, moving it up and down slowly
until the exact place is found. A more complete levelling
rod is provided with a round target which slides up and
down. The surface of the target is divided into four equal
sections painted alternately white and red; there is an
opening in the centre to admit of reading the number of
feet and inches indicated.

The Y-level is quite an expensive instrument used for the
same purpose, and in the same manner as the water-level,
being of course more exact and more useful for important
work. It consists of a telescope with a tube of brass or
gun-metal, and lenses provided with a haircross of spider's
webs, allowing very accurate observations. It is levelled
with the aid of two air-bubbles in glass tubes, and by means
of screws acting upon a pivot, placed loosely in the socket.
A tripod is always used in connection with this instrument.
It requires a very careful adjustment and cannot be used in
a satisfactory manner without some practice. The theodo-
lite combines the qualities of the compass and the Y-level.

It is expensive, but where it can be had no other instrument is necessary.

A measuring rod ten or fifteen feet long is handy for practical work; it should be divided into feet and inches. In laying out walks and drives, flower-beds and borders, it is used for measuring distances, as the width of a drive or the space between shrubs and other plants. Borning-rods[1] sometimes take the place of more exact instruments in every-day practice. They are simple stakes five feet long; one of the three generally used together is somewhat longer than the others, with a sight-hole at the upper end. To the other two short cross-pieces may be attached at the

FIG. 15.—HOW TO PLACE GRADE STAKES BY MEANS OF TWO BORNING-RODS AND MEASURING ROD.

upper ends, at exact right angles. Grade stakes for a gradually inclined plane may be placed by this means in the following manner: drive a stake at each end, one to mark the highest, the other the lowest part of the slope; let one man hold a rod vertically on one of the stakes, remain at the other end and direct a third man with another rod to drive grade stakes in a straight line between the two end stakes to the proper level. When, in looking through the sight-hole, the tops of the two rods are on the same plane, the stake is properly placed. Proceed in the same manner

[1] A horticultural term.

with the rest.   Figure 15 shows a nice method of placing
grade stakes for an undulated surface. A, A.′ are two rods of
equal length pushed into the soil to the same depth and
standing five feet above the surface.   B is a measuring rod
with a sliding cross-piece for a sight or target.   Supposing
the desired height of the stake at B to be 2 feet above the
shaded line, the cross-piece is placed at 3 feet on the measuring rod and the stake is driven in until the cross-piece
and the tops of the two rods are on the same plane, the
measuring rod, as a matter of course, being held vertically
on the top of the stake.   In like manner any number of
grade stakes may be placed.   A straight-edge, a plain
board of seasoned wood six inches wide and ten or fifteen
feet long, is sometimes used in combination with a carpenter's level and plumb-line for determining the rise of steep
hillsides; and in practical work, in road-making, construction of bridges and other rustic structures, its use and purpose are too evident to need any explanation.

The garden line is of great practical use in road- and lawn-
making, hedge-planting, and drainage work,
in laying out and planting beds and borders in
the vegetable garden and other parts, where
straight and formal lines are required.   A
plaited hempen cord about a quarter of an
inch in diameter and a hundred feet long
makes a neat and durable garden line.   One
end is attached to a reel, on which it is rolled

FIG. 16.—THE GAR-
DEN LINE.

up when not in use, and the other to a plain iron pin.

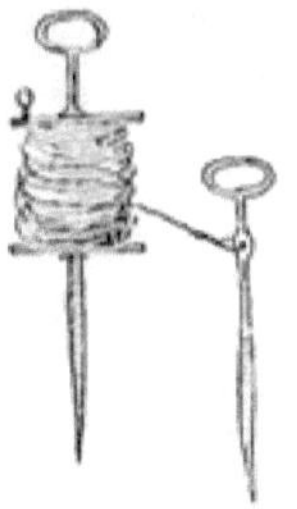

The spade is the most useful implement for working
and preparing the soil, and although much work is now

done with the plough and subsoiler, these implements cannot in any way compare in usefulness with the spade. In planting large grounds the soil can be worked tolerably well by these means, but for all more important work the spade is still used. Spades should be made of the best steel; they must be light and strong, with smoothly finished handles, and sharp blades that will remain clean and polished when in use. Spades of the best American manufacture are generally satisfactory. Shovels are used as adjuncts to the spade in digging and shifting loose materials and in surface grading of lawns. Those with long, smooth handles and comparatively small steel blades turned up at the sides, are the best for our purpose. Forks with flat prongs are handy for digging beds and borders, in preparing the vegetable garden for planting, or for digging in open shrubberies. Forks of light and strong make with spade handle and four or five elastic steel prongs are the best. Trowels are small tools for planting herbaceous plants and bulbs in rockeries and flower-beds. The blade is hollowed and pointed, made of a thin piece of steel about eight inches long joined to a short wooden handle five inches long. The pickaxe is employed in rough construction work for loosening soil, removing stones, digging trenches for drains, and in making cuts and excavations for drives and walks. For this purpose crowbars are also occasionally needed. The grubbing-axe is a similar tool, but has one end flattened into an axe-like edge. It is chiefly used in clearing land, and also in digging where many roots of trees are encountered. Besides this, where clearing is necessary, axes and brush hooks are required.

Steel rakes, with from six to fifteen more or less closely set teeth, are used in all surface finishing and for breaking up and levelling spaded soil. A rake eighteen inches wide, with fourteen strong steel teeth, is the best for ordinary use. The handle should be long and of light, strong material. Wooden rakes are chiefly used in cleaning lawns of leaves and other rubbish.

A sod-iron is the most handy and expedient tool for cutting grass-turfs, for edging lawns, for terraces and sloping surfaces. It consists of a heart-shaped steel blade, very thin, with a sharp-cutting edge. It is attached to a long handle in the same manner as a scuffle-hoe. In cutting sods, strips are first marked out in the lawn or pasture by means of a spade or verge-cutter. The verge-cutter or edging iron is further used in cutting clean the edges of a lawn after sodding. It is a simple steel blade with a rounded edge, attached to a straight wooden handle about five feet long. Another kind consists of a thin circular plate with a very sharp edge, and revolving on a steel axle fastened in a fork attached to a straight handle.

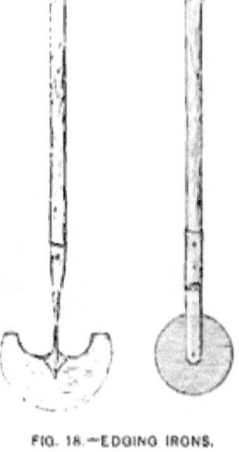

FIG. 17. TURF IRON.

FIG. 18.—EDGING IRONS.

The mallet consists of a rectangular piece of wood about eight inches long, six inches broad and four inches thick, and a short handle ten inches or a foot long. It is used in sodding for beating down the turf to the proper level. The sod-knife is handy for joining the edges of the separate turfs, and also for cutting off any unduly thick portion of the sod.

The turf-beater is used after all the sods have been placed in position to beat down and level the whole surface. It is simply a piece of wood, fourteen inches long, ten inches wide and three inches thick, supplied with a shovel handle.

A rammer is made of cast-iron, about eight inches square, with a socket for an upright handle four feet long. It is used for ramming down soil firmly, and in road-making for beating down the filling materials.

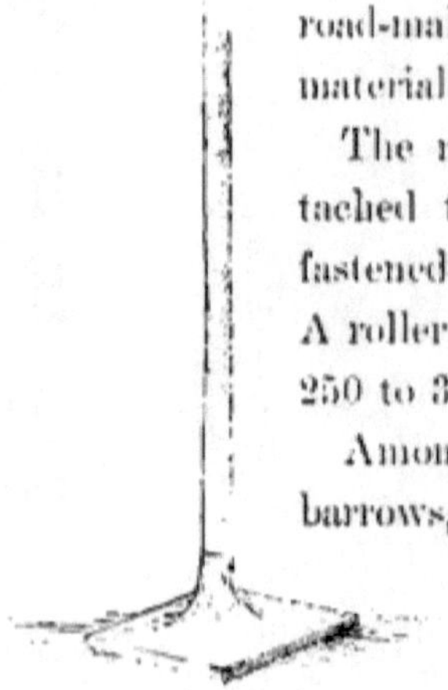

The roller is a cylinder of cast-iron attached to an axle, on which it revolves, fastened to a handle with a balance weight. A roller for hand power may weigh from 250 to 350 pounds.

Among other implements are: wheelbarrows, for shifting soil at short distances; scoops for horse power; carts, ploughs, subsoilers, harrows and pulverizers, and horse-power or steam rollers for extensive work;

FIG. 19.—CAST-IRON RAMMER.

a simple crane for hoisting stone and other heavy material, and specially constructed carts for the removal and planting of large trees.

III.

THE PLAN.

BEFORE beginning the work of improving the home lot, some definite plan of grading and planting should be adopted. The system of drives and walks must be determined upon, the character of the soil and surface noted, and all unsightly objects removed.

Be the grounds ever so small, steps should be taken to improve them in the best possible manner, and it is always prudent to ask the advice of a professional landscape gardener. There should be no hesitancy in investing a fair amount for the improvement of the home surroundings, and all investment of this kind will raise the value of the property far above the actual cost.

If the place is large and the ground greatly undulated, a topographic survey of the whole will be of great service in designing and laying out the garden. This is especially necessary if the landscape architect employed has no opportunity to supervise the work personally, but must convey all the necessary information in an intelligible manner in the plan and specifications. Even for small places a plan

48

is useful, but may be very simple, merely consisting of
the outlines of the grounds, buildings, walks, shrubberies,
and flower-beds, with the size and distance marked in plain
figures. When a place has been measured and surveyed as
directed in the chapter on implements, the rough map accompanying the field-notes is drawn to a scale either on
paper or cloth, the latter being best for practical use. The
drawing can be more or less finished, giving a perfect idea
of the appearance of the grounds after planting, or merely
indicate the general features. A working drawing must
show the exact position of shrubs and trees, each plant
being marked with a plain number; the width of drives and
walks, as well as the proper curves and grades; the number and position of specimen plants; outlines of rockeries,
borders, and flower-beds. Detail drawings, plans, and ele-
vations of rustic buildings, and all work requiring special
attention, should also be had. Any natural feature that
may be used to advantage, such as trees already growing
on the place, rocks, streams, and small ponds, should be
clearly shown. Trees to be removed are marked with a
cross, and any alteration of water margins by means of
dotted lines. Where the surface of the ground is designed
to be altered and graded, cross-section drawings, showing
the quantity of soil to be removed or brought on, are required if the work is of great importance.

In order to transfer the plan to the ground in every detail,
the working drawing may be divided into squares, as shown
by the dotted line in Fig. 20, identical lines being drawn on
the ground. From these lines all measures can be taken
and edges of walks and drives, shrubberies and trees are

4

then staked out according to the plan. In small places the measure can be taken from the sidewalk, the house, or any other fixed object. When locating trees and shrubs the

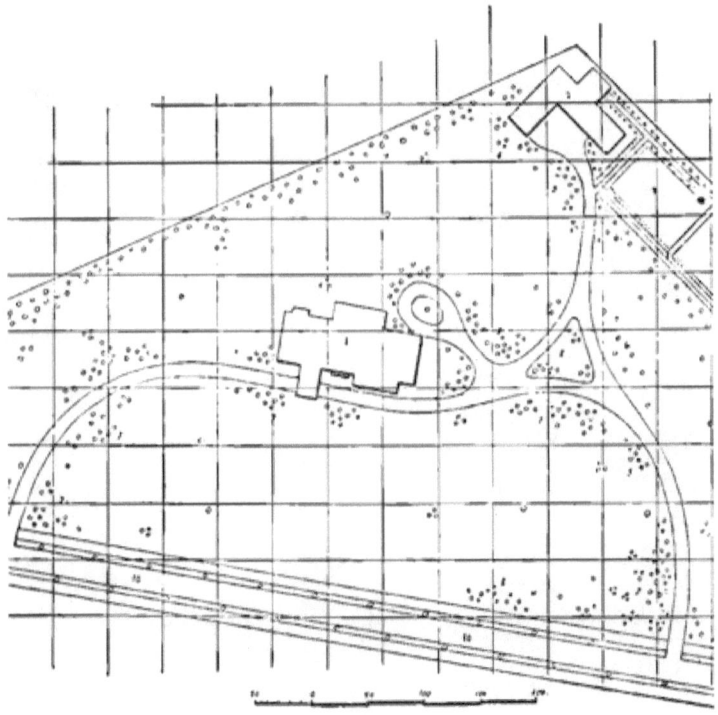

FIG. 20.—WORKING PLAN SHOWING HOW TO STAKE OUT DRIVES, AND MODE OF PLANTING
N. JÖNSSON ROSE, ARCHITECT.

1. Residence.   2. Stables.   3. Kitchen garden.   4. Avenue of fruit-trees.
5. Herbaceous borders.   6. Ornamental groups of fruit-trees and shrubs.
7. Composite groups of small ornamental trees and flowering shrubs.
8. Groups of coniferous trees.   9. Screen-planting.   10. Road.

name or number of each species should be plainly written in red chalk on the stake marking its future position. In this manner all mistakes in planting will be avoided.

The accompanying plans will serve as samples of plans for small home grounds. Fig. 21, A, represents a lot 50 by 200 feet, a rather small and insignificant piece of land

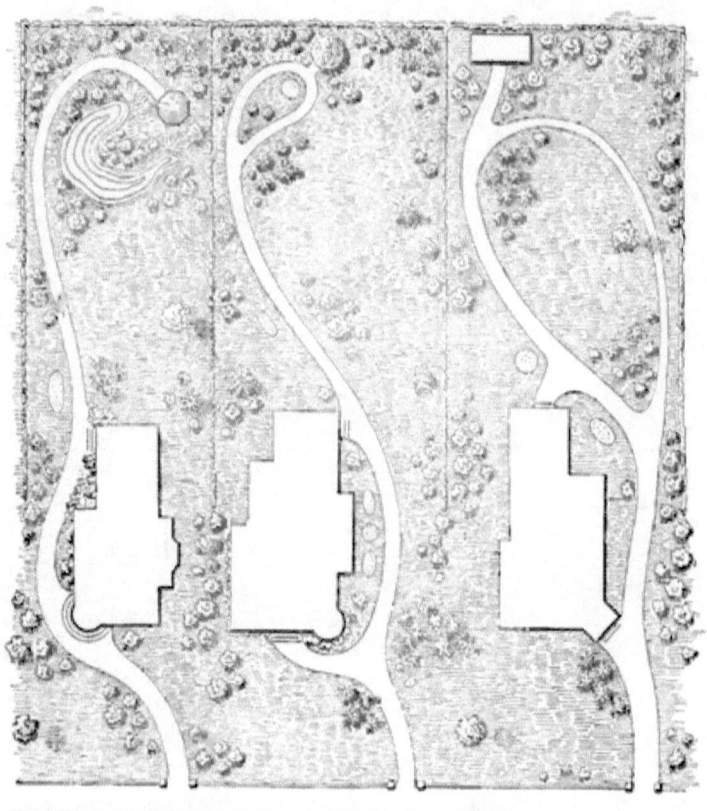

A.   B.   C.

FIG. 21.—THREE SMALL SUBURBAN GARDENS. N. J. ROSE.

which, however, can be rendered very attractive by proper planting. The building is placed lengthways on the lot, the entrance being at the left corner. The surface is slightly undulating. At the extreme back an unsightly gravel-pit has been made into a small, irregular pond with clean concrete bottom, so as to retain sufficient water at all times. The planting is simple and attractive. Here the lawn has been graded to form a somewhat rounded surface gradually sloping to the water's edge, thence rising into a small knoll on which a pavilion is erected. The front is open to the street, the lawn being continuous with those of the neighboring gardens. Behind the house the lot is enclosed by a thin, evergreen hedge. We have several open spaces of lawn, one quite large between the house and the pond, and a smaller one in front of the house. The groups are mostly of flowering shrubs with here and there a tree, a magnolia, hawthorn, or buckeye. Several hemlocks, firs, and other evergreen trees form a background behind the pavilion, and a smaller group is seen near the house. On either side of the kitchen entrance there is a small rockery for dwarf and choice plants only, sheltered from the strong sunshine during the better part of the day, and farther back on the opposite side of the walk a small bed for spring and summer flowers. The walk is a narrow one, six feet wide in front of the house, four feet behind, leading by graceful curves direct to the house and to the pond and pavilion. B and C in the same figure are plans of similar lots 60 by 200 feet. In the first of these there are a few beds for summer flowers, a rockery by the corner of the house, a bower of climbing roses, and several groups of evergreen trees and shrubs. The two plans differ but slightly, showing two ways of treating similar places. In C, a small workshop is shown at the back part instead of a pavilion. While the front of these three gardens is open to the street, the lawn is edged with a low stone enclosure surmounted with vases for flowering plants on each side of the entrance.

Fig. 22 shows one of the smallest of small gardens on a

piece of land 25' by 150', a size common in many suburban towns. Here we have a small piece of ground set apart for vegetables and flowers in the backyard besides the workshop. A flower-border runs along the south side of the house, and the whole is enclosed by a hedge, the straight lines of which are relieved by a few choice evergreen trees, and flowering shrubs.

Fig. 23 represents a city garden 50 by 150 feet. There is a stable behind, a drive entering the back-garden under

FIG. 22.—SMALL CITY GARDEN.

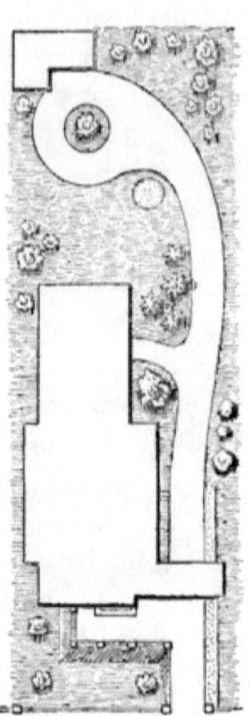

FIG. 23.—CITY GARDEN.

a porte-cochère, which shuts off the view from the street. The terrace in front is surmounted by a low stone wall with vases for flowering plants and vines. The lawn in front of the terrace is quite level and open to the street, edged with a stone enclosure similar to that on the terrace, with vases

on each side of the entrance. In this little garden there
are only a few choice flowering shrubs and evergreen trees:
a suitable place for flowers is provided in the border along
the drive, on both sides of the porte-cochère.

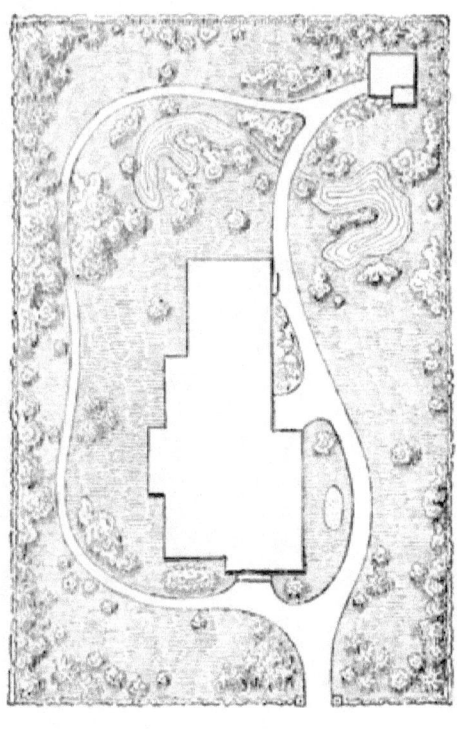

FIG. 24.—PRIVATE SUBURBAN GARDEN.

Fig. 24 is a more complete plan of a garden 100 by 150
feet. The place is screened and protected on all sides by
means of shrubberies, leaving the scenery within complete in
itself with open spaces of lawn and a small but beautiful
body of water. The pond being small, the bottom is made of

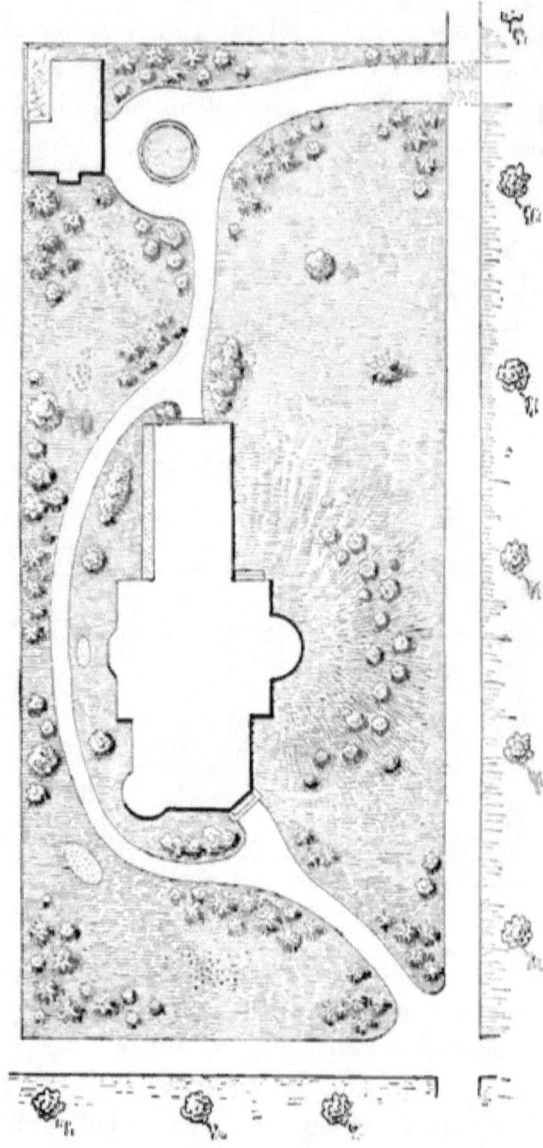

FIG. 25.—SUBURBAN VILLA GARDEN. N. J. ROSE.

concrete; it is supplied with water from the general water-works. The ground is slightly undulated; all the variety of the soil surface has been produced by means of the soil excavated from the pond, the walks, and in building the house. In one place the path leads through a shady grove of white birch, bordered by a few flowering shrubs, haw-thorn and viburnum, the ground being covered with various choice woodland flowers and ferns. There are rockeries instead of flower-beds near the pavilion, and by the side of the residence, and one single bed for flowers in front of the veranda. A small garden like this must be kept absolutely clean and trim to give a good impression. As nearly all external views are shut off, and the screen-planting breaks the force of high winds, the scenery within is secluded and peaceful, and many choice flowers and shrubs can be grown to perfection here. The whole is en-closed by means of a low, well trimmed hedge, and open-ings through the shrubbery give passers-by a glimpse of the scenery within.

Fig. 25 is the plan of a corner lot, 100 by 225 feet. The house stands on a slight elevation, which slopes gradually to the sidewalk. The hillside is girded by a few small flowering trees and shrubs. Besides this there are several groups of flowering shrubs and evergreen trees with a few specimens of shade-trees on the lawn, a purple beech and a white silver fir. Back of the house is a border for herba-ceous plants, and at some distance two flower-beds. The drive enters from the side street, and turns in front of the stable, in the upper left-hand corner, around a fountain. In the grass a few patches of spring flowers are marked by

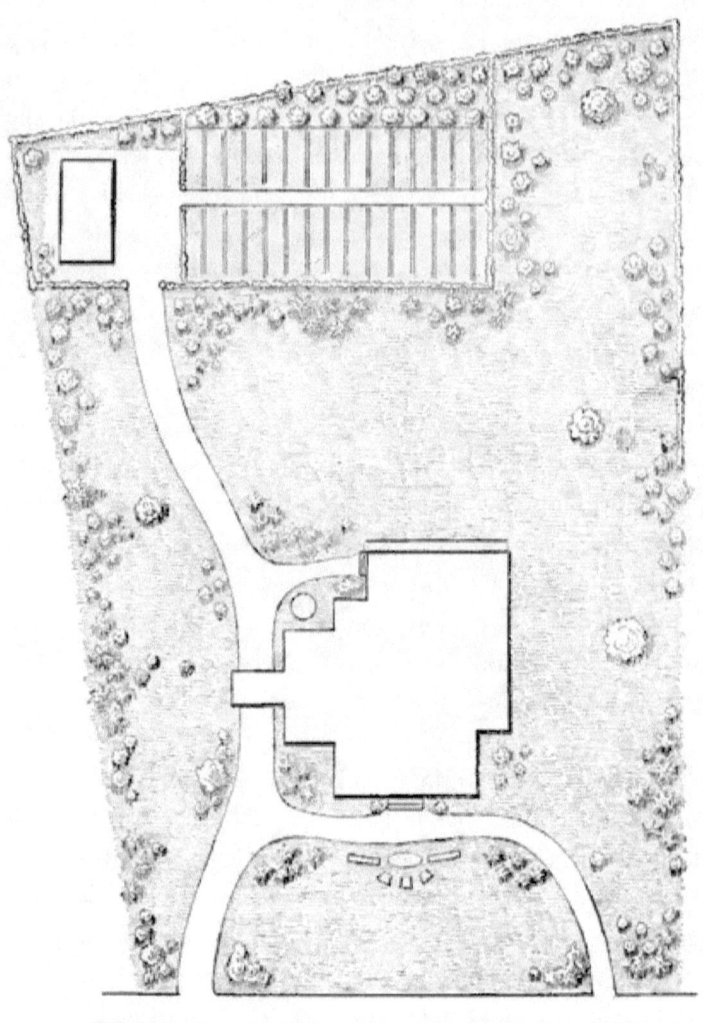

FIG. 26.—GROUNDS OF A SUBURBAN RESIDENCE. N. J. ROSE.

round dots or rings. These consist of crocus, snowdrops, two-leaved scilla, glory of the snow, and daffodils.

A somewhat larger and more pretentious place is represented in Fig. 26. This lawn covers nearly an acre of ground, with a frontage of 150 feet wide. In front of the barn, and enclosed by a hedge, there is a good-sized vegetable garden with a few choice fruit-trees on one side, and ample room for flower borders and small fruit. On the front lawn a few carpet beds are arranged in a semicircle around a larger one, and behind the house there is a border for herbaceous plants.

In Fig. 27 we have a plan of a villa garden of between four and five acres. The residence is simple and attractive, built of brick and stone. The grounds are more elaborate in design than is usual in this country, entailing more care and giving more satisfaction than the usual run of gardens. It is merely shown as an example of what can be done on so small a place. The vegetable garden is sufficient for a large family. Fruit-trees are planted here and there in the lawn near the vegetable garden and form quite attractive groups, especially when flowering. The drive to the stable is an avenue of red maples; it is bordered by flowering shrubs and herbaceous plants. There are wide open spaces of lawn, shady groves, and thickets or shrubberies with a variety of woodland flowers and creeping vines. On the north, the lake shore forms a very pleasing feature with small coves and bays and low woody promontories. The plan explains itself and needs no further comment.

In designing a garden or park there are certain qualities that must be taken into consideration. First of these and

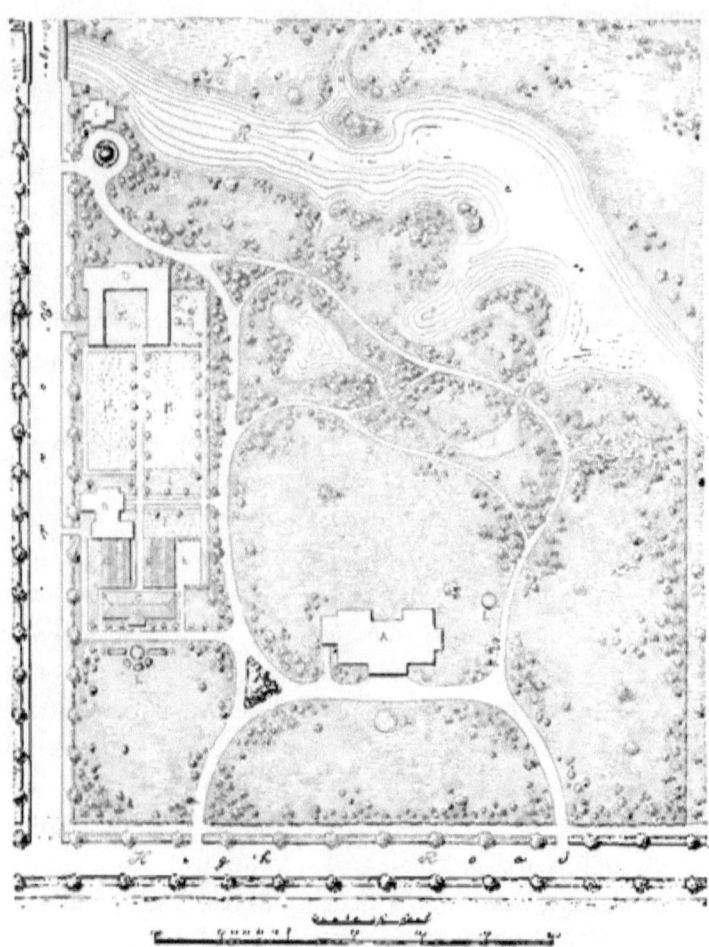

FIG. 27. HOME-GROUNDS OF A COUNTRY RESIDENCE. N. JÖNSSON ROSE.

A. Dwelling-house. B. Gardener's lodge. C. Conservatory and green-houses. D. Stables. E. Pavilion. F. Pavement. G. Place for composts and manures. H, H, Quarters for vegetables. I. Small Fruits. K. Children's playground. L. Flower-beds. M. Rocky knoll. N. Artificial modification of the river. O. Fruit-trees planted in natural groups.

most important is *Proportion*. It is necessary to make the
different parts proportionate in size with the size of the
grounds; small groups of smaller trees and shrubs for lesser
places, and larger groups of larger trees and shrubs for larger
places. And this rule, applicable to the plantations, must
also be observed in the construction of drives, walks, and
buildings. Another important quality is *Usefulness*. This
means that everything in the garden must have a meaning
and a purpose, not necessarily a material use. Every curve
in a walk or drive must have a reason for being and a purpose in leading to some object or other; every shrub and
tree must be pleasing and appropriate in its place. There
must be *Congruity* in the different elements composing the
scenery; no sudden breaks nor abnormal parts and positions
that cannot be accounted for, but gradual changes only; so
that one part is joined to another imperceptibly, shrubberies
vanishing in lawns and lawns losing themselves in glades
and groves. Without *Variety* and a proper difference in
the various parts that compose the scenery, the garden will
soon become flat and uninteresting to the common mind.
There should be something new and interesting every day
and season of the year. There must be no stereotyped
parts. Even the same groups should wear a different expression at different times of the day, and much more so
during different seasons; abounding in flowers in spring,
taking the glossy and sober hues of summer, changing into
blazing colors in autumn, and stretching picturesque and
graceful crowns to the sky in winter, followed by the tender
tints of bud and leaf, and rich with the various flowers
that form an undergrowth in early spring. Variety not

only in form and color, but in odors and sounds, in lights and shadows, is necessary to give the right impression. *Repose:* But although variety is the most salient factor in the planning of a garden, this variety must not be carried to excess, so as to give an impression of restlessness. Repose, dignity, and a peaceful expression are necessary for quiet rest and recreation. Wide open lawns, masses of trees, not too mixed, clear sheets of water—all embody this quality of repose. *Harmony* and *Contrast* go hand in hand; they are not antagonistic if rightly understood. There is often harmony between the most widely different forms and colors; scarlet, blue, and white, as represented in the field poppy, the ox-eye daisy, and the cornflower, combine the qualities of harmony and contrast. Two so widely different plants as the elm and the ivy, or the spruce and the prairie-rose, go in practice well together harmoniously; yet vastly different in form and color. By combining in intricate and inexplicable ways various forms and colors, nature sometimes creates the most enchanting scenery out of strongly opposing elements. Shadbush and hemlock, birch and pine, evergreen mountain laurels beside the deciduous azalea, are examples of such combinations.

It must further be remembered to take into consideration the quality and nature of soil and location, as one class of plants is especially adapted to one kind of soil, and another to quite a different one. We have seen that the seaside flora is quite different from that of a fertile plain or valley, and these, in turn, differ from the high mountain regions in the nature of their vegetation. But when a garden or park is a finished whole in itself, as the city park or garden must

of necessity be, we may quite properly introduce plants
from all regions, and grow them under as natural conditions
as is possible by artificial means. There we may have luxurious water-plants from the tropics, as the lotus, growing
naturally in ponds and lakes; and alpine plants flowering
freely on the sunny slopes of a rockery not far away. The
impression will be as pleasing as if the combination had
been made by nature itself. But when the garden is to be
a part only of a wide landscape, then it should be in entire
harmony with the whole, of which it possibly is the bright-
est and most beautiful spot.

The illustrations to this chapter give a fair idea of the
correct curvature of roads and walks, and the picturesque
outlines of shrubberies and other plantations. Drives and
walks must be as direct as possible, no bends or curves
being made simply for their own sake. A drive is naturally led around a knoll or hill and not across it, for the
grade would be too steep and the outline too stiff and
formal. In crossing a stream it must be done at right
angles, not obliquely or lengthways over the water; the
same rule must be observed when leading a path through a
hedge or other enclosure. The outlines of shrubberies and
groups of trees must never be too formal or rounded; a
slight irregularity will produce better effects of shade and
light and a more beautiful outline. Here and there stray
shrubs and trees should be planted to unite different groups
into larger masses, or to form specimens on the lawn. This
and like subjects will be more fully treated in subsequent
chapters.

IV.

GRADING.

GRADING is one of the most important operations connected with landscape-gardening. It is the plastic side of the art, just as planting is the pictorial side, one supplying form, the other color. By grading, a rough or broken surface may be made into softly undulating ground; if flat and characterless, it can be altered and hollowed out into shallow dells, or raised into low mounds, rounded slopes, and picturesque knolls. Grading means the creation of all the variety of the surface and the general improvement of the ground in both an artistic and practical sense. In small places there is, as a rule, but little grading to do, and that of the most simple kind, such as filling low ground, levelling the surface near the residence, and making terraces and lawns. In larger grounds it is often necessary to make quite important changes, as to alter the course of a stream, or to make the outlines of a symmetrical pond or lake sinuous and picturesque. If intelligently done, comparatively little work will produce good results. A slightly undulating surface may be made simply by using the soil excavated

from the drives and roads, as seen in Fig. 28. The low,
raised mound will form a good place for a shrubbery.
Supposing it is desirable to make the flat surface represented by the straight line in Fig. 29 into an undulated
surface represented by the dotted line in the same figure.
The difference in the level between A and B will be one

FIG. 28.—HOW TO UTILIZE SOIL EXCAVATED FROM A DRIVE FOR SLIGHT VARIATIONS
OF THE GROUND.

foot, yet we have only removed six inches of soil from A
to B; the result is the little rounded hill at B and the
shallow dell at A. This effect may afterwards be considerably heightened by means of judicious planting, as indicated in the diagram. If we increase the depth of the
excavation, indicated in this figure, from six inches to six
feet, and the length from sixteen to two hundred feet, we

FIG. 29. SHOWING HOW TO FORM GENTLE UNDULATIONS OF THE GROUND.

will have the same rolling surface on a much larger scale,
and the effect will be heightened. Instead of planting a few
dwarf, flowering plants on the little mound, we now have
the opportunity to plant a large and varied shrubbery on
the slope of a considerable hill. But while it would be perfectly safe to remove six inches of soil from A to B, if the
soil was of ordinary depth and fertility, by the removal

of six feet, all the fertile soil at A would be taken away, and at B it would be covered up beneath a considerable mass of subsoil, clay or gravel. Hence if so considerable a work was undertaken, the good soil would have to be dug away first, and put aside to be used as a surface soil again, after finishing the work.

FIG. 30.—HOW TO IMPROVE AND MODIFY LOW GROUND.

Supposing, too, we have a low, marshy piece of land in our grounds which must be either filled in or converted into a small lake. The straight line in Fig. 30 represents the water level, and the undulating line the surface of the ground. We desire to make our lake three feet deep, necessitating the removal of about four feet of soil from A, which we deposit at B, forming a nicely rounded slope fall-

FIG. 31.—OLD GRAVEL PIT TRANSFORMED INTO A SMALL ORNAMENTAL WATER WITH SLOPING SHORES.

ing gently to the water's edge. The result is better, and the effect is more varied, than if the same marshy ground had been filled in by means of soil brought from outside at great expense.

By intelligently grading the soil and taking advantage even of natural defects, we are able to produce good results economically. In another place there is a gravel pit, ragged

5

and unsightly, with a ditch of stagnant water at the bottom. The dotted line in Fig. 31 represents the actual surface. The solid line shows the grading after the work has been finished. It will be seen from the section in the figure that only a comparatively small quantity of material

FIG. 32.—METHOD OF MODIFYING STEEP SHORES.

has been handled to produce this effect. The result is a pleasantly sloping lawn, a clear, fresh-water pond surrounded by various ornamental trees and shrubs. Small streams and ponds are often found with steep banks, as seen in Fig. 32. In such cases an easy and natural slope to the water's edge should be made, as shown by the dotted

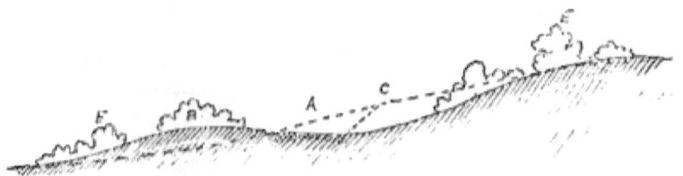

FIG. 33.—HOW TO MAKE A WALK ON SLOPING GROUND.

line in the same diagram. This, while not increasing the volume of water contained in the pond, widens the surface considerably, and gives a more natural and pleasing finish.

In the construction of walks and drives considerable grading is often necessary. Fig. 33 shows a sloping surface with a considerable fall. As it has been decided to construct a walk at A. it is clear that some grading must be done in order to make the roadbed perfectly level. It could be done in the manner indicated by the short, dotted line at C, but it is evidently better to make the surface as represented by the solid line. The soil excavated from A will be deposited at B to form a rounded slope, instead of a straight and angular one. If it is found necessary to make a deep cut for a drive or walk, as shown in Fig. 38, or if we want to modify an angular cut like that repre-

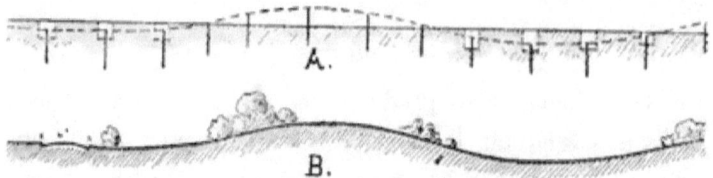

FIG. 34.—METHOD OF PLACING GRADE STAKES.

sented by the dotted line, here also we find that the rounded outline is the most pleasing and natural one, and we modify the angular surface, deposit the soil farther away, with a view to planting the shrubberies afterwards to heighten the effect. In all cases where deep excavations are necessary, a sufficiently deep layer of surface soil must be provided in finishing the work.

If it is necessary to grade according to a given plan, sectional drawings being supplied by the landscape architect, it is important to transfer the measures from the drawing to the ground. Fig. 34 shows how this is done. The shaded line represents the actual surface of the ground which it is desirable to change into an undulating lawn, as shown by the dotted line. By means of pegs driven into

the soil on the line A–B at given distances, we mark the
form of the new surface. Where excavations have to be
made, holes must be dug in the ground, in which the pegs
are driven to the desired depth, and where it is intended to
form a mound or knoll, the height of the pegs must cor-
respond with the height of the surface line, as shown in the
figure. The finished surface is shown in B.

Most of the work of grading on small places, where the
object is simply to round the surface of a lawn, or raise
low mounds for shrubberies or flower-beds, or to build terraces in front of a house, can be done by means of spade,
shovel, and wheelbarrow. Much of this work may be done
without wheeling or carting, as that shown in Fig. 29; the
soil from A may easily be thrown to B, where it can be
levelled and finished by means of a rake. But where the
work is considerable and soil has to be transported long distances, dumping carts are needed for the transportation,
and a man should be kept to level the soil as it is brought
on the ground. For shorter distances the use of wheelbarrows is more economical. If the soil is merely to be
shifted, to make slight variations in the ground, as in Fig.
34, it may be loosened by means of plowing, and scooped
from one place to the other. This is the most economical
manner of grading, if the soil is loose, or can be loosened
by the plow. As soon as one layer of soil has been removed in this way, another may be plowed up and scooped
away in its turn; and so on, until the desired result is
obtained, when the good soil put aside for covering can be
transported by the same means, and spread uniformly over
the surface.

As the roughest grading is done before the drives and
walks are finished, a kind of supplementary grading is
often needed before the lawns can be sodded and sown. It
is desirable to have all lawns smooth and finished, and the
surface soil must be well broken up: in small places, by
means of rake and shovel: in larger fields, by means of
harrowing and rolling. If the surface soil can be worked
thoroughly and enriched with dressings of manure and fillings of good loam at the time the grading is done, the extra
work of digging and plowing is not necessary. But as it
is only in certain places that the surface of the ground has

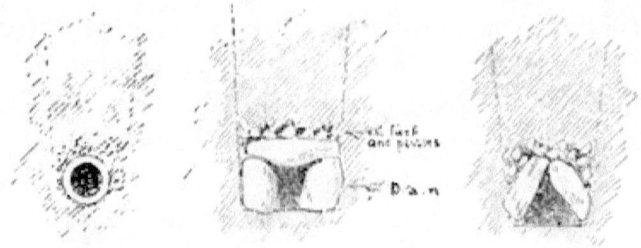

FIG. 35.—DRAINS OF ROUND TILES AND STONE DRAINS.

been altered, the whole ground should be thoroughly
spaded or plowed, and worked in the most approved manner to make the soil open and porous. If the subsoil consists of heavy clay, and the surface soil is rather light, or
vice versa, subsoiling for shrubberies and choice trees will
be well repaid, by a more luxurious and rapid growth than
could be expected without such work.

In close connection with grading comes the draining of
the ground. It is not always necessary except where land
is stiff and low. The best drains for a lawn or garden are

illustrated in Fig. 35. Round tiles are apt to become filled and clogged by the roots of trees and shrubs; they are best used in open places, where they are in no danger of being rendered useless.

On land with a stiff and clayey subsoil, drainage is a most important operation which must receive special attention. If the area to be drained is large and a number of trenches must be dug, a main drain with an easy flow to some large, open ditch or river is constructed. With this all the lateral drains are connected. Such drains should unite with the main drain at an acute angle, and can be from twenty-five to fifty feet apart, or more, according to the need of the ground. Ordinarily, a main drain of round tiles from four to six inches in diameter, will carry off all the superfluous water of several acres. For lateral drains the one and a half or two-inch size is sufficient. Round tiles when laid are put end to end, but not joined. A minimum fall of six inches in one hundred feet is necessary, and may be had on the most level ground. No drain should be nearer the surface than three feet. Hence if the ground is almost level, as most watery land is apt to be, the drains at their outlet must be several feet deeper than at the other end. For instance, in digging a drain six hundred feet long on flat land, it is necessary, in order to ensure the proper fall of six inches in a hundred feet, to make it six feet deep at its outlet, while at its opposite end it is only three feet deep. In a garden, larger and deeper drains, and a greater fall is needed than in an open field. If the drains are made very shallow, a greater number are needed to drain a given piece of land. The depth and distance must

of necessity be in accordance with the more or less watery
nature of the soil. In digging the drains it is well to begin
at the lower end. Any ordinary workman can then easily
see for himself if the fall is sufficient, as there is always apt
to be more or less water at the proper depth, which, if the
fall is right, will easily flow away. Drains thus roughly
dug must, however, be gone over afterwards by a skilled
workman. It is well to employ the most skilled and expert
workman to lay the drain, whether it be of stone or of
round tile.

V.

DRIVES AND WALKS.

DRIVES and walks are necessary for comfort and convenience, and are chiefly intended for use and not for ornament. Still they should be as ornamental and symmetrical as possible, with a regularly rounded surface, raised somewhat above the level of the lawn, and with edges slightly lower. They must be uniform in width and as direct as possible. Straight walks, such as those common in old French gardens, are seldom used at present. A winding path is more to the purpose, as in its course it leads to more objects of interest than a straight one. But all curves must be simple and have a reason for being, such as an object to which they lead, or an obstruction of some kind or other that must be avoided. And, even without such an obstruction, the walk is never laid straight, but a shrubbery, or a flower-bed, or some other object is placed so as to form an apparent reason for the sinuous windings, which are essential in order to avoid straight and formal lines. In Fig. 36 the walk leads between A and B, and while it could have been made perfectly straight when constructed, it is advan-

tageous to have it as it is for several reasons. First, it is
now in harmony with the grounds; secondly, as the walk
winds in and out among trees and shrubberies, the scenery
appears more rich and varied than it would otherwise do.
Furthermore, the reason for this curve, which did not exist
at the time the path was made, is now very tangible in the
form of a considerable shrubbery.

Fig. 37 represents the plan of a mound or knoll with a
pavilion, which it is desired to reach with a path from A.
The most direct route is too steep, and in order to have an

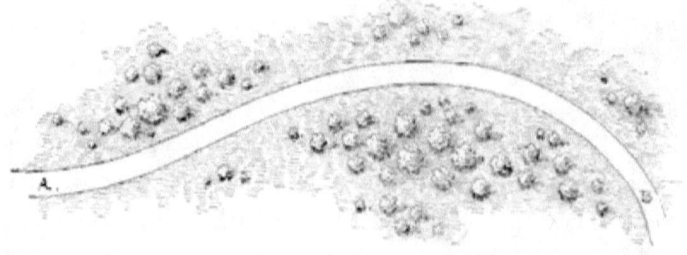

FIG. 36.—CURVED ROAD ROUNDING A SHRUBBERY.

easy ascent, we make the path as shown in the diagram.
Behind the same hill there is a bathing-house on the shore
of a lake. Here again we abandon the most direct line, to
make the descent as gradual as possible, and the path in its
winding course brings us, first opposite a sloping lawn to
the north, then, northeast to groves and shrubberies; and
lastly, east and south, a transparent sheet of water bursts
upon our view. The width and size and number of
walks must vary according to the size of a place and be in
accordance with the actual need. When the paths divide,
as shown in some of the plans submitted in a previous chap-

ter, the main path should always be broader than the by-
paths. The manner in which one road joins another is also
illustrated in these plans. Intervening lawns must not be
too narrow, and two paths should never be laid on parallel
lines close together. In large parks, a walk or promenade
may run alongside of a drive, as they are intended for
different uses, and may in that case be separated by narrow
strips of lawn, with here and there a tree or shrub.

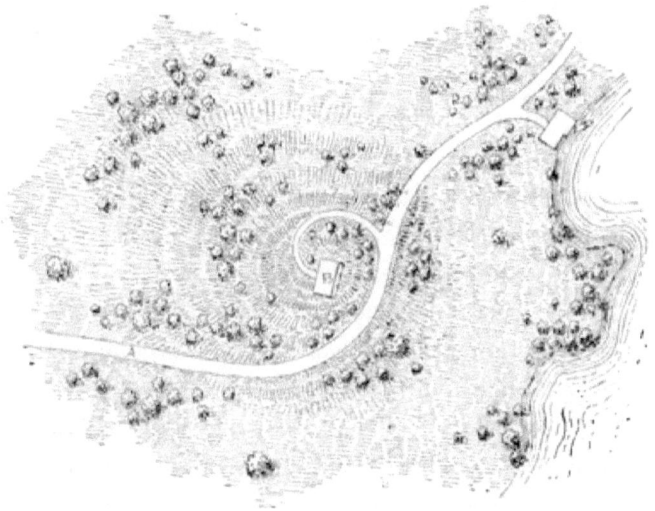

FIG. 37.—WALK LAID TO THE TOP OF A HILL. HOW TO AVOID STEEP GRADES.

As soon as a plan has been accepted, and before any
other work is done, the drives and walks should be staked
out according to the plan, and if the surface is to be raised
or sunk, this must be indicated by means of pegs placed in
the middle at a suitable distance. If the road is to be considerably lower than the surface of the soil, as in Fig. 38,
holes must be dug, in which the pegs are driven, and the

correct height must be fixed by means of instruments.
The exact location will be found by measuring the distances
on the working drawing, and transferring them to the
ground with precision. When the curves are long, stakes
may be placed ten or more
feet apart, but when the turns
are short and rounded, the
distance should be less, so
that the exact outline will be

FIG. 38.—GRADING THE SIDES OF A SUNKEN
ROAD.

well defined. If the roads are to be made of asphalt or
cement, a specialist must be employed. The making of
macadamized drives and walks is, however, well understood
by most gardeners and may be left to them. The diagrams supplied herewith illustrate the different methods of
constructing a drive or walk.

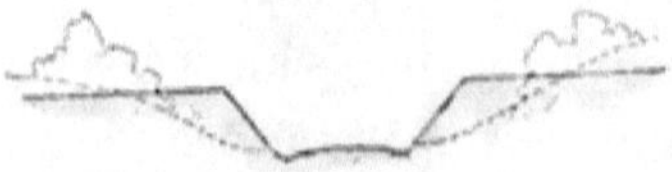

First, the outline should be marked by means of a line
laid on the curve indicated by the stakes, and the edge
cut out with a spade. Then the soil is dug away to
the desired depth, the road-bed being made equally broad
and deep from end to end, with the surface slightly rounded
and a couple of inches higher in the middle than at the sides.
If the soil is loose and uneven after digging, it must be
broken, trodden, and beaten down, so as to form a solid
bed.

If the drive is large, and intended to be used frequently,
a good and solid foundation must be made. From four to
eight inches of broken stone or small pebbles should be put
in the bottom and well packed together with a rammer, or
it may be rolled. Over this, when in a proper condition, a
layer of about two inches of sandy clay or other binding

material, will be necessary to fill up crevices, and to join the
whole together. This layer in its turn must be spread,
and packed into the mass beneath, by ramming or rolling.
For surface covering, about three inches of coarse gravel
should be used, from which the larger stones and the finer
sediment have been removed, or can be raked off afterwards. When this is raked uniformly over the surface and
rolled or beaten down, the main part of the road is finished.
The finish of the edge requires some skill and precision. As
a rule, the edges of walks and drives—that is, the grass
edge—should be finished before the top layer of gravel is
put on. These should be firmly and solidly made of tough
and even sods. The sodded edges on both sides of the walk
must be on the same level, no matter how different the
general surface of the lawn.

A piece of board cut out as shown in Fig. 39, is used to
make the surface of the walk uniformly rounded and to
mark its exact width.
By means of this board
we can also easily find
out whether the oppo-

FIG 39.—GAUGE USED IN ROAD-MAKING.

site sides of the walk are on the same level, by placing a
common spirit level on the straight upper edge. Of course
this gauge must be equally wide at both ends and perfectly
straight.

In different places the material obtainable differs greatly. In many stoneless countries, oyster shells, hard clay,
and other materials are used in road-making. Oyster shells
make good, dry, and solid walks for a garden, especially if
covered with a thin layer of fine pebbles. Small pebbles of

uniform size, as large as peas or hazel-nuts, up to an inch in diameter, are often found in large quantities on the sea-shore. These are excellent for the construction of all kinds of walks and drives in a garden. If the walk is small and the road-bed has been made perfectly solid by means of ramming, a layer of these, about two inches deep, spread over the ground and beaten down firmly, will make a dry and durable path in most places. On low ground it is practical to make road material

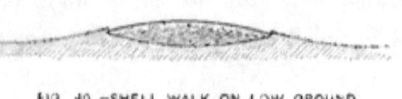

FIG. 40. —SHELL WALK ON LOW GROUND.

thickest in the middle, as shown in the diagram, Fig. 40.

Fig. 41 shows a section of a drained walk on clayey soil. As the clay prevents the water from sinking, the drain is necessary to carry away the water after heavy rains. After draining through the covering, or making its way from the edge of the walk along the scooped-out surface of

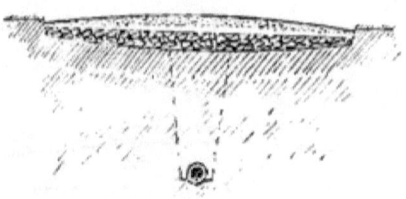

FIG. 41 —DRAINED WALK OR DRIVE ON LOW GROUND.

the bed, it sinks without difficulty to the drain. Special drainage for drives and walks is needed only on flat and low land, or where the subsoil is stiff and impenetrable. In all places where the subsoil is gravelly or porous, drainage is superfluous. If the

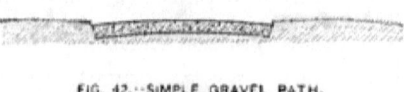

FIG. 42.--SIMPLE GRAVEL PATH.

incline of a drive is very steep, the edges are likely to be

cut, or washed away in places during heavy rains. To
prevent this, shallow gutters, about eighteen inches
wide, made of cobblestones from three to five inches in
diameter, are needed on both sides of the drive. The
stones should be set in sand, and the finished gutter
must be slightly lower than the edge of the drive or walk,
as shown in the diagram, Fig. 43. Simple gravel paths of
coarse material are solid enough for most small gardens and

FIG. 43.—LARGE DRIVE WITH SURFACE DRAINAGE ; *a a*, GUTTERS.

will generally keep dry and comfortable. Paths of flag-
stones and boards are ugly and unsigthly—out of all harmony with a garden ; but asphalt and cement walks are
both nice and comfortable.

In the construction of walks, besides such common tools
as the spade, shovel, and rake, a rammer of hard wood or cast
iron, as shown in Fig. 19, is needed. It is used in the road-
bed for making the soil firm, and afterwards to ram down
stones and gravel. For marking the edge a strong line is
necessary, and to cut out the edge of the sod an edging
iron is better than a spade, as it cuts cleaner and with
greater ease.

The walks may be kept clean either by sweeping, if the
surface is perfectly solid, or by using a short-toothed rake.
Cement and asphalt walks can be washed when necessary
by means of the garden hose.

VI.

GROUPING AND MASSING OF TREES AND SHRUBS.

F we examine the composition of some of the most beautiful scenery in a young wood or copse, where the majority of trees and shrubs have sprung from seeds, we find they are generally formed in the following manner: A young tree, just reaching maturity, is standing alone in an uncultivated field; numerous seedlings spring up around its base, and in a few years we have a small group around the mother tree. The younger trees vary in size according to age, and the group has a picturesquely rounded appearance. In the course of time the younger trees reach maturity, and in their turn become centres of new groups. The result is an irregular, compound group, with taller trees here and there, surrounded by smaller ones, and apparently scattered without order, but in reality placed according to a very natural law. Primarily these groups consist of only one species; in that illustrated in Fig. 44, of scarlet oak; having their origin in the one mother tree, by-and-by seeds of flowering shrubs lodge among the fallen leaves, and in their

turn grow up and form centres of new groups among the
trees, or on the outskirts of the wood.   After a while, various herbaceous plants take the place of the grass and cover
the ground with a carpet of flowers.   Now we have a composite group of trees, shrubs, and flowering plants, the out-

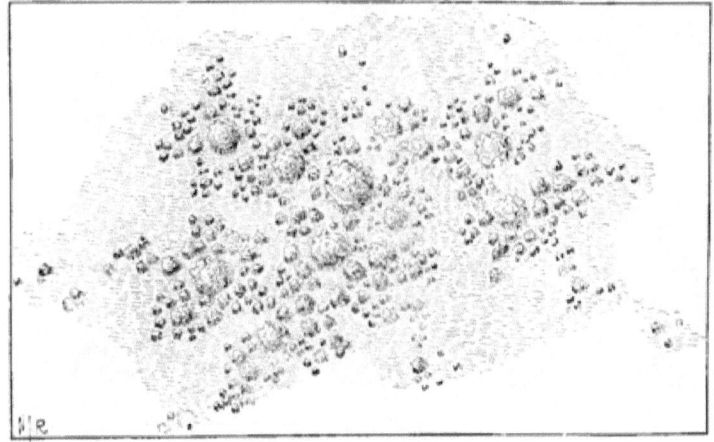

FIG. 14.—NATURAL GROUP OF OAKS.

lines of which are sinuous and undulating, here advancing,
there retreating, and formed after the manner shown in the
figure.

All minor groups consist chiefly of one kind of variously
sized plants, which later on unite into larger masses.   Groups
of various species are finally brought together, and the result
is a mixed wood of trees and shrubs differing greatly in
form and habit.   But the distribution of the various kinds
is regulated in the nicest manner; for, as some species
thrive best in the bright sunshine, others in partial
shade, and some prefer the dry ground, while many seek
the moist and swampy land, the groups of trees and flowers

of the various localities differ greatly and are characteristic
of each.   On the open borders of wood and copse we find
the sun-loving thorns, in the shade of trees in high and dry
positions, the mountain laurel, while the swamp honeysuckle seeks shade and moisture.

From this superficial analysis of a small wood we may
gather some practical hints on the grouping and massing of
trees : first, how to make the outline varied and picturesque,
by uniting many small groups of different size into larger
ones : secondly, how to make the sky-line pleasing to the
eye and in harmony with the general formation of the
group: and, finally, how trees and shrubs should be dis-

FIG. 45.—COMPOSITE GROUP OF TREES AND SHRUBS SHOWING PICTURESQUE SKY-LINE.

tributed in a shrubbery according to their nature and
habit, in order to develop their best qualities.

The smaller groups should preferably consist of one
kind only, or of several varieties of one species.   But similar
forms, as the different species of lilac, may be brought together in the same group, when the taller kinds, such as the
common lilac, should be surrounded by the smaller Chinese
or Persian varieties.   In a composite plantation the taller
groups must be placed in the more central parts, and in
the simple group the tallest tree or shrub should be in the
middle, both for practical and æsthetic reasons.   The simple groups may consist of three or more individual plants,

which should be placed at a sufficient distance to allow each
the fullest possible development. One plantation should
not consist of too many species mixed without order, but
the different groups should mingle in a natural manner to
form a united whole. Coniferous trees make the best impression when planted by themselves in groups and masses,
in the same manner as deciduous shrubs and trees. When
two plantations meet, one evergreen and the other deciduous, the transition should be gradual; spruce and birch, and
other trees will mix together, and the plantation in such
places must be less dense than in the main groups; glades

FIG. 46.—MIXED PLANTATION OF DECIDUOUS TREES AND EVERGREENS.

and vistas and open patches of grass should alternate with
the scattered groups.

There must be harmony of form and color between the
different plants that compose the shrubbery, but monotony
should be avoided. If plants with light foliage are placed
in front of dark ones the effect is much better than if they
were planted in an opposite way, hence the beautiful effect
of flowering shrubs with a group of spruce and pine for a
background. Trees with ovate or cordate leaves, such as
the different varieties of birch and beech, may be placed in
one group. Others with sinuous or incised leaves, such as
the many forms of oak, in another, and pinnately leaved

forms of all shapes and sizes will unite well into groups
and masses of their own.

As a rule, each individual plant should have sufficient
room to develop its full beauty, and to allow of a growth
of grass beneath. But when planting is done for immediate effect, the trees and shrubs must be planted much
closer together, and then the superfluous plants should be
removed as soon as the group becomes crowded.

Coniferous trees especially must be watched in order to

FIG. 47. - SCREEN PLANTING.
PSEUDOTSUGA DOUGLASII.   ABIES NOBILIS GLAUCA.   PICEA PICHTA.

prevent the loss of the lower branches, and all superfluous
trees must be removed without hesitation, as soon as this
becomes necessary.

In order to provide shelter, or for the sake of excluding
disagreeable views, or to render a place more secluded and
private, dense plantations are often formed around the
entire garden. The outlines of this screen-planting should

be as irregular and varied as the space will allow. In some places, where the space is sufficient, it should be composed of taller trees, edged with larger and smaller shrubs, and finished off towards the lawn. In other parts it should be much lower, consisting only of a dense mass of shrubs. In such plantations grass will seldom grow to perfection, and the ground is generally kept bare and forked every autumn and occasionally enriched with a heavy covering of manure. In that case the ground is kept perfectly clean during the summer months by means of frequent raking, and the grass edge along the border must be cut in the same manner as around a flower bed. In many gardens all the shrubberies are planted and treated in this manner, and only a few specimen trees and shrubs on the lawn stand free in the grass. This way of keeping a shrubbery involves a considerable amount of labor, and it is far better to have the ground in dense shrubberies and groves covered with woodland flowers, of which there are so many exquisitely beautiful kinds. A choice selection of these should be planted indiscriminately in groups, in places where they are most likely to succeed, and they will generally spread over the whole surface if left alone. If it is desirable to introduce any special kind that requires a different soil from that of the garden, deep layers of leaf soil or peat may be dug in in suitable places, to form irregular beds for such varieties. From sylvan scenes of this nature all coarse weeds must be excluded; the principal masses should consist of windflowers, sweet woodruff (*Asperula odorata*), lesser celandine, fumitory (*Dicentra formosa* and *eximia*, various species of *Corydalis*), Alp-violets (*Cyclamen Europeum*), and many kinds of orchids. Under the shelter of trees with light foliage, such as the birches, rhododendrons, mountain laurels, mahonias, euonymus, and hollies find an ideal home. Many climbers and creeping plants may also be introduced into the shrubbery, and where the ground is low and rich various kinds of ferns should be planted. As a

FIG. 48.--RHODODENDRON DAURICUM AS UNDERGROWTH IN A WOOD.

background for these there may be some scattered and partly buried rocks and stones. Narrow woodland paths should lead from the freer and more open parts of the garden into these secluded spots where the landscape gardener's art clasps the hand of nature.

The delicate work of properly arranging trees and shrubs
—the most severe trial of the designer's knowledge and
ability—must never be neglected or left to chance or accident. Complete detail plans should be furnished as guides
to planting, with the positions marked and the name of each
species appended. Afterwards it is important that the
place of each plant be properly located on the ground and
marked by means of labelled sticks or stakes.

If this preliminary work is completed, the ground having
been previously dug or subsoiled, the planting may take
place either in the fall, if the weather is good and the soil

FIG. 49.—GROUP AND SPECIMEN SHRUBS NEAR A WALK.

is sufficiently moist, or very early in spring as soon as the
frost has left the ground and the soil is in a workable condition. If the planting is left till spring, the holes may nevertheless be dug during the autumn or winter; they should
be made considerably larger and deeper than is actually
necessary. The frost will have a most beneficial and disin-
tegrating effect on the soil; it will be light and friable
during the earliest dry weather in spring, and will fall with
greater ease around the tender roots of the plant.

On receiving shrubs and trees the roots should be ex-
amined, and all broken or mutilated parts must be cut clean

with a sharp knife. They are then heeled in—that is, put close together in a trench, until the time of planting. Just before planting, the top must be pruned, the extreme tips of the young shoots being cut off above an eye, and if the tree is large, a branch or two may have to be entirely removed so as to reduce the top sufficiently. For evergreen trees of all kinds, the roots must be fully preserved and left undisturbed in a clump of soil, which should be unbroken at the time of planting. Conifers, especially spruce and pine, would be entirely ruined by pruning. As a rule, the top of evergreens cannot be reduced without bad results. Coniferous trees and shrubs may be planted in August and September, or early in spring before the commencement of growth. They must be planted with extreme care; failures are common on account of ignorance of this fact.

The actual planting is best done by two men, one to dig and throw the soil about the roots, the other to hold the plant in position, to imbed the roots in a natural position, and to trample down the soil firmly. When it is intended to move and plant very large trees, a trench should be dug around the roots at a sufficient distance from the stem before frost sets in, and the clump must be undermined so as to allow of removing as soon as the soil has frozen to a solid mass. The excavation for planting must be done at the same time. Smaller ones may be shifted at almost any time during the planting season, and the root-clump may be boxed up or wrapped in canvas. Specially constructed carts are used for transportation. Newly-planted subjects require an occasional watering if the summer is dry; whenever this is necessary the soil should be thoroughly soaked.

The selection of plants is hardly less important than the actual arrangement, as certain species are best adapted to special soils. The willows and poplars, without exception, are found in rich alluvial soil, and often near water. Other species grow best in rocky ground, as the beech and hornbeam. Most birches and many coniferous trees do well in poor and gravelly soil.

The most thrifty, healthy, and vigorous plants should be chosen in preference to any showy variety, which is subject to the ravages of insects or disease. For small places it is necessary to select the choicest material obtainable, as an abundance of flowers, neat and compact species of evergreens, and the general beauty of the few plants used is of more importance here than in large places, where good effects are produced by an artistic arrangement of a higher order.

Form and color must also be considered, and in order to produce a good effect the various shades of green must be arranged so as to make the most beautiful contrast. If light or glaucous-leaved species, as the buckthorn or oleaster, or flowering trees like the magnolia or flowering dogwood, are placed in front of dark evergreens, or vice versa, the impression will be better than if both foreground and background were of the same shade.

Most wonderful results are obtained by properly arranging species which assume showy autumn tints. The beauty of the foliage in autumn is unsurpassed by any other phenomenon in the world of plants, the height of the flowering season not excepted, and it is therefore quite proper to select species which, in addition to other attractions, possess this quality, as the season of autumnal coloring is far more lasting than that of spring in this country.   Most beautiful are birches, elms and tulip-trees, which turn pure yellow; scarlet oaks, red maples and cockspur thorns, which have foliage of the most brilliant scarlet, intermingled with orange and yellow.   Pepperidge, liquidambar, and, under favorable conditions, the beech, assume rich crimson tints which last for a considerable time.

The ripe fruit, abundant in many species, is also a factor, especially in the winter landscape.   Species with red or scarlet fruits, like the spindle-tree or the cockspur thorn, arranged among evergreens, form a very attractive feature of the scenery in winter.

VII.

DETACHED GROUPS AND SPECIMEN PLANTS.

O N the borders of shrubberies, smaller detached groups and specimen trees, must form a gradual transition between the denser plantation and the more open spaces of lawn. There should be no sudden change from one scenery to another, no rigorously marked borders of any kind. A better impression will be made if narrow stretches of lawn run far in among groves and shrubbery and finally vanish in an undergrowth of shrubs and flowers.

FIG. 50. FINE PLANTING, SHOWING EFFECT OF LIGHT AND SHADE.

To create this appearance is the chief purpose of detached groups and specimen trees. Specimens should also appeal

to our sense of beauty individually, through exquisite forms
and colors.

In planting these groups, three or more shrubs may be
arranged together in a free manner, so as to form a beautiful outline. They should consist of the very finest flower-

FIG. 51.—WEEPING BIRCH AS A SPECIMEN TREE.

ing plants: lilac, mock orange, roses, golden bells, hydran-
geas, many spireas, and tree-pæonies.

Flowering and other ornamental trees are generally
placed singly, but of some of the smaller kinds several may

be planted together, so as to make two or more stems spring, as nearly as possible, from the same place.

Among flowering trees, the showy magnolia, the halesia, red bud (*Cersis chinensis*), double-flowered hawthorns, with white and red flowers, sophora, Japanese crab (*Pyrus floribunda*), and the double-flowered plum (*Prunus triloba*) make exceptionally beautiful specimens.

There are several classes of lawn trees, differing in habit in shape of leaf, and in color. Some of the most picturesque ones, with slender, drooping branches, are the so-called *weeping trees*. These are available for no other purpose, but are very ornamental when placed on a wide, open lawn or near the margin of a lake or stream. There are two classes of weeping trees: deciduous and evergreen. The deciduous trees are : weeping beech, birch, willow, ash, elm, and sallow, the pendulous sophora and some others. There are only a few evergreen trees with drooping branches, one desirable and picturesque form being a variety of the Norway spruce.

Another and equally unique class of trees is formed by the *fastigiate* or *columnar* varieties of poplar, oak, birch, and some coniferous trees. These, while useful as specimen trees to a limited extent, are also very picturesque in a shrubbery.

Differing in the shape of the leaf only, but similar in habit to the species, are the many beautiful *cut-leaved* varieties of trees and shrubs. These varieties occur among the same class of trees that produce weeping and fastigiate forms, but are more numerous. There are cut-leaved varieties of birch, beech, alder, sycamore, and Japanese maple, all of which are very graceful and attractive as specimen trees.

A most remarkable and often very showy class of trees and shrubs are the almost innumerable varieties with *variegated*, or highly-colored foliage, ranging in color from silver-margined leaves, in a form of box elder, bright yellow, in golden elder and poplar, to a reddish color in red-leaved plum (*Prunus Pissardii*), and a black purple or coppery color in the purple-leaved varieties of birch and beech. All these, because of their unique habit or color, are especially well adapted to the embellishment of the lawn. They are all of garden origin.

The evergreen conifers, especially species of spruce and pine, such as the Spanish silver fir (*Abies Pinsapo*), the white silver fir (*Abies concolor*), the Nordmann fir, the stone pine (*Pinus cembra*), dwarf mountain pine (*Pinus Mugho*), and in places where they are hardy, the Japanese cypress (*Cryptomeria elegans*), the deodar (*Cedrus deodara*) and, umbrella pine (*Sciadopitys verticillata*) are extremely fine for the same purpose. Small groups of coniferous trees may form a special feature of the garden. They are especially appropriate on hillsides and declivities, on little knolls and in rockeries.

Many of the larger herbaceous plants, as goats' beard (*Spiraea aruncus*), oriental poppy, bocconia, and peony, form nice specimen plants for use along walks and drives.

These are the chief subjects for permanent planting. During the summer, tropical plants—palms, tree-ferns, and cycads—are frequently employed to produce unique and beautiful effects. In the South many of these may be

planted out permanently, besides various fine flowering
trees and shrubs of a sub-tropical nature, such as the
crape myrtles (*Lagerstraemia*), cape jessamine (*Gardenia*),

FIG. 52.—BOLD GROUPING OF TREES. LOMBARDY POPLAR AND PINE.
ROYAL GARDENS, KEW.

the camellia, Cattley's guava (*Psidium Cattleyanum*), and
coniferous trees of the genus Araucaria.

To select proper places for specimens on the lawn requires good judgment, as they, according to their position,
will make or mar the whole effect.

VIII.

ON THE PROPER USE OF HERBACEOUS PLANTS.

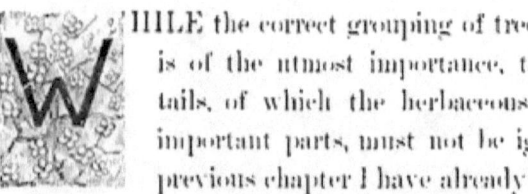HILE the correct grouping of trees and shrubs
is of the utmost importance, the lesser de-
tails, of which the herbaceous plants form
important parts, must not be ignored. In a
previous chapter I have already hinted at the
proper use of woodland flowers; but not only the woodland—every field, every sea-shore and meadow, bogs, river-
sides, and rocks all have their own characteristic flora, which
it is useless or undesirable to plant except under natural
conditions.

For our purpose it is best to consider severally the
proper use of each of these classes of herbaceous plants,
and to see under what conditions they may be naturalized
in parks and gardens:

1. *Woodland Flowers.*—Sylvan plants generally delight
in more or less shady positions, and in comparatively
light and moist soil, chiefly consisting of decayed leaves.
Some grow in scattered masses covering the whole expanse
of a wood with leaves and flowers. Among these are the
white anemone and the spring beauty. Others form well-

defined masses in shady thickets, as the May-apple: close
to the roots of trees, as the hepatica; in more open places,
as many lilies; or in sheltered positions among crumbling
rocks, as Solomon's-seal and maiden-hair fern. Ferns thrive
best in moist and shady woods on alluvial soil.

The richest herbaceous flora is generally found in the
most sheltered positions, where the soil is moist and loose,
and where the leaves of deciduous trees collect, as among
the low undergrowth of shrubs common in all well preserved woods. It is comparatively easy to establish plants
of this class, and success is most certain among such trees
as birch, dogwood, and oak, the roots of which penetrate
deep into the soil and which enrich the surface annually
with a new covering of leaves.

Besides our own wild flowers many exotic species are
excellent for naturalizing in woods and thickets, such as
oxlips, wild tulips, Turk's-cap lily, golden anemone, and
lesser celandine. Plants of a spreading habit producing
seeds in abundance may be sown late in autumn in the
place where they are to flower, or they may be planted in
scattered groups in spring, and once introduced will spread
naturally under favorable conditions. Species which grow
in clumps or in small groups should be planted in prepared
beds of well decayed leaf-mould. It is necessary in all cases
to be sure that the roots are perfect, and to press the soil
firmly around the plants. In rocky woods many delicate
and beautiful species may be grown in deep crevices of
rocks filled with moist vegetable soil.

The smaller the species, the greater the masses necessary
to produce a good effect. Groups or masses of wild flowers

FIG. 53.—TYPICAL WOODLAND FLOWERS, THE WOOD ANEMONE (A. SYLVÉSTRIS).

must in no case have any definite outlines; they should mingle with others, and gradually disappear in near-by groups, or advance in places on adjoining lawns. The following are a few of the best plants for naturalizing in woods and thickets: *In moist and shady ravines:* baneberry, false Solomon's-seal, mitrewort, golden anemone, Dutchman's-breeches, and many ferns. *On high rocky knolls:* Arnica, columbine, catchfly, wild pink, fire pink, saxifrage, stone-crop, and polypody. *Along woodland streams:* Blue violet, horsemint, omphalodes, wild geranium, pennywort, loosestrife, daffodils, and flowering ferns. *On rocky hillsides in rich woods:* Hepatica, vetch, everlasting pea, catchfly, several columbines, four-leaved silk weed, shield ferns. *In rich alluvial woods:* Orchis, moccasin flower, cowslip, shooting star, oxlip, lily-of-the-valley, harebells, bluebells, wood hyacinth, beech fern, and spleenwort.

2. *Meadow Plants.*—Some of the most beautiful of all herbaceous plants are found wild in meadows and in rich, moist ground generally. Like the woodland flowers, the meadow plants are either found in small groups among the grass or scattered over the whole area, the smaller species generally most abundantly. Many grow readily from seeds, others may be planted without fear of failure provided the roots are good.

Among the most beautiful plants for this purpose are: *For mixing with the grass in moist lawns:* Cowslips, violets, bluets, meadow cress, spring beauty, blue-eyed grass, meadow saxifrage, and germander speedwell. *For planting in simple groups or in smaller patches:* Globe-flower,

meadow-sweet, blue-buttons, many lilies, tall meadow rue,
and sweet Cicely. All grow well in a rich sandy loam.
Where flowers of this latter kind are planted in a moist
lawn, mowing, except once or twice a year, is out of the
question.

3. *Flowers of Fields and Hillsides.*—Sunny fields and
hillsides are very rich in highly-colored flowers, and similar
effects may be produced on the lawns of large parks and
pleasure-grounds, where many desirable field plants can be
sown with the grass when making the lawn; or, late in the
fall, in established lawns and pastures. Such troublesome
weeds as the dandelion and evening primrose must, of
course, be excluded if possible.

Some of the rarer species may be planted by means of a
spade or trowel very early in spring; others, as many bulbous plants, including Canadian lilies, crocus, meadow
saffron, squills, and snowdrops, with the aid of a strong,
pointed stick, care being taken to place all bulbs right side
up. Special beds may also be prepared for many bulbous
plants, as rec-
ommended in
the chapter on
Lawns; but
when the soil
is moderately
good no such
preparation is required. Large plants, such as lilies, lark-

FIG. 54.—PRIMROSE GROWING IN OLD PASTURE.

spurs, and bellflowers, should be planted singly and far
apart, forming thin, scattered masses; but small species
with fine leaves, such as birdgrass, germander speedwell,

English daisies, violets, and primroses, may be sown thinly over a large area.

The following are some of the best field plants : *For roadsides, along drives and walks :* Mouse-ear, ox-eye daisy, field poppy, cornflower, dropwort, meadow-sweet, yellow daisy, yarrow, soapwort, chamomile, Sedum telephium, harebell, aster, and solidago. *For open fields and pastures :* Bluets, primrose, birdgrass, germander speedwell, maiden's pink, bird's-foot trefoil, larkspur, yellow daisy, pin-cushion flower, red clover, and sweet-scented herbs. *For sheltered fields and orchards :* Daffodils and narcissi, wild hyacinth, St. Bruno's lily, Star of Bethlehem, maiden pink, lilies, wild tulips, checker lilies, crown imperial, and sweet Cicely.

4. *Plants of Sandy Fields and Seashores.*—Sandy fields, shores of lakes and rivers, and barren hillsides can be made very attractive by the liberal use of maritime plants. The flora of the seashore and of many sand-fields, while poor in species, is exceptionally interesting. Many species of thrift form low, tufted masses of narrow leaves, and produce an abundance of flowers in summer, covering long stretches of sandy shores. Golden eternelle grows in mat like masses in other places, and is very effective when in flower. Few maritime plants are of any importance as individuals. The best for general use are : *On sandy shores :* Thrift, sand pink, wild thyme, golden eternelle, arenaria, sea-rocket (among sea-weeds),—all dwarf and attractive, producing numerous flowers in summer,—sea-kale, sea-holly, Marianna thistle, with large glaucous or variegated leaves. *For sterile, sandy fields :* Many of the previous forms, bird's-foot violet, heart's-ease, lupine, sand clover, Hieracium, mouse-ear,

field stone-crop, alkanet, and Rudbeckia. *For barren hill-sides:* Candytuft, rock cress, alyssum, cat's-paw, field bind-weed, wild thyme, house leek, and many annual plants of the mustard family.

5. *Riverside Plants.*—A great variety of beautiful wild flowers are found on the shores of brooks and rivers, some growing on the margin of the water, as the forget-me-not of the old world and the cardinal flower; others are common on high grassy banks. Many meadow plants are also found along water courses, and species with fine leaves, such as sweet Cicely, valerian, and Heracleum, are not uncommon. All can be established in similar positions in parks and gardens with the greatest of ease, either by planting or by sowing fresh seeds among the grass early in spring. Some species take a couple of years to reach a flowering size.

The following grow on grassy banks: Bugle, penny-wort, buttercups, blue-buttons, globe-flower, trumpet-weed, tall meadow rue, meadow-sweet, day lilies, great ox-eye daisy. *On the margin of water:* Forget-me-not, spearwort, cardinal flower, bee balm, mimulus, marsh marigold, water trefoil, and flags (*Iris*) of several species.

6. *Bog Plants.*—These are common plants of moist peat-bogs, which may be grown in rich and low ground on the shores of a small stream, or in specially prepared beds in a rockery. The bird's-eye primrose and the grass of Par-nassus may be sown or planted in large masses among the grass in moist lawns, but larger species such as wild calla, veratrum, many orchids and ferns do best in boggy ground near a river or lake. Other beautiful plants of this class are golden senecio, Jeffersonia, Welsh poppy, and the bog

bean or water trefoil, which is best grown on the margin of
a shallow stream.

7. *Water Plants.*—Ornamental water plants may be divided into three distinct classes according to their habit
and place of growth. 1. *With floating leaves:* water-lily,
Hydrocharis, Aponagaton, Alisma natans, Limnocharis, and
Nuphar—all growing in more or less deep water. 2. *With
erect leaves:* Sagittaria, water violet, flowering rush
lotus and the water-flag, which grow in more or less
shallow water near the shore. 3. *Species not rooting in the
ground:* bladder wort, Eichornia, and several unimportant
floating plants. The first two kinds delight in rich, muddy
soil composed of decaying vegetable matter, but will also
do well when planted in beds of good loam. The upright
forms are generally found growing in small tufts here and
there in shallow water.

8. *Rock Plants.*—Rock plants are among the most
beautiful of all herbaceous plants. They are generally of
dwarf and compact habit, with large flowers and comparatively small, often fleshy, leaves. Some grow in the deep
shade of rocky woods, as those mentioned among woodland
flowers; others enjoy the full sunlight and grow profusely
in Alpine regions in crevices of rocks or in deep pockets of
soil formed by decaying vegetable matter. Many are found
in moist and shady places along mountain streams where
the spray of running water keeps them continually moist
and cool. No park or garden should be without rock
plants. In hot countries species which naturally grow in the
bright sunlight and pure air of mountain regions require
partial shade and abundant watering in summer, and can

FIG. 55.—TYPICAL RIPARIAN VEGETATION, GREEN HELLEBORE (VERATRUM VIRIDE).

hardly be naturalized. But they well deserve to be grown even at the expense of considerable labor, for the sake of their delicate beauty. Many rock plants, on the other hand, may be naturalized in crevices of rocks filled with deep layers of leaf mould or in rocky woods as previously shown in this chapter. Among the most desirable for naturalizing are: *In sunny positions:* Stone crops, saxifrages,

FIG. 56.—DWARF MULLEIN (RAMONDIA PYRENAICA)   A TYPICAL ROCK PLANT.

houseleek, rock cress, Erysimum, whitlaw grass, Alyssum saxatile, creeping phlox, purple rock cress, Erinus, champion, candytuft, Linaria alpina, several columbines, and Opuntia. *In half shady positions:* Silene, several species, Dianthus, aster, Hieracium, yellow chamomile, bellflowers, Epimedium, Heuchera, many anemones, potentillas, ranunculus, several species of Primula, Tunica, Ramondia, and numerous ferns.

IX.

THE LAWN.

BEAUTIFUL lawn should be the most important feature of every city and suburban garden. Where the space is limited, little can be done in the way of planting and beautifying the ground, but if there are only a few square feet of soft, velvety grass in front of the city residence, the place looks so much the more pleasant and homelike. In making a lawn, the first thing to be done should be to examine the surface soil, and if necessary improve it to a sufficient depth. We take it for granted that the drainage and grading of the soil have been done according to previous instructions, and that it is only with the surface itself we have to do at present. At the same time, the condition of the subsoil and the more or less pronounced variety of the ground have a great deal to do with the permanence and beauty of the lawn. Where the subsoil is very light and gravelly, the ground is apt to dry up more suddenly than where it is of a more or less clayey nature. High knolls if exposed will dry up more quickly than a plane or but slightly undulating surface. Grounds situated on a natural meadow or in a level field near a lake or river are less liable to suffer from drought than those situated on a higher level or on a hillside. As to the nature of the surface soil itself, a sandy loam will make the best and most durable lawn. Where the soil is sandy or gravelly, too much cannot be done to enrich it by means of additions of rich loam and thick dressings of manure. The surface soil should be rich and friable to a depth of at least eighteen inches. The more liable a place is to the exposure of excessive heat and drought, the more thoroughly should the ground be worked and prepared before sodding and sowing, as a porous, well-worked soil will retain moisture much longer than a badly-worked, close, and heavy soil. It is therefore a good practice to dig and break up the soil to a sufficient depth, after the grading has been done, without disturbing the general surface of the ground. The soil must be worked fine by means of a stout iron rake. Of course where deep fillings of good soil have been deposited this digging is seldom necessary, but where the fillings are thin it is essential that they should be worked in and mixed with the old soil, as they would otherwise form a layer by themselves insufficient to resist even short spells of dry weather. By subsoiling, during which operation plenty of manure is dug in and mixed with the soil to a depth of two or three feet, even the poorest and least promising soil may be improved. Light soil is made more solid in this way, and heavy clay, if mixed with turfy loam, decayed manure, and sand or gravel, may be made quite porous.

If the soil is considered satisfactory in every way and has been thoroughly worked, and the trees and shrubs are planted, we may proceed to make the lawn by means of sodding and sowing. Sods may be procured from an old clean pasture, or from a good lawn. They should be cut in long narrow strips about ten inches wide, two inches thick, and five or six feet long, which can be rolled together as shown in A, Fig. 57. They must be cut quite even and with clean edges throughout their length. A large number

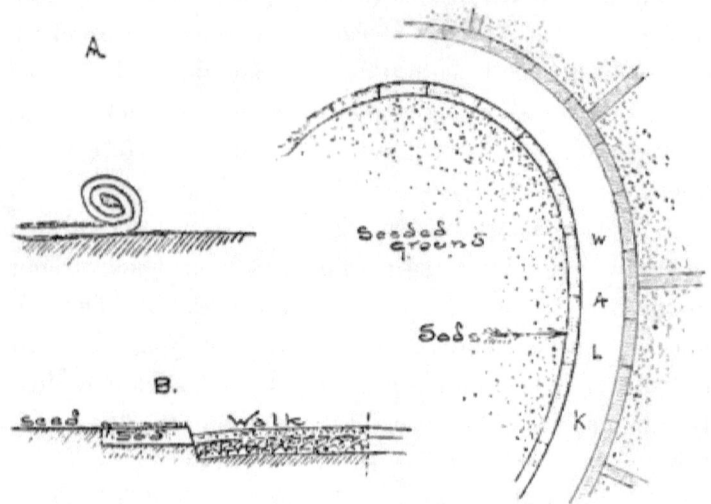

FIG. 57. A.—METHOD OF CUTTING AND ROLLING SODS. B.—SECTION OF THE EDGE OF A LAWN, SODDED.

may be marked out at a time, and a straight board or a line may be used in guiding the spade. A special thin iron with a sharp edge is best for the cutting, but if this cannot be had an old and sharp steel spade may be used. Sod-cutters drawn by horses are used by many if an unusually large quantity is required, but sods cut by means of an iron are better and easier to handle. In sodding the edge of a

lawn as shown in B, Fig. 57, care must be taken to make
the edge equally high above the surface of the walk at all
parts. If the sod is uneven, loose soil must be put in
under all thin places, and the soil may either be cut away
where the sod is too thick or scooped out of the ground
beneath the turf. A thin and sharp knife is used to fit the
edges together, and for loosening the soil a rake with a
short handle is useful. Before the sods are placed in position the surface to be sodded must be quite firm and even.
When a number of sods have been put down, the shovel
or rammer should be used to make the surface perfectly
level. A mallet may be advantageously used for the same

FIG. 58. SECTION OF A TERRACE. A.—SODS. B.—SEEDED GROUND. C—WALK

purpose. Sodding is chiefly done to make edges along
walks and drives or around flower-beds and shrubberries,
but if a lawn is wanted quickly the whole surface may be
covered in this manner. Terraces and steep inclines should
be sodded if it can be done. The manner of sodding a
terrace and along the edges of a walk is shown in several
diagrams (Figs. 57 and 58). The surface of the sod when a
lawn is finished should be on a level with the seeded
ground.

The grade of a terrace or other sloping lawn ought not
to exceed an angle of forty-five degrees, and here the strips
of sod should be placed from top to bottom, not lengthwise.

Sometimes, on very steep grades, it becomes necessary to fasten the turfs by means of pegs driven through them into the ground. Such places, which are liable to dry up very quickly, should be thoroughly watered occasionally, until the grass is fully established.

If all edges have been made in the above manner, we may proceed to sow the remaining parts of the lawn. It is imperative that the soil should be perfectly firm, with an even surface. It must have been thoroughly worked previously, but if it is spaded immediately before sowing, success is doubly certain, for then it will retain sufficient moisture until the grass has commenced to grow nicely. The sowing should take place on a calm day, as, if the weather is windy, the smallest and lightest seeds will be blown in all directions.

Some kinds of grasses grow best in shade, others in open places: a few will do well on sandy and sterile soil, while the majority are found in rich fields and meadows. The varieties commonly used for lawns are: English rye grass (*Lolium perenne* and *Lolium perenne tenuum*): the Kentucky blue or meadow grass (*Poa pratensis*), the smaller meadow grass (*Poa trivialis*), wood meadow grass (*Poa nemoralis*), timothy (*Phleum pratense*), tufted hair-grass (*Aira cæspitosa*), the crested grass (*Cynosurus cristatus*), the sweet-smelling spring grass (*Anthoxanthum odoratum*), and orchard grass (*Dactylis glomerata*), all growing in rich and fertile soil. The red-top (*Agrostis vulgaris*), the hard fescue (*Festuca duriuscula*), the sheep-grass (*Festuca ovina*), and the bent-grass (*Agrostis stolonifera*), do well on light and gravelly soil. Besides these the white clover (*Trifolium repens*) is used to a limited extent in all lawn-grass mixtures. If it is desired to form a meadow or field with a number of flowers growing among the grass, many dwarf and fine-leaved herbaceous plants may be sown at the same time as the grass. Among the best of these *for open and sunny positions* in rich soil are: the bluet (*Houstonia cœrulea*), the milkwort (*Polygala vulgaris, P. comosa*), the yellow star-grass (*Hypoxis erecta*), the maiden-pink (*Dianthus deltoides*), bird's-eye primrose (*Primula farinosa*) in moist ground, and the blue speedwell (*Veronica chamœdrys*): *beneath trees and shrubs:* the lesser celandine (*Ranunculus ficaria*), the harebell (*Campanula rotundifolia*), spring beauty (*Claytonia virginica*), purple phlox (*Phlox divaricata*), babes-in-the-wood (*Polygala pauciflora*), white windflower (*Anemone nemorosa*), golden windflower (*Anemone ranunculoides*), lily-of-the-valley (*Convallaria majalis*) and the cowslip (*Primula veris*); *in gravelly soil, open and sunny positions, sandy shores, etc.:* the sea-pink (*Armeria vulgaris* and *cephalotes*), sand-pink (*Dianthus arenarius*), bird's-foot trefoil (*Lotus corniculatus*), mouse-ear (*Cerastium Biebersteinii*), golden eternelle (*Helichrysum arenarium*), sandwort (*Arenaria*), wild thyme (*Thymus serpyllum—Thymus chamœdrys*) and creeping leadwort (*Plumbago larpenta*).

The following is an excellent lawn-grass mixture *for ordinary use:* two parts English rye grass, one part Kentucky blue, and one part red-top; *for moist ground:* one part English rye grass, two parts Kentucky blue, one part smaller meadow grass, one part meadow fox-tail (*Alopecurus pratensis*), and one part spring grass; *for dry*

ground: one part English rye grass, two parts hard fescue,
two parts red-top, one part tufted hair-grass, and one part
each of bent and crested grass; *for shady positions:* one
part orchard grass, two parts wood meadow grass, one part
bent grass, and one part Milium effusum, with a good
admixture of harebell and other fine-leaved and tufted
flowers. To all these mixtures may be added a small
quantity of white clover. The different seeds which vary
greatly in size must be thoroughly mixed before sowing.
One acre of ground requires fifty or sixty pounds to make

FIG. 59.—LAWN WITH ROUNDED SURFACE.

a good lawn, or in smaller areas a pound and a half to a
hundred square yards—a plot of land ten yards by ten.

If the lawn has been properly made and the weather is
favorable, the grass will soon grow and require cutting
The first cutting should be done with a sharp scythe, as
carefully as possible, after which a good rolling is beneficial. Watering or sprinkling when needed should be done
in a thorough manner; no merely superficial sprinkling will
benefit the grass. The watering is best done by means of
lawn-sprinklers, and the water pipes should be laid so as to
admit of easy access to all parts of the lawn and garden.

When the lawn after some time becomes worn and impoverished, dressings of artificial manures thinly sown over

the surface in spring, or dressings of stable manure late in fall, will be needed. Blood and bone, fish guano, bone dust, and nitrate of soda are among the best for this purpose, and should be applied in spring after the lawns have been swept clean of leaves and other matter. If after an un-

FIG. 60.—LAWN FORMING A SHALLOW DELL.

usually severe winter bare spots should be found on the lawn, sodding or sowing to cover up these defects should be done as early as the weather permits.

To a great extent the character and beauty of a garden depend on the lawn. A level lawn gives an impression of

FIG. 61.—UNDULATED LAWN.

peace and quiet ; an undulating one wears an expression of cheerfulness. Gardens with well trimmed, close and velvety lawns are beautiful and attractive, but, nevertheless, they

are not more natural than were formerly the creations of
old Maitre Lenôtre. But when the lawn adopts the choicest
flowers of field and meadow, and shrubberies and thickets
are filled with woodland blossoms, then the garden becomes,
as far as our impressions are concerned, a part of nature itself. Then the lawns should mingle with thicket and grove
to produce rich effects of light and shade, and, as in nature,
small groups of trees and shrubs and single specimen plants
should be found on the lawns, like so many outposts of the
wood. For such specimens we select the choicest of plants

FIG. 62. CROCUS, GROWING IN THE GRASS.

at our disposal, weeping beech and birch, trees with finely
incised foliage, and the most beautiful flowering shrubs, or
rare varieties of evergreen trees. But the lawn must not be
encumbered with too many plants: large trees especially are
apt to injure the grass. When such trees are found on a
place and it is not desirable to remove them, effective woodland scenes may be established in the thin grass below.
Ivy, wintergreen, periwinkle, and such bulbous plants as
scillas, daffodils, wild hyacinths, and dog-tooth violets are
especially useful for this purpose. In sunny spots on the

8

lawn irregular patches of snowdrop, crocus, and meadow saffron may be planted before sowing the lawn. For such plants the soil must be made as rich and light and porous as possible to the depth of a foot or eighteen inches. The flowers should be more crowded in the central parts of the group and become less numerous towards the edges where the group mingles with the lawn. When the flowers are out of season in such places the surface should present the appearance of a common lawn. These little patches of various bright colors heralding the approach of summer form as pleasant a feature of the lawn as any.

X.

ROCKS AND WATER.

AMONG the most attractive natural effects which it is possible to produce artificially in a garden are those enchanting glimpses of rocks and water frequently seen in mountain regions along streams and rivulets.

Rocks and water form a most happy combination in nature; wherever a stream cuts its way through a narrow ravine, the eroded and crumbling rocks form themselves into masses of the most picturesque beauty, and sustain a varied and wonderful vegetation.

In designing rockeries, it is vain for us to attempt to construct any of the larger masses that appeal to us more through their grandeur than through their beauty. The chief object is to create a pleasing variety within a limited area, and to provide a congenial soil for alpine plants. In minor places, rockeries may be formed on a very small scale on a narrow sloping piece of lawn, on the sides of a mound, or where a slight cut has been made for a drive or walk. In a more complete state the rockery should provide many opportunities for the display of water; here a

mountain rill falling over a narrow ledge and forming
glassy sheets of water below, rivulets bursting forth among
stones and boulders, streams with pebbly bottom surrounded by small bogs and meadows.

To make this scenery attractive in a limited area requires considerable skill and a thorough knowledge of the
materials used, whether it be plants or stones and building
materials, as also a taste cultivated by a close and intimate
study of nature.

The site must be selected where the rocks and water
will be in entire harmony with the surroundings.   If the

FIG. 63.—ROCKY SUMMIT OF A KNOLL.

rockery is constructed on elevated ground, as shown in
Fig. 63, water is out of the question, and the work should
be of the most simple nature.   A few rocks may rise in a
natural manner as if forming the skeleton of the hill.   For
rockeries of this isolated kind plants of a rigid habit and of
a sunloving nature, such as yucca, sunrose (*Helianthemum,
Cistus*), rock cress (*Arabis*), savin, and wild thyme are preferable to all others.

An excellent place for a rockery is a glen or ravine

overgrown with a wood of trees of light foliage. The rocks may here be imbedded on the steep sides as if tumbled down from time to time during the formation of the ravine, and loose bowlders may be placed in the bottom, forming imaginary remains of a river-bed. Here ferns of all classes and such delicate plants as the diadem flower (*Tiarella*), the

shooting-star (*Dodecatheon*), mitre-wort (*Mitella*), hepatica, Solomon's-seal (*Polygonatum*), and flowers of rocky woods, such as the ginseng (*Aralia racemosa*), will find a

FIG. 64.   SANDSTONE ROCKS PRO-TRUDING THROUGH A HILLSIDE.

natural home, besides many of the finest vines and creepers.

More extensive rockeries can be built on a steep hill-side, or on the banks of small lakes or rivers, where the necessary material is easy to obtain. A hillside will form a

natural and suitable back-ground, and the work may be made to imitate nature in the best way possible, for it is on such declivities that

FIG. 65.—SECTION OF A SUNKEN WALK WITH ROCKY SIDES.

cliffs and masses of broken rocks are most often seen in mountain regions.

If no such background can be had, and the rockeries are to be built on almost level ground on the sides of a slightly sunken walk, dark-leaved evergreens, such as rho-dodendrons, pine, spruce, and hemlock, should be planted to form the necessary background, to make a connecting link between the smooth lawn and the picturesque rocks, and to modify the contrast between the two.

In small places, rockeries may be built about the corner

of a house or on both sides of the steps with the foundation of the house for a background. These would, however,

FIG. 66.—SMALL ROCKERY AGAINST A WALL.

look out of place if the walls of the house were built of wood. Such miniature rockeries should be simple, unpretentious affairs that can be built in a day or two without any heavy outlay. A cart-load of stones a foot in diameter or less, stones left by the masons after the construction of a house, clinkers, and pieces of brickwork from an old wall are among the materials that can be used.

Rockeries should have a thorough drainage and congenial soil for all classes of dwarf herbaceous perennials and rock-plants, from the stone-crops, that delight to grow in an imperceptible crevice of a calcareous rock, sending

FIG. 67.—ROCKY BANK OF A RIVULET

their roots below to some hidden source of moisture, to the prim auricula that seeks a moist, mossy place by the edge of a mountain stream. The materials used in the actual construction are of various nature; granite bowlders, sandstone blocks, masses of overburnt bricks, and segments of old walls—mortar and all—can be used to advantage. For the borders of cisterns and small sheets of water generally, tuff stone and coral are excellent materials when they can be obtained. Sandstone and calcareous rocks are most desirable, as all classes of plants will succeed best on and among these; they form many cracks and crevices in which numerous rock-plants will lodge and grow to perfection in a moist place. Tree roots and large stems are hardly in keeping with the nature of a rockery; to most people they are ugly and objectionable, even when moderately used. A slight mound of soil forms the main body of the rockery, and in this the various bowlders and stones should be imbedded more or less deeply, closer together here, there, far apart and in different positions. The elevation must not be uniform. Isolated blocks should form bold masses in places, and dark caves may be constructed in wider and higher parts among the rocks. Such caves are often desirable for the culture of certain classes of ferns. In other parts the rockery may be quite low and depressed, formed of smaller and scattered stones only. Vertical rocks may be made to enclose wet and boggy ground in which moisture-loving plants will thrive and form a special feature. Plants desirable for this purpose are moccasin-flower (*Cypripedium*), purple orchis, Dentarias, flower of parnassus (*Parnassia palustris*), Gentians, and forget-me-nots. A tiny stream of water may wind in and out among the flowers, either falling over the cliffs or welling forth from beneath a block or stone.

A heavy and characterless heap of stone, filled in with ordinary soil, is satisfactory neither in an ideal nor a practical sense. The separate crevices or "pockets" should be filled with specially prepared soil, different for different classes of plants. For most true rock-plants a light,

FIG. 68. SECTION OF A ROCKERY.

sandy soil mixed with old mortar and brick rubbish is satisfactory. Others require a richer and lighter compost with plenty of peat or leaf-mould mixed in. This soil, when used, must be firmly packed down to the surface of the bottom soil, as it will dry up very quickly if it is separated in the least. The crevices and pockets should be vertical or oblique, capable of catching rain and of letting off superfluous moisture.

In planting the rockery, none but suitable and characteristic species should be selected. All the coarser herbaceous plants are better excluded, the dwarfer forms being preferable, and these also should be proportionate in size and in harmony with the position of the rockery, as it may be located either in a shady wood or in a perfectly open and sunny place. Shrubs and subshrubs of a dwarf habit are appropriate, such as berberis, cotoneaster, many of the choicest ericaceous plants, dwarf conifers; and among vines and creepers, ivy, periwinkle, matrimony vine, periploca, and climbing roses. No plants should be allowed to entirely overgrow and hide the picturesque outlines of the rocks.

Water in a small garden cannot, as a matter of course, be very elaborate in design. A transparent miniature lake, or a pebbly stream, oval or circular cisterns with a more or less regular outline, and playing fountains, may all be formed artificially. But when the ground has such natural advantages as a lake or river shore, or a small brook, much can be done to enhance their beauty and to modify the banks and shores if they are too steep or too formal. Such modification may involve considerable work, but as a rule much can be done by taking advantage of any depression in the ground that may be deepened without too arduous labor and by filling in the excavated soil in near-by places where the shore is higher.

The shore may be either a gradual, grassy slope or an abrupt and rocky declivity or a combination of both. Where the water widens into small bays the shores are generally low and level, forming soft lawns or grassy meadows. A considerable sheet of water when formal and rounded in outline will look small and insignificant especially if bordered by a tall growth of trees, whereas small bodies of

FIG. 69.—PONDLIKE CISTERN WITH FOUNTAIN.

water will look much larger than they really are if the shores are of a sinuous outline and hidden from view in parts, and if the surface of the soil is but slightly elevated above the water, with very gradual slopes. The effect will in all cases be modified either favorably or unfavorably, by plantations of trees and shrubs. The trees must of necessity be proportionate to the width and extent of the water. Low and bold promontories may be planted with such light-foliaged trees as birch or willow with the trunks exposed to view in places and admitting of glimpses of water through the foliage and between the trunks; open lawns unincumbered with trees and shrubs should descend to the edge of coves and bays. In other words, the plantations should chiefly be on the protruding bluffs of land, and where the land retreats few or no plants should be seen.

Among trees that are especially effective on shores are the numerous varieties of willow including the weeping willow, dogwood, white alder, arrowwood, elder, and Andromeda, while vines such as the virgin's bower, wild cucumber, bryony, and honeysuckle may be planted among the shrubbery to form natural thickets. The shore, if muddy and slimy, should be covered with pebbles, gravel, or coarse sand, and wide stretches of sandy shore may be made on which the choicest of maritime plants and many showy bulbous flowers will be at home.

The bottom of small artificial ponds can be made of solid

concrete. This should be hidden by coral, tuffstone, and pebbles and the grassy or rocky banks may be

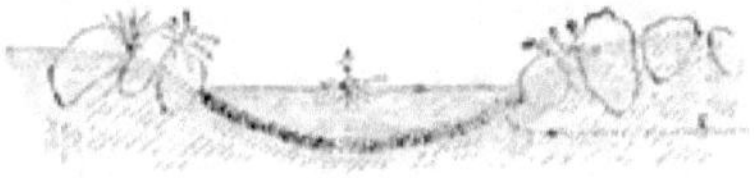

FIG. 70. SECTION OF SMALL ARTIFICIAL STREAM WITH CONCRETE BOTTOM; ROCKY BANKS.

made to hide its artificial construction. The edges must here be built with care as the whole impression depends upon a natural appearance. Inlets and outlets must be provided for the water which can be supplied by the general waterworks in the ordinary way; it will then be possible to renew the water occasionally. Round cisterns so often used

in small gardens must be emptied in autumn before the frosts set in, and may be converted into beds of evergreen shrubs and

FIG. 71.—SAME AS 70; WITH GRASSY BANKS.

creepers for the winter season.

N. Rose

FIG. 72. LAKE AND WATERSIDE PLANTING, RED MAPLES AND OAKS.

123

As a special and important feature of water scenery the exquisitely beautiful flowers of pond and stream should be grown in suitable places. But they must never be allowed to cover up the surface entirely or to form too thick and crowded masses. Some of the finest of all flowers grow in water or on lake and river shores; the yellow flag and many other forms of iris, the wild calla, the cardinal flower (*Lobelia cardinalis* and *fulgens*), the water violet (*Hottonia palustris*), and forget-me-not will grow on moist shores; the many varieties of pond lilies, the lotus (*Nelumbium*

FIG. 73.—SECTION OF ARTIFICIAL WATER WITH CONCRETE BOTTOM, ROCKY BANKS, AND FOUNTAIN.

speciosum), the water poppy (*Hydrocharis Humboldtii*), the water crowfoot with its feathery and three-lobed leaves and numerous white flowers, and the fragrant water hawthorn, in more or less deep water. In large ponds and lakes many kinds may be established permanently, while the choicer varieties should be planted in separate tubs and sunk to the requisite depth near the shore. There is a subtle charm about all water plants, the lily resting on the bosom of a lake, the golden flower-de-luce bathing its feet in limpid water, and the blue-eyed forget-me-not—all have been loved and sung by a thousand poets.

XI.

FLOWER-BEDS AND BORDERS.

LOWER-BEDS are chiefly used on smooth and well-kept lawns near the residence to produce bright and cheerful effects by a judicious display of summer flowers. These groups should be a source of interest and enjoyment from the earliest spring days till late in fall.

The first flowers to expand in early spring are the innumerable forms of bulbous plants with flowers of the most exquisite and brilliant colors, such as tulips, squills, crocus, hyacinths, and daffodils.

Bulbs for spring display are planted late in fall in well-prepared beds of light and rich soil. Tulips, hyacinths, and daffodils are planted from five to six inches apart in regular rows and in separate beds. Crocus, glory of the snow (*Chionodoxa*), and snowflakes may be placed several together and in little clusters three inches apart. When the beds are prepared and the rows marked on the ground showing the place of each bulb or cluster of bulbs, the planting may be done by means of a trowel, a dibbler (pointed stick), or simply by the hand, care being taken to place all bulbs equally deep in the soil. The covering, varying in depth for different classes of bulbs, should never be less than three inches. After finishing planting, the beds should be dressed with a thin layer of clean horse manure or tanner's bark, to protect the soil against sudden changes of temperature. This covering may be removed in spring as soon as the bulbs show signs of growth; the edge of the bed must then be cut clean and the surface raked, as in all formal bedding neatness and cleanliness are necessary to produce a good effect.

Bulbs are sold in both separate and mixed colors and also in named varieties; the single ones are preferable to the double for all out-door use. Mixed beds of scarlet and yellow tulips are very pretty. Crimson and white varieties also make a fine display. Hyacinths may be mixed, but the varieties should flower at the same time to make a good show, and as there is a marked difference in their time of flowering it is best to select a few good varieties that flower simultaneously and arrange them with some reference to the harmony of color. Crocuses look best when mingled together in a confusion of tints and colors, and as for narcissi and daffodils, they are all yellow or white and yellow. Oxlips, cowslips, primroses, and daisies may also be used with excellent effect for early spring bedding. These, as well as all bulbs, should be removed carefully after flowering and planted close together in a shady place in a border or shrubbery where they will finish their growth and ripen.

As soon as bulbs and other spring flowers have been removed the material for summer display should be ready for planting. For large places the plants may be grown in a greenhouse or warm frame; for smaller cottage and city gardens a sufficient number of geraniums, heliotrope, Paris daisy, coleus, verbenas, pyrethrum, pansies, and lobelia may be raised in flat boxes in a light and warm cellar or basement, or in a kitchen window, and where this is impracticable they can be obtained from a florist at a very moderate cost.

Of course the beds have to be prepared before the planting is done. Then the middle is first filled, row after row, the border being left to the last. Large plants, such as geraniums, are placed from eight to ten inches apart, and smaller ones from three to six inches apart, according to size. These plants require little or no care after planting, except an occasional watering, pinching, or trimming. The beds should be mulched with a thin layer of well-decayed horse manure.

Annual plants may also be used with advantage for summer bedding; they are very numerous, and some are exceedingly fine. The most permanent ones are: Stocks, Indian cress, asters, zinnias, phlox, three-colored convolvulus, California poppy, Nemophila, scarlet flax, poppies, lupins, Brachycome, the white rocket, larkspurs, marigolds, and pinks of various kinds. None will form a permanent display throughout the season.

A beautiful effect may be produced by the proper use of inexpensive foliage-plants such as Whitlavia, Solanum, Perilla, Ricinus, Artemesia, Nicotiana, golden feather pyrethrum, and young seedlings of blue gum (*Eucalyptus*), arranged according to size in circular or oval beds and bordered by some flowering plant such as lobelia or bedding violets.

In the arrangement of beds of these different kinds, a charming effect may be produced by planting low or trailing plants with dense, dark-colored foliage or flowers as an undergrowth for taller light-colored plants; as, for example, the black-purple Perilla in a bed of blue gum; blue or violet verbenas in a bed of white geraniums; Sanvitalia procumbens in a bed of Nicotiana affinis; Gnaphalium lanatum, Centaurea maritima or Ageratum in a bed of Salvia splendens, and so on. In all such beds the taller plants must never be allowed to grow too closely together, but the bottom growth should be visible all over the bed. Plants suitable for summer bedding will be fully described in a subsequent chapter.

The border is a special place set apart for herbaceous plants, annual and perennial, bulbs, etc., and is generally located in an out-of-the-way place in the vegetable garden, in the front of a shrubbery, or by the side of a house. The border may be from three to four feet wide, seldom more, and the plants are arranged according to their size, the taller behind, the smaller in front, in a free and easy manner, with sufficient space for the development of all. A border, if the plants have been selected with care and intelligence, will produce a continual supply of cut flowers from early in spring until frost sets in. They should if possible have a suitable background of dark-leaved trees or shrubs, a hedge or wall, and this will also afford shelter and protection. Every fall the soil should be mulched and spaded carefully so as not to disturb bulbs or other plants. Bulbs should be marked in some manner by stakes, or otherwise. In spring the surface should be stirred and raked even and level, and when the hot summer begins to scorch the ground a good mulching of clean, decayed manure is absolutely necessary in some localities. Some of the taller plants will need staking, and this should be done as neatly as possible, green-painted garden stakes and bamboo canes being preferable to any other.

As early as March or April the border will begin to be a source of interest. Christmas roses and winter aconite bloom during these months. Later on we have the many varieties of oxlip, cowslip, and primrose, the early spring bulbs, Lenten roses, spring Adonis and Lenten lilies. In May we have the anemones and windflowers; in May and June, columbines, poet's narcissus, bleeding-hearts, peonies, foxgloves, night violets, some bellflowers, pinks, and lark-spurs, followed by an endless succession of poppies, lilies, hollyhocks, Lychnis, lupins, Pentstemons, and Ptarmicas, and in the late summer months by marshmallows and the thousand and one forms of composite plants.

A flower-garden of more or less complex design, in symmetrical style, with narrow walks at straight angles and square or rectangular beds for summer flowers and carpet beddings, is sometimes desirable. It is generally located near the residence, enclosed by low hedges of box or by stone borders in harmony with the architecture of the house. Where there is a conservatory or greenhouse the flower-garden should form a part of the design around these structures. Here the neatest and choicest of exotic plants should be used; the dwarfest and most floriferous kinds of

9

flowers, highly colored foliage-plants of compact habit, and
subtropical plants of luxurious growth; palms, bananas,
cycads, and tree-ferns to a limited extent.

Mosaic or carpet-bedding is a special class of summer
display. The plants being dwarf and compact with highly
colored leaves of a silvery white, bright yellow, vivid green
or various shades of red, are planted so as to form patterns
of mathematical figures: the circle and the square, with
numerous modifications, are the chief forms. It requires
both skill and expense to produce good results, and is only
kept up through continual care. Several carpet-beds showing the mode of arrangement are reproduced in the accompanying figure. As examples of the plants used the following are interesting: *Gray or silvery white*—Gnaphalium,
Mesembryanthemum cordifolium var., Santolina incana,
Centaurea ragusina, Cineraria maritima, Cerastium, and
Artemisia; *yellow*—Pyrethrum golden feather, several
coleus, Alternanthera p. aurea; *rose and bright tints of crimson*
mixed with other colors—Acalypha, Coleus, Alternanthera,
Irisine, and Achyranthes; *black, purple, or maroon*—several
Coleus, Perilla, red-leaved Oxalis and clover; *succulent
plants*—Echeveria, Sempervivum, Sedum, small century
plants, Yucca, Cordyline, and cactus; *flowering plants*—
Lobelia fulgens (scarlet), Lobelia erinus (blue and white),
and Ageratum (blue and white); *subtropical plants*—Grevillea, Acacia lophanta, crotons, abutilons, screw pines, and
palms.

Somewhat distinct and extremely beautiful effects are
produced by large-leaved plants of quick and robust growth
such as Musa ensete, Wigandia caracasana, Aralia papy-

rifera, Canna, Ferdinandia, Jacaranda, Ficus, Melianthus, Grevillea, Acacia lophanta, Aralia chinensis, Lea amabilis, and white variegated Lavatera. Even maize, giant hemp, Ricinus, and Artemisia are useful and effective for this purpose. In

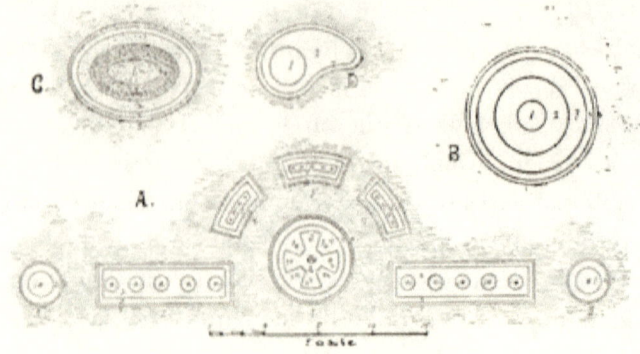

FIG. 74.—FLOWER BEDS.

Explanation : A. Parterre.

1. A central bed planted as follows : 1. Areca lutescens (specimen palm). 2. Rose-colored Begonia. 3. Grevillea robusta. 4. White ageratum. 5. *Viola cornuta.* 6. Echeveria.

2. Two rectangular beds : 1. Specimen *Dracœna indivisa ;* bottom, blue Ageratum. 2. Verbenas. 3. *Lobelia crinus.* 4. Echeveria.

3. Circular beds : 1. Centre, Chamæpeuce in a bed of red Alternanthera. 2. *Mesembryanthemum cordifolium cariegatum.* 3. Red-leaved oxalis.

4. Two beds : 1. Scarlet geranium. 2. Rose-colored geranium. 3. Blue lobelia. 4. Sempervivum.

5. One bed : 1. Heliotrope. 2. Scarlet geranium. 3. Dusty miller. 4. Sempervivum.

B. Circular bed : 1. *Salvia splendens.* 2. *Salvia patens.* 3. Rose-colored Begonia. 4. White Ageratum. 5. *Lobelia crinus,* blue stone.

C. Oval bed : 1. Acalypha. 2. Red coleus. 3. Yellow coleus. 4. Dusty miller. 5. Arenaria.

D. 1. Variegated maize. 2. Wigandia or Solanum. 3. Pyrethrum golden feather.

such foliage groups the plants must never be crowded, as the effect is most beautiful when sober and dignified. Groups of this nature may be joined, in an apparently natural manner, with the rest of the scenery to produce distinctly

subtropical effects.   It must be remembered that the
majority of plants grown at the present time for summer
bedding are greenhouse plants and do not properly belong
to the landscape, as every garden may be complete without
them.   They are beautiful accessories, which rightly handled
will greatly enhance the beauty of a place, but when mis-
used are worse than useless.

The most important flowering plants used for bedding are tender greenhouse plants.   Most important are
the many varieties of Abutilon, red, white, or yellow, excellent for central parts; Begonia semperflorens, various
shades of red and pure white (*Vernon, coccinea, Erfordii*),
dwarf, compact, and ever-blooming; tuberous-rooted Begonias of all colors, Calceolaria rugosa, Cuphea, heliotrope,
Libonia, zonal pelargoniums, single varieties of all colors,
Salvia, Streptosolon, Torenia, and Vinca rosea.   For combination with these, numerous hardy annuals are used for
summer effect, most of which are described in a subsequent
chapter.

XII.

HEDGES.

LIPPED hedges with straight and formal outlines are sometimes desirable for protection
against wind and dust, and injury from dogs
and other animals running about. A hedge,
although formal in appearance, can be made
a very useful as well as ornamental object. Of course,
when straight lines are used in a garden, they must be
exactly straight and uniform from beginning to end. The
contrast between these smooth-cut rows of vegetation and
the free and graceful shrubs and trees within is rather
pleasing than otherwise, and if a small place is isolated it
looks forlorn without such an enclosure. When an entire
street is planted upon a uniform plan a hedge is out of
place, because the effect is there one united whole, and as
such, ornamental. But even here the back of the lot may
be enclosed without disturbing the general character of the
lawns and the street. In bleak and windy positions, especially far north, a screen planting becomes indispensable in
addition to the hedge.

Hedges may be planted either on flat ground, when the

soil is of ordinarily good character, or on raised ground,
when the soil is moist and liable to inundation, or in the
bottom of shallow trenches, when the ground is unusually
dry. When the hedge is planted in such trenches a deep
layer of soil must cover the bottom, or the bottom may be
subsoiled and improved by means of a liberal addition of
manure. Hedges of this kind may be used both by farmers

FIG. 75. WELL-KEPT HEDGE; FORMAL LINES BROKEN BY FINE PLANTING.

and gardeners for enclosing fields, orchards, parks, and
gardens.

In planting a hedge a trench is dug from end to end for
its entire length; to make it perfectly straight a line must
be used. The trench should be sufficiently deep, varying
according to the size of the plants, but never less than a
foot in depth and diameter. The soil must be trodden
down firmly after planting, while the plants are kept in a
perfectly straight row and at an equal distance.

For small hedges, solid and impenetrable for most animals, the hawthorn, and the wild apple (seedlings of *Pyrus malus*, any variety), which is commonly used by nurserymen for stock, are better than almost any other kind of plant. They should be planted when two or three years old, about six inches apart, in a single row, and cut even with a pair of garden shears immediately after planting. These should in a few years form a hedge ten or twelve inches wide and several feet high. Two clippings are necessary every year—one in winter or spring before the commencement of growth, and one in summer. Among other deciduous trees and shrubs used for this purpose are the white mulberry, common oak, beech, and hornbeam, as well as the small-leaved elm and field maple. These latter kinds are more robust, forming, when well planted, very strong hedges. The distance should be somewhat greater than in the case of the hawthorn. Smaller hedges, chiefly for divisions in the garden, may be made of privet and box. Osage-orange and Christthorn are sometimes used for rough hedges. Among evergreen trees the holly, yew, Norway spruce, arbor-vitæ, and hemlock form close and beautiful hedges for protection both winter and summer. The hedge-row must be kept absolutely clean and free from grass and weeds, but many beautiful climbers may be grown in the hedge, and are there quite at home. The virgin's bower and purple clematis, cucumber vine, morning-glory, and many other annual climbers with light foliage, will not interfere with the growth of the hedge proper. When sown, small circular beds must be dug for each alongside the hedge. There are numerous fine and dwarf bulbous plants that will do well in a hedge-row. Our common wood lilies, dogtooth violets, Smilacina, star-grass, and several European plants, such as squills, yellow star of Bethlehem (*Gagea*), winter aconite, snowdrops, and meadow saffron are admirable subjects for this purpose. It will be seen that even so formal a thing as a hedge-row can be made beautiful by a little thoughtful and intelligent work. To reduce the monotony of a long and smoothly cut hedge, small trees and shrubs may be planted on both sides of the hedge at irregular intervals and a safe distance, as shown in the illustration on page 134. The combination is one of great beauty, uniting the qualities of ornament and utility in a happy manner.

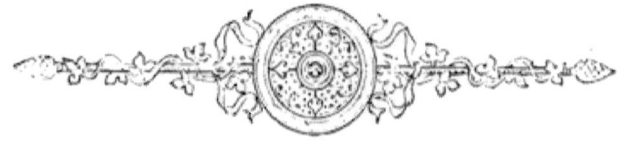

XIII.

BUILDINGS AND ENCLOSURES.

 PARK or garden should never be encumbered with buildings or other structures foreign to its nature. All buildings should be for the sake of use and convenience only, not mere ornaments devoid of all other interest. Shelters and places of rest are necessary in every large park; bowers and pavilions are desirable places for spending holidays and summer evenings in pleasure or study. In botanic gardens and city parks, museums, gymnasiums, boat-houses, and other structures are in keeping with the purpose of these places, and while intended for use only, should be of simple and artistic design, and as ornamental as possible.

A pavilion in the shape of a Swiss cottage in a suitable position, or a simple rustic shelter, like the one illustrated in Fig. 76, and bowers of creepers and vines, are in perfect harmony with the nature and use of a garden, but besides these, temples in pure Grecian or Roman style may be erected on high bluffs and knolls to serve the same purpose. The rustic pavilion shown in the illustration can be con-

structed by any experienced carpenter. The material is
white or red cedar in a natural state, which has been
stripped of bark to make it more durable. The columns
support a square roof thatched with shingles, and supporting a lantern in which bird's-nests are provided. The sides
are covered with honeysuckle, wistaria, and trumpet-flower,
while inside, seats are made all around. The little rocky
knoll, with its sparse and scattered vegetation, is in perfect
harmony with the building, and sets it off to advantage.
This is only a modest example of that class of structures.

FIG. 76.—RUSTIC SHELTER; EFFICIENT WHEN COVERED WITH CREEPERS AND VINES.

A bower may be made entirely by planting trees, hedge-
row fashion, in a circle, and allowing the tops to grow
together eight or ten feet above the ground. Beech and
hornbeam are excellent for this purpose, and will make a
close wall of greenery if properly treated. For the first
few years they should be cut like a hedge, but as soon as
the wall is perfectly close it may be allowed more freedom.
But when it is intended to make a bower of flowering vines,
such as the wistaria or trumpet-flower, a screen or trellis-
work must be made to support these rambling plants; the

branches should be tied at equal distances from each other, and distributed uniformly over the whole.

When the grounds border on a lake or river with facilities for bathing and boating, convenient structures will be needed, but they should never be made out of proportion with the grounds. These, like all buildings, must be in harmony with the surroundings, and ornamental in design.

Rustic seats, when used, should be simply made, of light and strong wood in as graceful proportions as possible.

FIG. 77. WOODEN BRIDGE.

Red cedar and juniper make excellent materials for this, as well as for all kinds of rustic work. Fig. 77 represents a bridge across a small stream. Piers of rough stone are built on both sides of the water, and round timbers are simply thrown across from side to side and bound together by means of cross timbers at each end. The wood is painted with creosote and covered by a thin layer of gravel to make the surface of the bridge uniform with that of the walk. The handrails, made fast to the outside timbers, are also of natural wood, quite strong and simply joined together by means of wooden pins. The bridge may also be made by nailing round sticks, two or three inches in diameter, crosswise on top of two timbers thrown across the water. Bridges form picturesque parts of a landscape, whether they be of stone or wood, pretentious, or as simply constructed as the one shown in the illustration. The style

FIG. 78.—STONE BRIDGE.

may differ greatly, and such structures cannot be fully treated here. A great mistake often committed in designing bridges for public parks and gardens is to make the design too heavy and elaborate. All carvings or architectural affectations are decidedly out of place. Simple bridges just large enough to serve their purpose, either of natural wood or something after the manner shown in Fig. 78, are best in harmony with natural scenery.

Steps are sometimes needed on very steep grades or
terraces. In formal gardens and near a dwelling-house
they should be of hewn stone, but where the garden is free
and natural the steps may be made of rough stones without
mortar or cement, bordered by a few scattered rocks and
stones half buried in the adjoining lawns. Wood can also
be used, and in that case a board six or eight inches wide
is simply put across the walk and nailed to posts driven
vertically into the ground. Gravel is then filled in to the
top of the board, and another step is made a foot or more

FIG. 79. IRON FENCE AND GATES

behind, and so on for the required distance. The face of
the board should be covered with split sticks of a uniform
size nailed vertically to the front.

Fences and enclosures, if any, must be of neat design
and proportionate in size. One that affords every necessary protection, and at the same time leaves the garden
exposed to the view of the passers-by, is shown in Fig.
79. It is made of round iron bars run through flat top
and bottom pieces, and placed firmly on a low stone foundation with stone pillars on each side of the entrance to which

the gates are hung. The pillars are in this instance
surmounted by flower vases. A stone enclosure suitable
for rural suburbs is represented in Fig. 80. It may be
made either with or without mortar, and in the latter
case will furnish good places for ferns and rock-plants.
This enclosure needs to be covered with strong vines and
climbers. Brambles, climbing roses, trumpet-flower, and
wistaria can be used for this purpose. Another rural en-

FIG. 80.—STONE ENCLOSURE AND GATEWAY PILLARS COVERED WITH TRUMPET-CREEPER
(TECOMA RADICANS).

closure, as illustrated in the following figure, is made of
sticks of juniper or red cedar. To make the wood more
durable it must be stripped of bark at the time of cutting.
The sticks are firmly inserted, diagonally, in a sill of some
strong and durable wood, which is placed on top of a
low stone foundation or firmly attached to low locust posts.
This fence, besides being strong and durable, affords good
opportunities for growing flowering vines and climbers or
rambling shrubs, such as many honeysuckles and jessamines.

The English, and many people of continental Europe, make their gardens absolutely private by means of walls eight or ten feet high. In a crowded city it is perhaps desirable to make the residence as private as possible, but aside from this, such walls afford a good protection for all plants grown in the garden. Neither is it disagreeable to see a rich and luxuriant vegetation bearing clusters of leaves and flowers over a garden wall

FIG. 61.—RUSTIC FENCE.

across the sidewalk. If the grounds are large and the wall can be hidden by means of plantations, at least on the inside, without hiding all external views, low stone or brick walls may be used to advantage in windy and exposed positions and where some protection is necessary.

XIV.

ON THE EMBELLISHMENT OF THE DWELLING-HOUSE.

N city and suburban gardens, where the ground area is limited, many plants may be grown for the embellishment of the dwelling-house and other buildings. Around and between the columns of a porch or veranda, climbers and vines may be trained to form a rich and luxurious effect. The plants, however, must never be allowed to grow too thickly. Thinning and pruning must often be resorted to in the case of strong growing woody climbers, and the whole should be kept neat and trim by careful attention. On the wall itself the Boston ivy will make a nice display of greenery in summer, turning into exquisite autumn tints before the leaves fall, and leaving a tracery of slender branches in winter. The ivy, more constant, clings to the support in a similar manner, but its persistent foliage makes it still more valuable for covering the bare walls of a house. But while these are the principal and most interesting plants of their kind, there are numerous very pretty shrubs and flowering vines that may be trained on wires or trellises against a wall. Among these are the evergreen Japanese spindle-trees (*Euonymus japonicus* and *E. radicans*), the deciduous Actinidia, climbing roses, honeysuckles and clematis. The evergreen thorn (*Crataegus Pyracantha*), with its orange-scarlet berries in winter and white flowers in spring, is also a very interesting plant for a wall. It must not be supposed that each and every kind of climbing plant can be used together indiscriminately to produce a good effect. It is better to choose a few good ones and cover a large space of wall with one kind, and another part with a different but similar kind, or to cover the entire surface with one kind only. No plants must be allowed to interfere with the architectural beauty of the house; they should merely be introduced to add a touch of finish and permanency to the structure, if possible setting off to greater advantage the carvings on lintels and cornices, and other devices of the architect's art.

In planting climbers for a wall or veranda, a border must be dug along the entire front of the wall which it is intended to cover, and new soil must be procured when the ground near the house is mixed with stone and gravel to a great extent. A narrow border should be left open after planting. This border may be used in spring and summer for flowering plants. The after-treatment merely consists in thinning the shoots once or twice in a year, and in training and tying the plants that need support.

The stoop of a porch or veranda may be beautified by means of vases filled with an assortment of summer flowers and trailing plants, such as begonias, heliotropes, mesem-

10

bryanthemum, periwinkle, trailing verbena and Indian cress, or with a combination of these and subtropical plants; dracenas, palms, and American aloe. While such vases are also available for the embellishment of other parts of a garden, they are chiefly used in connection with the house. A pretty custom is the use of window boxes filled to overflowing with vines and flowering plants. The window box to be practical in a hot climate should be constructed so as to protect the roots from overheating and drying during hot days, and to allow for drainage in wet weather. While the drainage cannot be carried outside the box, as it would soil the building, the bottom of the box may be filled with a couple of inches of cinders or crocks. The outside may be made of wood, slate, or enamelled earthenware, and the inside should consist of a tight zinc box, fitting in so as to leave an air space of half an inch between the zinc and the outer covering. This construction prevents any sudden drying of the roots or overheating of the soil from exposure to the sun. The soil, which should be light and rich, must be firmly packed in planting. The boxes, after planting and watering, are placed on the narrow sill outside the window, and if this is too narrow it must be supported by means of brackets or bands fastened to the wall. Boxes may also be placed on top of the balustrade or balcony between the columns, if the character of the building admits of such display. Besides these, hanging baskets may be suspended from the roof directly above the boxes, one between each pair of columns. The plants used for vases and boxes are also amenable to basket culture; they include such sorts as geraniums, ivy-leaved geraniums, German ivy, musk, coleus,

FIG. 82.—PORCH COVERED WITH JAPANESE HONEYSUCKLE (LONICERA HALLEANA).

wandering Jew, Aaron's-beard, Torenia, and several succulent plants and trailers.

These suggestions, somewhat foreign to the plan of a work of landscape-gardening, are simply for the benefit of the many whose existence is mainly passed between the narrow walls of a city; but they are important to a certain extent as showing how to beautify the *city landscape*, so much in need of vegetable life and color.

XV.

THE ORCHARD AND KITCHEN-GARDEN.

N places where the size of the ground admits of a small vegetable garden and orchard, these will add materially to the use and pleasure of the garden. Not only can a better and fresher supply of fruits and vegetables be provided for home consumption than it would be possible to obtain in any other manner, but there are many opportunities for healthful exercise and recreation valuable in themselves. The beauty of the trees in the flowering season, the odor of sweet-scented fruits and vegetables—all help to make the garden a source of pleasure and interest.

The site for a kitchen-garden and orchard should be well-drained, and the soil must be of a tolerably good kind—light, sandy loam being preferable to any other, as it is easily worked and may be enriched to suit any kind of fruit or vegetable. The ground should be thoroughly worked and subsoiled before planting, if possible. Where the entire plot cannot be prepared in this manner a sufficient space around each tree must be dug two or three feet deep to provide a well-worked soil for the young roots.

The orchard may be laid out in grass afterwards, the soil around each tree being kept open for about two feet on each side of the trunk. The grass in the orchard may be allowed to grow freely; red clover, myrrh, daffodils, lilies, wild tulips, maiden pink, and many other sweet-scented and beautiful flowers should be allowed to run wild among the grass. Small fruits such as strawberries, raspberries, gooseberries, currants, and grapes may be grown in special quarters in the kitchen-garden. The orchard can also be planted so as to form a part of the pleasure-ground without any sharp dividing lines. In that case the trees should not be planted in formal rows, but in irregular groups, the taller ones being placed in the middle, and the plantations may be rounded off by means of near-by specimens in the grass, either small trees or fruit shrubs. The distance between the trees varies for different kinds from ten to twelve, fifteen, and twenty feet. In small places it is most practical to place all trees closer together than they are to be when fully grown, and thin out superfluous trees some years afterwards. The least permanent fruit-trees are peaches, plums, and apricots; the most lasting, pears and apples, and as these latter grow much larger than any other fruit-trees they should be planted farther apart.

The following is a select list of the best fruits for general culture: *Apples, early*—Early harvest, pale yellow, of medium size; red Astrachan, deep crimson, spotted, medium size; early strawberry, red dotted, medium; Tetofsky, yellow, striped red, medium size; yellow transparent, greenish-yellow or yellow. *Autumn*—Alexander, yellow and crimson, very large; Fameuse, deep crimson, medium size: Gravenstein, yellow and orange, medium size or larger; Duchess of Oldenburg, striped red and yellow, large; wealthy, dark red, brighter on one side, medium. *Winter*—Baldwin, red, quite large; Jonathan, red and yellow, medium size; Newton pippin, greenish, red on one side, medium; northern spy, greenish-red, dark crimson on one side, striped, medium; Rhode Island Greening, dull green, medium size. *Pears, Summer*—Bartlett, greenish yellow, large; Clapp's Favorite, medium or large; Petite Marguerite, greenish yellow, dotted, darker on one side, medium; Summer Doyenne, greenish, small or medium-sized. *Autumn*—Duchesse d'Angouleme, very large; Beurre Bose, russet, large size; Flemish Beauty, large, excellent variety; Hardy russet, quite large; Seckle, small or medium. *Winter*—Beurre d'Anjou, one of the best varieties, large; Clairgeau, greenish yellow, red on one side, very large; Winter Nelis, russet, small or medium; Easter Beurre, yellow and red, quite large; Josephine de Malines, pale yellow, medium size. Apples and pears are grown as *standards*, with a high trunk, or as *dwarfs*, which branch near the ground. Dwarf trees are best adapted to growing in the kitchen-garden along the walks as seen in the accompanying plan. The two forms in combination may be used in groups on the lawn.

The following are a few good *Cherries.*—1. With acid flesh: Belle Magnifique, red, rather late, quite acid; Early Richmond, red and acid, very early; Montmorency, quite large, red, later than the previous kind; Morello, very dark crimson or nearly black; Reine Hortense, red, large, of excellent quality. 2. With sweet flesh: Black Tartarian,

reddish-black, quite large; Elton, red and yellow, large;
Knight's Early Black, quite large; Coe's Transparent,
amber-colored and red, medium size; Napoleon, pale yellow
and red, very large, flesh firm; Windsor, reddish-brown,
large, with firm flesh.

Plums.—Coe's Golden Drop, pale yellow, large; Green
Gage, greenish, of good quality but small; General Hand,
yellow, very large; Yellow Egg, a very fine variety; Brad-
shaw, very large, dark violet-red, early; Wild Goose, small
or medium, reddish, a useful wild species. Plums and
cherries may be grown for hedges enclosing the vegetable
garden or at regular intervals in a trimmed hedge. The
smaller growing kinds are especially useful for this purpose,
as the Wild Goose Plum and the acid cherries. They
thrive in a lighter soil than apples and pears, which do best
on rich ground.

Peaches.—Alexander, pale whitish-green suffused with
red, medium size; Crawford's Early, rich yellow, very large;
Princess of Wales, creamy white suffused with rose, large;
Snow, cream-colored, medium; Waterloo, whitish-green suffused with rose and crimson on one side, rather large.
Peaches may be grown for avenues in the kitchen-gardens
for which purpose they are better adapted than any other
tree. The surface soil should be kept free and open.

Apricots.—Early Golden, orange-colored, small size;
Breda, orange suffused with red, small; Moorpark, yellow
and red, large; St. Ambrose, large and beautiful. Apricots
are best grown on a south wall. They should be protected
from the sun's rays in spring.

Grapes.—Clinton, black, rather small; Concord, bluish-black, large; Catawba, red, rather large; Delaware, light red, small; Moores' Diamond, greenish-white, medium size; Niagara, pale yellowish-green, bunch medium size, berry large; Pocklington, yellow, rather large irregular bunches, berry large. Grape-vines may be grown to cover a straight walk in a kitchen-garden or for arbors. The soil should be kept open and cultivated.

Gooseberries.—Industry, dark red, hairy, very large; Downing, whitish-green, large; Triumph, golden yellow, rather large. Gooseberries are best grown for edging a walk in the kitchen-garden or in open borders from three to five feet apart.

Currants.—Black: Black Naples, Black Champion; red: Cherry, Fay's Prolific; white or amber: White Grape.

Blackberries.—Early Cluster, Lawton, Wilson Jr. Blackberries may be grown in rough places on sunny slopes to form a part of the garden scenery or for low hedges enclosing the kitchen-garden.

Raspberries.—Champlain, whitish-amber; Fontenoy, purplish, red, late; Hornet, crimson, quite large; Cuthbert, deep crimson; Golden Queen, amber; Marlboro, red, quite early. Raspberries should be grown in beds in the kitchen-garden; they require cultivation.

Strawberries.—Bubach, bright crimson, large, early; Cumberland, rosy-red, large size; Haverland, light red oval, early; Sharpless, rosy-red, very large. Strawberries should be grown in beds in the kitchen-garden, planted in rows and cultivated all summer. The little "Alpine Wood" strawberry may be planted all over in the grass among the trees in the orchard.

The kitchen-garden should be laid out somewhat after the manner shown in the plan, viz.: in square or rectangular quarters varying in size according to the size of the garden.

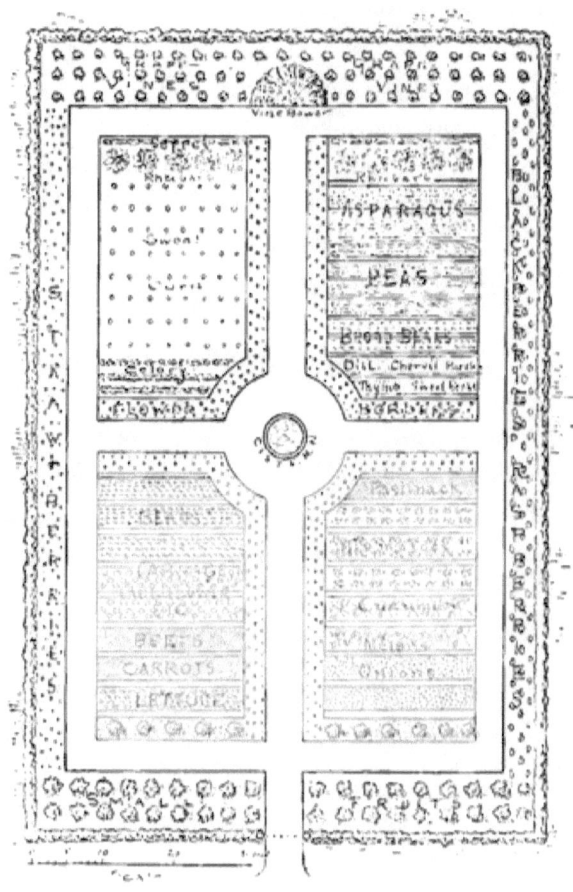

FIG. 83.—PLAN OF A KITCHEN-GARDEN.

The principal walk may be lined with a border of hardy herbaceous plants from three to four feet wide, and planted at regular distances with standard rose-trees, standard currants, or similar plants. It can be separated from the vegetable quarter by means of a hedge of gooseberries or currants and edged with box or lavender. If the walk is broad, say over six feet wide, we may plant an avenue of small fruit-trees as stated above. It is best, for many reasons, to have the kitchen-garden enclosed by a low hedge or plantation; in no case should it open upon a lawn, as the effect would be very incongruous. On the other hand, the quarters set apart for vegetables should not be crowded in among too many trees; they must be fully open to light and sunshine. Trees with running roots are not suited to planting in or near a kitchen-garden. The common hazel- or cob-nut is excellent for hedges around the orchard and vegetable-garden, being profitable as well. Among other suitable shrubs and trees are lilacs, privet, arbor-vitæ, sweet brier, crab-apple, and dwarf cherries. Thus a great variety of useful or ornamental plants may find a place in or near the quarters set apart for economic purposes only.

XVI.

AFTER-TREATMENT.

S everything in a garden is subject to constant
change, brought about by growth or decay, it
is necessary to watch every development with
jealous care, and either to check or encourage
the growth of individual plants as circumstances may
warrant. As the trees increase in size, many of the
weaker individuals are apt to suffer, no matter how carefully they were arranged in the beginning. Hence the
necessity of thinning and pruning, and the occasional removal of too rapid-growing specimens in order to preserve
the grace and beauty of groups and other plantations.
When this becomes necessary, the offending object must be
removed without hesitation; no matter how valuable it may
be as an individual tree, if it mars the beauty of the scenery
it must be sacrificed in the interest of the whole. But as a
rule very severe measures are not necessary in this respect.
There are generally many plants to choose from, and the
least valuable ones are removed if it serves the purpose
equally well. In many places a great number of trees and
shrubs are planted to produce an immediate effect, and it is

understood from the beginning which are to remain and which must be removed; and to make this arrangement doubly safe, each class should be marked on the working drawing in a different manner. From an economical point this may not come amiss in places where woods are scarce; in fact, in such localities the park and garden could be made to supply all the wood needed for home consumption.

In pruning flowering shrubs the branches must not be mutilated so as to destroy the spray or the flower-buds. It is better simply to remove older and more or less useless branches, as the natural grace of trees and shrubs is often totally destroyed by severe pruning. The object of pruning is to regulate the growth and to increase the vigor of young plants, or simply to remove offending or decayed parts, or to keep strong growing specimens within proper bounds, for a time at least. Summer pruning is best for all flowering shrubs and for many fruit-trees. It consists in the nipping off of very vigorous shoots which threaten to absorb all the nutriment, and to force such nutriment into the weaker shoots which are left undisturbed. This will encourage the formation of fruit-spurs in such trees as apples and pears, and the setting and ripening of flower-buds in many ornamental shrubs. Winter pruning, as far as shade-trees, flowering shrubs, and fruit-shrubs of the currant family are concerned, consists merely in a thinning out of crowded and crippled or old and sterile branches, and can be done at any time in winter. Where it is necessary to remove large branches the wound should be covered with tar or some other sticky matter to prevent the stump from rotting or splitting. To some trees, such as plums and cherries, pruning is not only useless but absolutely injurious and should not be resorted to after planting.

While some parts of the shrubbery have to be thinned out, the development and growth of trees and shrubs may cause a need of more planting in other parts, and thus the material removed may be utilized to advantage for this purpose. This also applies to specimens on the lawn, whether trees or shrubs.

FIG. 84.—GROUP OF TREES AND SHRUBS SHOWING ONE-SIDED DEVELOPMENT TO BE REC-
TIFIED BY AFTER-PLANTING.

If the soil was properly worked and prepared before planting, no nutriment will be needed for a long time, but sooner or later an occasional heavy dressing of barn-yard manure will be necessary; this should be put on in fall and dug in without disturbing the roots. If the shrubs are all planted as specimens in the grass, the manure put on to fertilize the lawn will also benefit these. The lawn requires a more constant care than the shrubberies. In summer the grass must be frequently cut and thoroughly watered during dry spells by means of lawn sprinklers,

This is especially necessary near the residence and around flower- and carpet-beds where the grass must be kept green and velvety all summer. The lawns should be cleaned and rolled in spring, and all dead spots must be re-sown or sodded over in a proper manner. When the soil becomes impoverished, good dressings of clean manure in winter, or, better still, a sprinkling of some concentrated fertilizer in spring, must be resorted to. Fish guano, wood ashes, blood and bone, bone dust and nitrate of soda are among the most useful for this purpose; they must be applied in spring just before the grass begins to grow.

The drives and walks if properly made need very little or no care except cleaning, which should be done as often as necessary.

The flowers that form a part of the natural scenery will, if properly selected and planted in suitable positions, for the most part grow without attention. If a stronger sort should usurp too much space and crowd out rarer varieties this should be kept in check. From time to time new and interesting kinds may be introduced in lawns and shrubberies. The flower-beds and borders should be kept absolutely clean and neatly trimmed, and no weeds must be allowed either there or in other spaces of bare ground as in shrubberies and open ground around specimen trees. Hedgerows and lawns must be kept free from weeds of all kinds such as dandelion, docks, evening primroses, and thistles. The weeding of the lawn should be attended to the first summer, and afterwards very little attention is necessary to keep weeds away.

Hedges, when intended to be cut, should be clipped

regularly, so as to make the growth dense and impenetrable, and the refuse must not be left in or around the hedge after clipping. A narrow strip of soil should be kept open and cultivated on each side of the hedge for a few years at least, and no coarse weeds must ever be allowed to get a foothold there, as it will be almost impossible afterwards to get rid of them.

In this, as in all phases of gardening, cleanliness is very important ; borders of shrubberies and flower-beds, edges of lawns, especially along the main path, should be cleanly cut, and no refuse must be allowed either on the walks, the lawn, or among flowers and shrubs.

Much supplementary work is needed to give the garden a touch of finish in summer, such as filling of vases, planting and sowing of flower-beds, shifting of specimen palms and cycads from greenhouses or conservatories to proper places on the lawn, all of which requires care and judgment. A pond or other body of water is apt to become filled with leaves, the decaying foliage of water plants and other matter, and when it is not too extensive, or if the water can be let out at will, the bottom should be cleaned annually or once in two or three years. Large ponds and lakes are not apt to become filled so soon, and very often no cleaning is necessary. Water-lilies and other plants must be kept within proper limits, so as not to mar the beauty of the surface or to accumulate too much decaying matter in the water.

From these concluding remarks on the making and planting of the pleasure-ground we will turn briefly to the study of the most important plants that form, or can be

made to form, characteristic features of the scenery. They
will be considered from a landscape-gardener's point of
view only; their natural habitat, the soil they prefer, their
size, form, and color—all will be pointed out as fully as it
is possible to do in a space so limited.

PART II.

SELECTION AND DESCRIPTION OF THE BEST HARDY ORNAMENTAL PLANTS FOR THE TEMPERATE ZONE OF NORTH AMERICA.

I.

DECIDUOUS TREES,

Chiefly planted for Shade and Shelter.

THE deciduous trees brought together under this heading are chiefly trees of considerable size, with broad, umbrageous crowns. Some are excellent street trees, such as the larger maples, box elder, lindens, and elms, and they are also used for larger plantations in pleasure-grounds and parks, or as shade-trees in smaller places. They include the most useful of ornamental trees, but the larger species, when planted in small grounds, must be used with discretion, so as not to crowd out the dwarfer and choicer vegetation. Most of them have elliptical crowns or present a rounded or obovate outline. They are destitute of conspicuous flowers, with the possible exception of the lindens, which have large quantities of fragrant, yellowish blossoms in July, and the chestnut, which is white with flowers in June. Still they are essentially grown for the sake of shade and shelter. Many of them assume the most beautiful autumn tints, such as the scarlet oak, the red maple, the pepperidge, the sassafras laurel, and the sweet gum. In their autumn garbs they excel the best spring effects of flowering trees, painting hill and dale in exquisite tints of gold and scarlet. Species that possess the special merit of changing into fine autumn colors should be selected in preference to others, as they introduce a new element of ornament and beauty into the garden.

THE LINDEN FAMILY.

Linden, *Tilia.*—The species of this genus are fine trees with very regular, rounded crowns and cordate leaves, bright green or silvery beneath; foliage very dense, giving a heavy shade. Both the European lindens, the two varieties of *Tilia Europea,* and the American linden (*T. Americana*), are fine trees for avenues. While flowering in summer the sweet odor of the innumerable flowers add to their general attractiveness. The silver lindens (*Tilia argentea* of Europe, and *T. heterophylla,* an American species) are very ornamental in a young state and suitable for the embellishment of lawns as specimen trees. The lindens do best in a moderately dry and fertile soil; they are rapid-growing trees, useful for shade and shelter.

THE QUASSIA FAMILY.

Tree of Heaven, *Ailanthus glandulosa.*—An elegant and quick-growing, medium-sized tree with long pinnate leaves, similar in appearance to some species of ash. It forms a dense, globular crown, producing nice effects of shade and light. The species will thrive in almost any soil; its long searching roots are apt to impoverish the ground, and its weed-like propensities make it less desirable than it would otherwise be.

Maple, *Acer.* —The maples are very numerous, scattered over a large part of the northern hemisphere, throughout America, Europe, and Asia. They vary in size from shrubs to tall forest-trees. All have more or less palmately-lobed leaves. Their foliage turns into a beautiful bright yellow, scarlet, or crimson in autumn. The flowers are racemose or corymbose, sometimes conspicuous, as in the American mountain maple, a tall and beautiful shrub.

The sycamore maple (*Acer pseudo-platanus*) is a fine tree with an elliptical crown and five-lobed leaves. The flowers are produced in pendulous racemes. The Norway maple (*A. platanoides*) is similar in habit, but the flowers are produced in upright corymbs. There are several varieties with variegated foliage of each species. The best forms of the sycamore maple are *A. Schwedlerii*, with bronzy-red foliage, *variegatum*, with white variegated, and *laciniatum*, with incised green and yellow leaves. The Norway maple has a white variegated form, *albo variegatum*, and one with yellow-margined leaves, *flavo variegatum*. Among other large forms is the silver maple (*A. dasycarpum*), with the under side of the leaves silvery white. It forms a moderately large tree with slender branches and an obovate outline. The large-leaved maple (*A. macrophyllum*) has the largest leaves of any and a regular habit. It is seldom seen in cultivation, but has no rival for beauty and utility. For high and rocky ground the sugar maple (*A. saccharinum*) is excellent. It has a dense, globular crown and a formal appearance. Of the smaller forms, very suitable for parks and gardens, the red maple (*A. rubrum*) is a most elegant tree. The leaves are of medium size, whitish beneath, and turn into bright yellow and scarlet tints in fall. This is the best maple for general use in small grounds. The striped maple (*A. Pennsylvanicum*) is a small tree with elliptical crown, large leaves, and light, beautifully striped bark. Field maple (*A. campestre*) has small five-lobed leaves. It is a tree about twenty feet high with globular crown and corymbose flowers. Tartarian maple (*A. tartaricum*) is similar in size and habit, but has almost cordate leaves with very superficial lobes.

Among forms that may be considered as large shrubs only, the vine maple (*A. circinatum*) and the mountain maple (*A. spicatum*) are very beautiful; the last one in particular is very showy when in flower, the erect racemes stand well above the foliage, and the yellow color contrasts well with the tender green of the leaves. From the extreme east of Asia come the beautiful dwarf varieties known as Japanese maples, which are somewhat tender in the north. There are several forms with more or less deeply cut or highly colored foliage, varieties of *Acer palmatum*. *Acer Japonicum* and *Acer Ginnala*, which are distinct species, are also known by the same popular name. They form broad masses of highly colored leaves in autumn if not injured by early frosts.

All maples will grow in a moderately rich and moist ground; some, as the Tartarian, the field, and the sugar

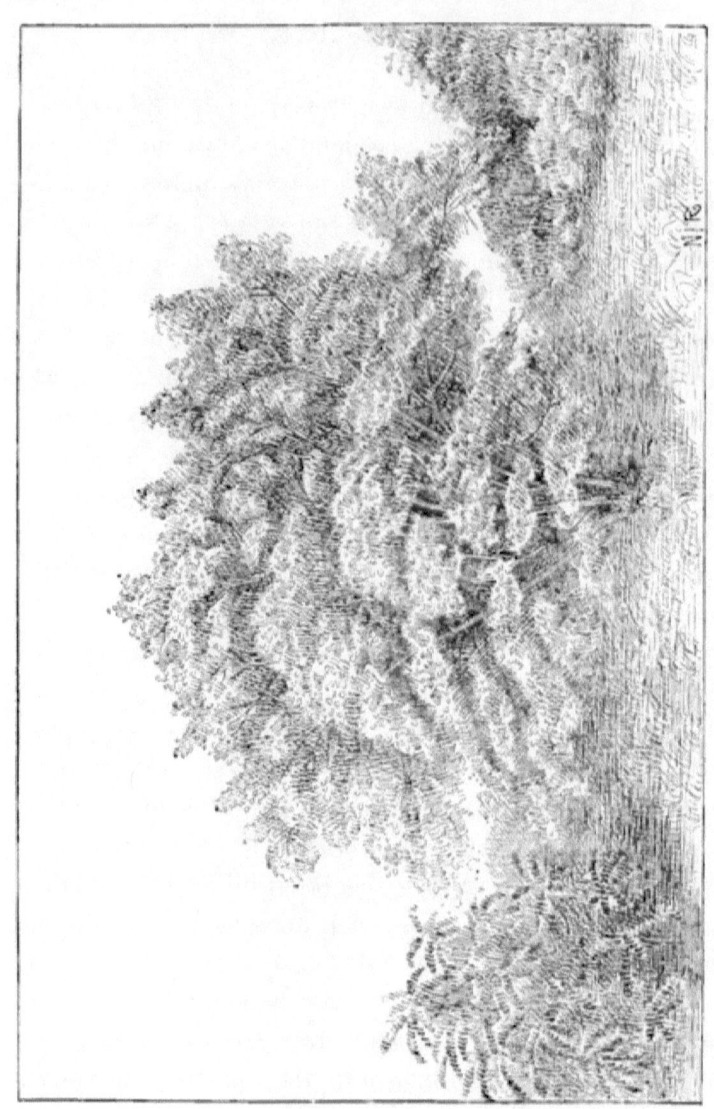

FIG. 65.—TARTARIAN MAPLE (ACER TARTARICUM).

maple will also do well in poor and stony soil. The maples are the most useful and ornamental of our deciduous trees.

Box Elder, *Negundo fraxinifolium.*—This is a moderately large tree with pinnate leaves and roundish crowns. It is an ornamental and valuable tree for avenues. The silver-leaved variety—with white margined leaves—forms an exceedingly fine lawn tree.

THE WITCH-HAZEL FAMILY.

Sweet Gum, *Liquidambar styraciflua.*—The foliage of this beautiful tree is five-lobed like that of the maples, but the texture is firmer and the lobes more acute. The habit is regular, broadly pyramidal in outline. Beautiful in summer with dark glossy leaves, changing into a deep crimson in autumn. It is common on moist ground and in old fields in moderately good soil. One of our best ornamental trees, fine for specimens on the lawn when young.

THE DOGWOOD FAMILY.

Pepperidge, *Nyssa multiflora.*—A small tree of irregular habit, twisted branches and horizontal sprays. This is a very elegant and picturesque tree with fine glossy leaves in summer and bright crimson autumn tints. It grows well in any light and open soil, in the outskirts of woods and frequently in old fields. Deserves to be used abundantly in landscape-gardening.

THE EBONY FAMILY.

Persimmon, *Diospyrus Virginica.*—A common tree of the South and Middle States with ovate leaves of a firm texture, upright habit, and irregular crowns with rounded outlines. It grows in any kind of soil in moderately moist positions.

FIG. 86. PERSIMMON (DIOSPYRUS VIRGINICA).

THE OLIVE FAMILY.

Ash, *Fraxinus excelsior.*—The European ash is a noble and picturesque tree with dark shining green foliage, ample rounded or ovate crowns, and straight grayish stems.

The leaves are pinnate. It grows on the shores of highland rivers, sometimes in dry ground but often on the water level among rocks and stones. Cultivated, it thrives well in any moderately rich soil. There is a variety with pendulous branches which when grafted on the common ash forms small, shady arbors in a short time. The ash retains a beautiful green and luxuriant foliage until late in fall.

THE LAUREL FAMILY.

Sassafras Laurel, *Sassafras officinale.*—A small but

ornamental tree with irregular crown of rounded outlines and s t r a i g h t, slender stems. Grows in rich or moderately gravel-ly soil either in moist or dry positions. Finest in old fields and on the outskirts of woods. The obo-vate, three-cleft leaves a r e very handsome glossy green in sum-mer, changing into a dull red and crimson in autumn. The tree

FIG. 87.—SASSAFRAS LAUREL (SASSAFRAS OFFICINALE).   is very effective on

account of its characteristic and picturesque habit.

THE NETTLE FAMILY.

Elm, *Ulmus montana, U. campestris, U. Americana.*— These are well-known trees with obovate crowns, very broad at the top, oblique sprays and sometimes slender, pendulous branches. The elms are excellent trees for avenues, but often become easy prey for insects which strip them of every leaf in dry summers. They prefer rich, loamy soil with a gravelly subsoil. *Ulmus campestris* is excellent for hedges. Of this species there are several good

FIG. 88.—NETTLE TREE (CELTIS OCCIDENTALIS).

varieties, one with yellow leaves. The majority of its numerous forms are of little or no importance. The same may be said of the varieties of the Scotch elm (*U. Mon-*

tana). There are two very distinct forms, one with fastigiate the other with pendulous branches. The white elm, (*U. Americana*) is of a more elegant habit than the rest, with more slender branches.

Nettle Tree, *Celtis occidentalis.*—An elegant tree of medium size growing in rich, moist ground. The leaves are more narrow than those of the elm. The crown is irregular, rounded, broadest at the base. It will grow in any moderately good soil.

Mulberry, *Morus.*—The mulberry trees are seldom used in ornamental gardening, but they are very ornamental when young. The most useful species for this purpose is the red mulberry (*M. rubra*), which has the finest foliage. All are useful for hedge-planting. The black mulberry gives a well-known fruit.

Paper Mulberry, *Broussonetia papyrifera.*—A small shade-tree with very ornamental three-cleft leaves, hardly, south of New York. For ornamental purposes this is better than the common mulberry trees. Will grow in any moderately good soil.

Osage Orange, *Maclura.*—A coarse, spreading, rapid-growing tree, with spiny branches and ovate lanceolate leaves. It is excellent for strong hedges and enclosures and of great ornamental value. It multiplies by means of running roots and is apt to become a weed.

THE PLANE-TREE FAMILY.

Sycamore or **Plane,** *Platanus.*—Large and beautiful trees with truncate, five-angled leaves, which are of a leathery texture and downy on the lower side. The crowns are

irregularly rounded, somewhat broader at the base than at
the top, with beautiful effects of light and shade. The
stem is grayish and, in places where the old bark strips off,
silvery white. The Oriental plane (*Pl. orientalis*) has
leaves more lobed and also broader crowns than the
American plane (*Pl. occidentalis*). The sycamore is common on the river-banks and in low fertile soil. While
small it is a most beautiful tree for any garden, but being
of rapid growth it will in time grow too large for smaller
grounds. Under cultivation it thrives in any moderately
good soil.

THE WALNUT FAMILY.

Walnut, *Juglans*.—These are large trees, with spreading, rounded crowns and fine pinnate leaves. They are
all ornamental, especially when young; grand and imposing when old. The English walnut is chiefly planted
for the sake of its well-known fruit. The black walnut is
a large American tree, and the butternut (*J. cinerea*) a
somewhat smaller but ornamental species. The walnuts
prefer rich soil with a light and open subsoil.

Hickory, *Carya*.—The hickories are large and beautiful
trees with more elongated crowns than the walnuts. The
leaves are long, pinnate. They are all well-known American trees common in deep and fertile soil. The butternut
(*C. amara*), the water hickory (*C. aquatica*), and pecan-nut
C. olivæformis) delight in low alluvial soil along rivers and
swamps. The shellbark hickories (*C. alba, C. sulcata*) grow
on higher ground in rich woods.

Caucasian Walnut, *Pterocaria caucasica,* is a beautiful hardy tree with broad, spreading crowns, and much smaller than the hickories and walnuts. It has long pinnate leaves of a glossy green with about nineteen leaflets. The fine

FIG. 89 —CAUCASIAN WALNUT (PTEROCARIA CAUCASICA).

specimen illustrated grows in 56° N. latitude in Sweden on moderately high, fertile ground. This is the most ornamental tree of the walnut family.

THE OAK FAMILY.

Oak, *Quercus.*—The oaks are among our most beautiful trees and very plentiful in American woods ; in fact, they form the main body of most mixed woods, both here and in Europe. The American forms grow more rapidly than the common English oak, and many species have exquisitely beautiful leaves. The English oak (*Q. robur*) grows in high and fertile ground on clayey subsoil. It is one of the largest and handsomest of European forest-trees, deserving universal planting for the sake of ornament as well. The chestnut oak (*Q. prinos*) is a smaller but not less beautiful species, very valuable as an ornamental tree for small

FIG. 90.—PIN OAK (QUERCUS PALUSTRIS).

grounds. The crown of this is less broad and more regular than that of the English oak. The leaves are obovate or oblong, with large, wavy teeth. The scarlet oak (*Q. coccinea*) is remarkable because of its beautiful autumn tints and glossy, sharply pinnatifid leaves. Other desirable species are the pin oak (*Q. palustris*), the white oak (*Q. alba*), and the willow-leaved oak (*Q. phellos*). These are among the best for general planting, but all oaks deserve to be planted extensively, both for pleasure and profit. In the South the live oaks form the feature of many a wood, on rather moist and rich ground. They are comparatively low and broad in outline, and on the spreading branches the Spanish moss grows in abundance. In northern latitudes, the oak woods are remarkable for the rich and varied herbaceous flora that finds a shelter beneath the fallen leaves in winter, and a pleasant shade in summer. This is partly because the roots of the oak go deep and do not rob the surface soil of its nutriment, while the fallen leaves make it richer year after year.

Chestnut, *Castanea.*—The chestnuts are very beautiful trees when young, and in old age they become rugged and picturesque. The leaves are very long, lanceolate, sharply toothed, smooth, and green. The crown is generally more broad than high, with an irregularly rounded outline, the stem stout and tapering in old trees. The chestnuts grow in deep, fertile woods on undulating ground, sometimes among rocks and stones; when cultivated, a sandy loam with well-drained subsoil suits them best. The innumerable white flowers, produced in long catkins, make the trees beautiful in summer.

Beech, *Fagus.*—The beech is the most beautiful of all forest-trees; it forms large woods in middle and northern Europe, chiefly on high and rocky ground and hillsides. The stem is smooth and grayish. The spray light, horizontal, and the crowns almost globular. In spring, when the silky leaves unfold, the beech woods are in their most attractive condition. Unlike the oak, the beech casts a very heavy shade, and the abundance of flowering plants of the oak-wood is not seen among the beeches. A few orchids, chiefly *Habenaria chlorantha*, and the star anemone (*Trientalis Europea*), are the most common plants. Mountain ash and hagberry grow here and there on the outskirts. The European beech (*Fagus sylvatica*) differs chiefly from the American beech (*F. ferruginea*) in having larger and

FIG. 91.—CUT-LEAVED BEECH (*FAGUS SYLVATICA LACINIATA*).

brighter leaves and a more horizontal spray. The copper beech is a well-known form of the European species, as are also the cut-leaved variety often seen as a lawn tree, and the weeping beech. These varieties form beautiful specimens on a lawn. All assume splendid autumn tints. The beech grows best in a sandy loam with an open or stony subsoil. In a young state it is exceptionally beautiful for woods and coppices, and when too large for this purpose it may be cut down, and a new growth will follow quickly. Many of the larger forest-trees may be treated in the same manner in parks and gardens. When they have become too large they should be cut down and utilized, and a second and more rapid growth is sure to follow.

Hop-Hornbeam, *Ostrya Virginica.*—This is a fine and slender tree, with brownish bark and birch-like foliage, growing in rich woods, frequently among beech and birch.

Hornbeam, *Carpinus betulus.*—A medium-sized or, more often, a small tree with birch-like foliage and smooth grayish stems. The spray is light and beautiful. It grows along stony rivers in moist and rich soil, but will thrive in any moderately good soil when cultivated. This is one of the best trees for hedges and screen planting. Its elegant habit and moderate size make it a particularly valuable tree for smaller grounds. The American hornbeam is a smaller species, but grows under the same conditions and is available for the same purpose.

THE BIRCH FAMILY.

Birch, *Betula.*—All the birches are trees with comparatively light foliage and slender sprays of more or less cordate or ovate leaves. They are very fragrant in spring when the leaves unfold, and the tender green of their foliage makes them particularly attractive during that season. The white birch is very beautiful throughout the year because of its white trunk. It grows in poor and gravelly soil into medium-sized trees, with more or less bent and twisted stems and branches, and oblong crowns. There are many

FIG. 92.—WEEPING BEECH (FAGUS SYLVATICA PENDULA).

fine varieties, such as red-leaved birch (*B. alba purpurea*),
with coppery foliage; the cut-leaved birch (*B.a. Dalecarlica*),
with slender branches and laciniated leaves; and the weeping birch (*B. a. pendula*), one of the most beautiful lawn
trees. The white birch forms immense forests abounding
in a rich herbaceous flora. The American white birch
(*B. populifolia*) does not differ greatly from the common
white birch, except in having a stiffer and less elegant
habit. The paper birch (*B. papyracea*) has beautiful white
bark, which peels off in layers. It is almost similar in
habit to some varieties of the white birch, but the leaves
are broader and more heart-shaped. On the shores of
rivers, often growing in the water itself, the picturesque
river birch (*B. nigra*) is frequently seen in the Northern
States. The cherry birch (*B. lenta*) has denser crowns
than any of the preceding kinds. The spray is horizontal,
almost beech-like, and the globular crowns and grayish
stems make it resemble a small beech at a distance. The
bark is brownish gray, resembling that of a cherry-tree.
This species and the white birch are the most valuable from
an ornamental point of view. Birches are fine trees for
planting in masses in groves and copses, and where it is desired to introduce woodland scenery birch and oak should
be the principal trees, as their light foliage will allow a
luxurious growth of grass and flowers.

Alder, *Alnus.*--The alder grows in moist places in
meadows and on river shores. It has a tall elliptical crown,
grayish stems, and oval or ovate leaves. The common
forms are not very ornamental, but they are excellent for
very low and wet ground. The cut-leaved Alder (*Alnus*

glutinosa laciniata or *imperialis*) is the only really valuable tree of the genus. It has slender branches and beautiful fern-like foliage and forms a fine and very ornamental lawn tree.

THE WILLOW FAMILY.

Willow, *Salix.*—The willows are rapid-growing trees, found in moist places, in marshes and meadows on lake and

FIG 93.—WEEPING WILLOW (SALIX BABYLONICA).

river shores. They have all more or less narrow, lanceolate leaves of a glaucous or silvery color on the lower side. Their branches are gray or silvery, sometimes bright red or yellow, and many species are very attractive in winter because of the highly colored twigs. All are of a more or less bushy habit when young, but eventually grow into trees of considerable size.

Most common is the white willow (*S. alba*), with grayish branches and lanceolate leaves covered with white silky hair. The golden willow (*S. vitellina*) is only a variety of the white willow with golden yellow branches. *Salix fragilis* has beautiful shining leaves. All these grow into large-sized trees. The osier willow (*S. viminalis*) is a smaller but very handsome species. The laurel-leaved willow (*S. pentandra*) is a small but beautiful tree with ovate-lanceolate leaves. The most popular and useful of all is the weeping willow (*S. Babylonica*), a familiar tree on the shores of rivers and ponds.

Poplar, *Populus,* are rapid-growing trees useful for screen planting and for planting where it is necessary to cover bare spaces quickly. Most common are the Canada poplar (*P. monolifera*), with fine cordate leaves and a regular habit; the silver poplar (*P. alba*), with whitish silvery foliage; the balsam poplar (*P. balsamea*), with fragrant leaves in spring, and the Lombardy poplar (*P. dilatata*), with fastigiate branches and a columnar habit. There is a golden-leaved variety of the Canada poplar which is a very fine ornamental tree. All are beautiful when young, but some are undesirable because of their long running roots; the balsam poplar and the white poplar in particular.

Aspen, *Populus tremula.*—This is a small tree with rounded crown and grayish silvery bark, of no ornamental value. It grows in poor soil almost anywhere. The American aspen (*P. tremuloides*) is a more ornamental tree, of a regular habit.

II.

CONIFEROUS TREES.

HE importance of hardy evergreen trees in the North, where the deciduous trees remain bare for a long time of the year, can hardly be over-estimated. Unfortunately many of the finest coniferous trees and shrubs are too tender in the far North to be of general use. But among the pines proper, among the spruces, firs, and hemlocks there is so great a variety of beautiful trees, that with them alone a great diversity of evergreen groups and plantations may be had in any part of the country. Many of the finer spruces and firs, as the Nordmann fir, the Colorado blue spruce, the Cephalonian and Spanish silver firs can hardly be excelled by any other class of trees in dignity and beauty. Cedars are, unfortunately, tender in the Northern States, but they will succeed in most places south and west of New York. Coniferous trees are best planted in large, irregular masses, with closer plantations of the more common kinds and choice specimens on adjoining open lawns.

In forming a *pinetum* considerable time may be needed, and it should be planted upon a previously arranged plan. It is best to form a nucleus here and another there, in suitable places, of some larger trees already on hand, and as these increase in size plant younger trees about them or in separate groups, sufficiently far apart to allow a full development of every individual tree. In this manner the plantation will look finished and natural from the beginning and still be capable of enlargement by subsequent plantings. If a group of coniferous trees is wanted for immediate effect they may be planted quite close together, and as soon as the branches touch, the superfluous plants must be removed and planted elsewhere.

Coniferous trees are most attractive in spring, when the tender green of the young shoots is in beautiful contrast with the dark color of the older branches. In large plantations of spruce and pine fine effects may be produced by introducing choice flowering shrubs and herbaceous plants in open glades, and on small, irregular open spaces among the trees.

THE PINE FAMILY PROPER.

Pine, *Pinus.*—The pines are chiefly large forest trees, but are sometimes of a dwarf and compact habit. The leaves are more or less rigid, and vary in length from a couple of inches to more than a foot, mostly green, but sometimes of a beautiful glaucous color, disposed in clusters, two, three, or five together. Pines form vast forests, chiefly consisting of one species, and almost destitute of herbaceous vegetation except in open places. Most of the species grow in moun-

tain regions or on sandy plains, while a few, like the white
pine, are found in low and rich soil. All will do well
under cultivation in moderately good soil, in open and ex-

FIG. 94.--AUSTRIAN PINE (PINUS AUSTRIACA).

posed positions. Some are difficult to transplant on account
of their long and bare roots, and must be transplanted as
young seedlings in order to succeed.

Austrian pine (*P. Austriaca*) is the best species for general use and ornament. It forms a close and rounded crown with long, rigid leaves, grows rapidly, and is easily transplanted.

Scotch pine (*P. sylvestris*) is the most common tree of Northern Europe, with short, bluish-white leaves and reddish-brown trunks. Especially useful for screen planting on poor and sandy soil, on the sea-shore and in other exposed places. It is quite ornamental while young.

Northern pitch pine (*P. rigida*) is a beautiful American tree growing on poor sandy and rocky ground in exposed positions. A useful and ornamental tree. The white pine (*P. Strobus*) is one of the most beautiful species with long, glaucous leaves and an elegant habit. It is easy to transplant, and will grow in any moderately good soil. The Bhotan pine (*P. excelsa*) is a nearly related tree with much longer, slender, and drooping leaves of a whitish color, very numerous at the top of the branches.

FIG. 95. —WHITE PINE (PINUS STROBUS).

This species is less hardy than the common white pine.

The stone pine (*P. cembra*) is a dwarf and compact species of a regular ovate outline, slow growing, hardy, and ornamental, and one of the best for use in smaller places. The dwarf pine (*P. Mughus*) is a very compact and spreading form, with short rigid leaves. It is almost a shrub, forming broad and low masses when planted on a lawn.

Spruce, *Picea.*—Spruces, as distinguished from firs, have

FIG. 96.—DWARF PINE (PINUS MUGHUS).

pendulous, not upright, cones, and leaves spreading every way. They are of an upright pyramidal habit, with branches disposed in whorls at regular intervals along the stem. They grow in rocky and mountainous regions, and form the main forests in the far North, sometimes in the company of pines.

Norway spruce (*P. excelsa*) is a common ornamental tree with dark-green leaves, close, sometimes drooping, branches, and an upright, elegant habit. Very useful for screen-planting, and in a young state for groups and masses on the lawn and intermixed in large shrubberies. There

are several varieties, one very dwarf, another with drooping branches. White spruce (*P. alba*) is of a broader and
more compact habit, and has whitish leaves. A very handsome ornamental tree for groups or specimens. Black spruce
(*P. nigra*) has shorter and darker leaves. This is a small
tree growing in cold and damp soil. The Himalayan spruce
(*P. Morinda*) is the most beautiful of the spruces, with
comparatively long leaves, ample branches, and a very
regular, pyramidal habit.

Blue Spruce, *Picea pungens*, is a slow-growing, compact,
and rigid tree with sharp, needle-like leaves. Often very
beautiful on account
of its glaucous blue
color. A very attrac-
tive species for plant-
ing on rocky hillsides
or in small places as a
specimen on the lawn.

Fir, *Abies*.—The
firs are stately trees
with erect cones, most-
ly flattened branches,
and comparatively
long, glossy, green or
glaucous leaves. All
grow in mountain re-
gions, sometimes in
high altitudes on
rocky and precipitous

FIG. 97.—CEPHALONIAN SILVER FIR (ABIES CEPHA-
LONICA).

ground. They are the most ornamental of all coniferous

trees. The balsam firs (*A. balsamica, pectinata,* and *pichta*) are almost similar in habit. *A. pectinata* is the tallest and most valuable of them, while *A. pichta,* the Siberian bal-

FIG. 98.—WHITE SILVER FIR (ABIES CONCOLOR).

sam fir, is the most ornamental, with rather long, crowded leaves. The leaves of all are of a dark and lustrous green on the upper surface, and more or less silvery beneath. The

Spanish silver fir (*A. Pinsapo*) has very stout and rigid leaves pointing in every direction. It is a very ornamental tree of a broadly pyramidal habit and a dark shining green color. This species is less hardy than the Cephalonian silver fir (*A.*

FIG. 99.—NORDMANN'S SILVER FIR (ABIES NORDMANNIANA).

Cephalonica), which is almost similar in habit but with more glaucous leaves and perfectly hardy. The last two will form fine specimen trees on a lawn. The white silver fir (*A. concolor*) is one of the most beautiful of evergreen trees with spreading branches and long two-ranked leaves of a pale glaucous color. This is a perfectly hardy and very ornamental tree of a pyramidal habit, and one of the best specimens for small lawns where there is place for a few trees only. The great silver fir (*A. grandis*) is hardly less beautiful, but less glaucous. *A. nobilis* is another fine tree of an almost columnar habit with stout spreading branches and glaucous leaves. Nordmann's silver fir (*A. Nordmanniana*) is, however, the most common and popular of all these trees. It is of a narrow pyramidal habit, with short but ample branches and long leaves, of a dark, shining green color on the upper side, and slightly silvery beneath. This is an excellent lawn tree and comparatively easy to obtain.

False Hemlock, *Pseudotsuga Douglasii.*—A tree almost as common and popular as the Nordmann fir, of a less formal habit, with slender elegant branches, and two-ranked, light green leaves. Not hardy in the extreme North.

Hemlock, *Tsuga.*—These are well-known trees in rocky woods on hillsides and ravines, often seen among deciduous trees, forming little groups and scattered masses among birch and oak. They have slender, feathery branches and an elegant habit, with dark green or silvery foliage. Many varieties of the common hemlock (*T. canadensis*) are of a broad and bushy habit in a young state, and almost rival the Deodar cedar in beauty. *T. Hookeriana* is a species with more glaucous leaves than the common hemlock, a very graceful tree, but probably not hardy in the extreme North. The hemlocks are useful for hedges, for screen planting, and as an undergrowth in woods and copses. Small groups of young trees are very effective on the lawn, and they may be used with great advantage for mixed groups of coniferous trees. In ravines and among stones and rocks on high river banks is their ideal home, and they may be used to form a background for rockeries with the best result. They grow well in any moderately good and naturally drained soil. As the hemlock may be pruned without injury, the habit may be rendered more compact by judicious pruning of the young trees, but a free and natural growth is generally to be preferred.

Larch, *Larix Europœa.*—This deciduous tree is excellent in woods and shrubberies or in groups of evergreen trees where the tender green of its leaves in spring is very effective. In early spring, when the leaves unfold, the tree is very fragrant. The European larch is a large forest tree with valuable wood, and it is one of the best and most profitable species for forest-planting. It is of an erect and slender habit with an ovate, pointed crown and light feathery clusters of leaves. It grows in any moderately good soil.

Cedar, *Cedrus.*—The cedars are not quite hardy in the Northern States. They are very ornamental trees with broad, rounded crowns and horizontal branches of a dark green or glaucous color. The Cedar of Lebanon (*C. Libanotica*) is probably the most hardy. It will grow as far north as New York in sheltered positions, and probably much farther north. This species is of a more rigid habit than the Deodar (*C. deodara*), a Himalayan tree of great beauty, with a light feathery spray, slender arching branches, and glaucous leaves. The cedars are exceptionally beautiful trees for small clumps, and as specimens on the lawn. A high sandy loam and a somewhat sheltered position are essential to success in their cultivation.

THE CYPRESS FAMILY.

The trees of this family are distinguished botanically by their small and often fleshy cones, the scales of which often unite to form a dry berry as in juniper. They have more or less scaly or prickly leaves. Some of the largest known trees belong to this family, as the common redwood of the Pacific slopes. The dwarfest and smallest members of the coniferous family also belong here.

Japanese Cypress, *Cryptomeria japonica.*—This is a very picturesque tree with a slender stem, and few but large branches that descend from the stem and ascend again at the apex. The leaves are crowded and scaly, and the sprays are flat and frondlike. It succeeds best as an undergrowth in deciduous shrubberies and woods on hillsides, and on the sides of ravines in moderately good soil with an open or gravelly subsoil. Planted as a lawn tree in the full blaze of the sun, it will not endure in the North.

White Cedars, *Chamaecyparis* (*Retinospora*), a very large genus of dwarf or medium-sized trees and shrubs, of very varied aspect and habit. The majority are perfectly hardy, as they are inhabitants of high altitudes and of the North. The largest are Lawson's cypress, the Nootka cedar, and the Japanese cedar. The first one (*Ch. Lawsoniana*) is a well-known ornamental tree with flat, feathery sprays. It has numerous garden varieties, varying greatly in form and color. The best of these are: *albo-variegata,* with white leaves and branches among the green ones; dwarf and compact, of a conical habit; *aureo-variegata*, with the young

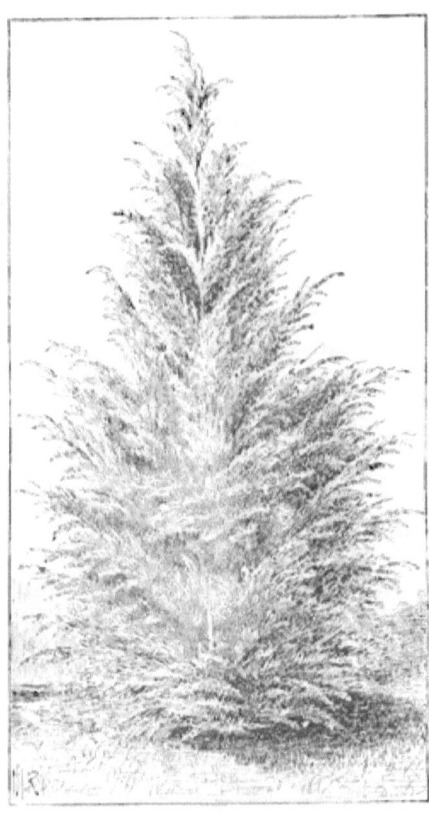

FIG. 103. LAWSON'S CEDAR (CHAMÆCYPARIS LAWSONIANA).

branches tipped golden yellow, very picturesque; *erecta viridis*, of a columnar habit and a beautiful green color; *gracilis pendula*, with long and slender, semi-pendulous branches; *nana*, a globular form, and *nana glauca*, a very beautiful glaucous variety. The Nootka cedar (*Ch. Nootkatensis*) is the finest and hardiest species of this genus. It is of a slender, graceful habit, with short arching branches and imbricated foliage, sometimes bright green, sometimes glaucous. There are several varieties of this species. The Japanese cedar (*Ch. obtusa*), which grows into a tree a hundred feet high, is quite common in gardens. The branches are slender, with ample, feathery sprays, and scale-like, adpressed leaves. The most common varieties are: *aurea*, with many of the sprays golden yellow, intermixed with green; *nana*, a very dwarf variety a couple of feet high only, broad and spreading; *plumosa*, with very large and feathery sprays of a fluffy appearance. There is a sub-variety of this cedar with yellow variegations (*plumosa aurea*), and one in which the young growth is creamy white (*argentea*). This species is one of the most useful garden plants. The smaller varieties are handsome in rockeries, and the larger ones in groups and as specimen trees. *Ch. pisifera* is a remarkable and picturesque species with very long, cord-like branchlets. It is of a compact habit and very beautiful and characteristic when well grown. In the variety *filifera*, this peculiar habit is more pronounced. *Ch. squarrosa* is one of the most common of the smaller coniferæ. It has fluffy, feathery sprays of a glaucous or silvery-gray color, and forms a small shrub or tree of a broadly columnar habit. These last kinds are excellent for rockeries. The American white cedar (*Ch. thuyoides*) is also a very fine and ornamental tree, useful for planting in deciduous woods and shrubberies as an undergrowth.

Arbor-Vitæ, *Thuya.*—Some of the arbor-vitæs are trees of considerable size, but many of the garden varieties are compact forms of a more or less globular or columnar habit. The American arbor-vitæ (*Thuya occidentalis*) is a common tree, growing in small colonies on almost any kind of ground, from rocky hillsides to cold swamps. The garden varieties are numerous and more common in cultivation than the type. The following are some of the best forms: *alba*, with the young shoots tipped with white early in the season; *aurea*, golden yellow; *Elwangeriana*, a dwarf bushy form; *Hoveyi*, a globular variety, tinted golden yellow; *Vervæneana*, oval, golden-tinted; *Warreana*, dwarf conical, a beautiful variety. The giant arbor-vitæ (*Th. gigantea*) is a tall and elegant tree with g r a c e f u l, irregular branches and flat, feathery sprays. This is a fine species for grouping with spruce and fir. Chinese arbor-vitæ (*Th. orientalis*) is a tree of a compact pyramidal or conical habit, less hardy than the common form. There are many varieties with differently colored leaves. The best are : *elegantissima*, with golden-tipped branches in summer ; *glauca*, a beautiful b l u i s h-white variety—one of the best ; *pyramidalis*, of a columnar habit, bright green color

FIG. 101.—GIANT ARBOR-VITÆ (THUYA GIGANTEA).

and robust growth. The American arbor-vitæ is very useful

for evergreen hedges; and choicer varieties for groups and as specimen trees, while some of the smaller kinds look fine in a rockery.

Japanese Arbor-Vitæ, *Thuyopsis dolabrata.*—This is a beautiful tree of a pyramidal habit with thick shoots and scale-like, fleshy leaves. It is of a fine green color, is probably the most ornamental of the arbor-vitæs, and very hardy. Fine for a specimen tree in a choice position on the lawn.

Juniper, *Juniperus.* The junipers are common trees on heaths, in barren and sandy soil, and—in America—in old fields. The common juniper (*J. communis*) is a very variable tree, generally of a fresh green color, with a more or less irregularly pyramidal habit. There are two common kinds grown in gardens—the Irish and the Swedish juniper. They are both of a columnar habit, with silvery or glaucous leaves. As an ornamental tree, the typical form is by far the best. Red cedar (*J. virginiana*) is a common tree on stony and sandy soil, on hillsides, and in old fields. Certain varieties of a columnar habit, and of a more or less glaucous color, are common all over the country. The Chinese juniper (*J. chinensis*) is also common in cultivation. The savin (*J. Sabina*) is a low, procumbent shrub, fine for rockeries.

There are a few singular forms, belonging to various divisions of the coniferous family, which are quite ornamental but rare in gardens.

The Umbrella Pine, *Sciadopytis verticillata,* is one of these. It is a dwarf, slow-growing tree with long, rigid leaves, collected in umbrella-like rosettes at the apex of the branches. It is a fine and hardy plant for a rockery or as a specimen tree on the lawn.

The Maidenhair Tree (*Ginkgo biloba*) is a large and ornamental, deciduous tree, with the habit of a common pear-tree, and fan-shaped, lobed leaves. It will form a fine specimen tree, and may also be planted in a shrubbery.

The Bald Cypress (*Taxodium distichum*) is more common; a deciduous tree of a pyramidal habit, growing in swamps and low ground generally. Fine for shores of rivers and lakes.

The Yew, *Taxus baccata.*—This is a very beautiful but slow-growing tree. It has flat sprays of dark olive-green leaves, and is generally of a broadly conical habit. It is often used for evergreen hedges, and in cemeteries, for which purposes it is excellent. There are several beautiful forms, now little known and seldom used because of their slow growth. All are fine for planting as an undergrowth in shrubberies and woods.

III.

FLOWERING TREES.

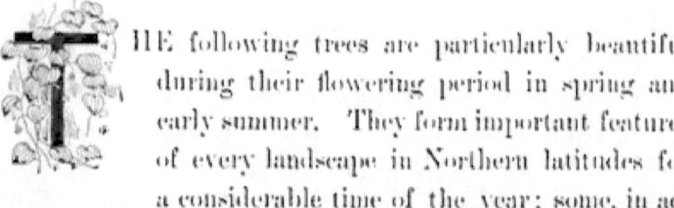

HE following trees are particularly beautiful during their flowering period in spring and early summer. They form important features of every landscape in Northern latitudes for a considerable time of the year; some, in addition to their attractive flowers in spring, change into beautiful autumn tints before the fall of the leaf, and many are covered in winter with showy clusters of fruit. The Siberian crab, American thorns, and the European mountain ash are a few of the deciduous trees that are ornamental in one way or another during the greater part of the year. Many of the species included under this heading are trees of considerable size, with large and beautiful foliage and shady crowns, useful as avenue and shade-trees, such as the horse chestnuts. The locust family contains a number of species with beautiful pinnate or twice-pinnate leaves; they are trees of considerable size, useful in landscape-gardening for every ornamental purpose. The locusts are fine trees for streets and avenues. All the species form beautiful and striking objects in masses of trees and shrubs. In many groups, such trees as the thorns, the hagberry, the buckeyes, yellow-wood and flowering ash may be used for the more central parts with good results. Catalpas, Paulownias, and Chinese magnolias are exceptionally beautiful for specimens on the lawn.

THE MAGNOLIA FAMILY.

Tulip Tree, *Liriodendron tulipifera.*—This is a well known, tall and handsome tree, with broad, lyrate leaves and showy, greenish-yellow flowers marked inside with rich orange, and resembling a tulip in shape. The flowers are produced in great numbers late in the spring. The tulip tree is found in different kinds of soil, but chiefly on moderately rich and well drained ground. As a small tree, twenty to thirty feet high, it is very ornamental with a broadly pyramidal or conical crown. It grows rapidly and must be removed as soon as it becomes too large for a place.

Chinese Magnolia, *Magnolia conspicua.*—A small tree with a rounded crown, smooth branches and obovate, pointed leaves about six inches long. The fragrant flowers are of a milky-white color, erect, six inches in diameter, expanding before the leaves in early spring. There is a variety or hybrid with purplish flowers known as Soulange's magnolia, which is equally valuable. The purple magnolia (*M. purpura*) is a Japanese shrub or small tree with obovate leaves and showy flowers, white inside, purple without. *Magnolia stellata* is also a very early flowering species of great beauty. These are fine trees for specimens on the lawn, and are among the best for small places. They will thrive in any moderately good soil that is not too wet.

FIG. 102.—CHINESE MAGNOLIA MAGNOLIA CONSPICUA.

Sweet Bay, *Magnolia glauca.*—A small American tree, very fine when cultivated, growing in swamps and low grounds generally. It has oblong leaves, green on the upper surface, glaucous beneath, and white fragrant flowers in early summer. Fine for groups and in shrubberies in rich, not necessarily low, ground.

Umbrella Tree, *Magnolia umbrella.*—This is a low ornamental tree with broad, spreading crowns and obovate-lanceolate leaves from one to two feet long, placed in rosettes at the apex of the branches, with a very large white flower in their midst. A very beautiful shade-tree for general use.

Great-leaved Magnolia, *Magnolia macrophylla.*—A small or medium-sized tree with extremely large leaves, two to three feet in length, and white flowers, sometimes a foot in diameter.

Cucumber Tree, *Magnolia acuminata,* is a large tree with oblong pointed leaves and greenish-yellow flowers. This is a fine shade-tree.

In the South, the large-flowered *Magnolia grandiflora,* with evergreen, leathery leaves, is one of the most important members of the magnolia family. All the magnolias do well in moderately good soil, but prefer a rich, sandy loam.

THE BUCKEYE FAMILY.

Kœlreuteria, *Kœlreuteria paniculata.*—This is a rare and beautiful tree with pinnate leaves consisting of numerous coarsely-toothed leaflets, and very large terminal panicles of yellow flowers. The crown is irregularly rounded; the habit, slender and elegant. An excellent small tree for shrubberies. Thrives well in common garden soil.

Horse Chestnut, *Æsculus Hippocastanum.*—This robust-growing tree, with its shady, conical crown, handsome fingered leaves and erect racemes of white flowers marked with yellow and purple, is one of the finest and hardiest of all shade-trees. It is of rapid growth and attains a considerable size. The red-flowered horse chestnut (*Æ. rubicunda*) is a smaller and more compact tree, flowering when quite small. The flowers are of a showy, rosy red. Preferable for small places in masses of trees and shrubs. Rich or moderately rich soil.

Buckeye, *Pavia.*—The red buckeye (*P. rubra*) is a small, handsome tree with a broad crown, smooth, fingered leaves smaller than in the horse chestnut, and loose racemes of bright red flowers. This is the finest tree of the family, and very ornamental when cultivated. It is excellent as a specimen tree, or in groups and shrubberies. The yellow buckeye (*P. flava*) is similar in habit, but larger, with less showy, pale yellow flowers. One of the most useful is the dwarf buckeye (*P. parviflora*), which is only a broad, leafy shrub. The small whitish flowers with conspicuous threadlike stamens are disposed in slightly branched, erect panicles ten inches long or more. It flowers late in the season and is then very ornamental for groups or as single specimens on the lawn. The buckeyes grow wild in rich woods, generally on high and naturally drained ground. Under cultivation, they do well in any moderately good soil. They are among our best ornamental trees.

THE LOCUST FAMILY.

Laburnum or **Golden Chain,** *Laburnum vulgare.*—A small tree with trifoliate leaves and long drooping racemes of yellow flowers early in May. The Scotch laburnum (*L. alpinum*) is similar in habit, but flowers later. Both are of an elegant habit and very ornamental when in full flower. Fine for shrubberies or smaller groups on the lawn. They thrive in any ordinarily good soil.

Locust Tree, *Robinia Pseudacacia.*—A fine ornamental tree of a very picturesque habit, with light rounded sprays of pinnate leaves and loose, drooping racemes of fragrant white flowers appearing late in the spring. A fine tree for

FIG. 103.- LOCUST (ROBINIA PSEUDACACIA).

small avenues, shrubberies and masses of trees and shrubs. It grows in high, often poor and gravelly soil. The rose-acacia (*R. hispida*) is a very small tree or shrub of a straggling and spreading habit, growing in rocky and stony soil on the banks of rivers and lakes. It has fine racemes of rose-colored flowers and pinnate leaves. The clammy locust (*R. viscosa*) is intermediate in size between the two. It has clammy branches, pinnate leaves, and pale rose-colored flowers in May or June. All the Robinias are excellent for rather poor and gravelly or stony soil, and for general use in ornamental gardening.

Yellow-wood or **Virgilia,** *Cladrastis tinctoria.*—This is a small, handsome tree, with regular, rounded crowns, smooth grayish stems, pinnate leaves with ovate, parallel-veined leaflets, and drooping panicles a foot or more long, of fragrant, creamy white flowers in early summer. It is without exception the finest of the small ornamental trees of the family, beautiful as a lawn tree and may also be used with good effect in mixed shrubberies. Thrives best in a rich, sandy loam.

Pagoda Tree, *Sophora Japonica.*—Small tree with rounded crowns, pinnate leaves, and drooping panicles of creamy white flowers late in summer. The weeping pagoda tree (*S. J. pendula*) is one of the finest trees of its class, with almost perpendicular branches. Both are beautiful for specimen trees on a lawn.

Red Bud, *Cercis.*—There are three very ornamental species of this genus which flower in spring before the leaves unfold. The reddish-purple flowers are produced in dense clusters along the bare branches, and the trees are very effective in that state. Leaves oval, rounded, or heart-shaped, undivided. The hardiest is the American red bud (*C. Canadensis*), a tree of an irregular, erect habit. The Japanese red bud (*C. Japonica*) and the Judas tree (*C. siliquastrum*) have larger and brighter blossoms and are suffi-

ciently hardy in most of the States. They are beautiful in
groups of flowering trees and shrubs, or in specimen groups
on the lawn, three or more together.

Kentucky Coffee Tree, *Gymnocladus Canadensis.*—A tall
and slender tree with spreading branches and twice-pinnate
leaves, from two to three feet long. Flowers white, in
terminal racemes, in early summer. A tree with a light
and airy appearance, irregularly rounded crowns, and slender stems, with rough, brownish bark. It looks best in
larger masses of trees, where it forms a very ornamental
object. Thrives best in moderately rich soil.

Honey Locust, *Gleditschia triacanthos.*—An erect, medium-sized tree with smooth, brownish stems protected by
clusters of long branched thorns, and rounded crowns of
light pinnate or doubly pinnate foliage. The flowers of
this tree are not conspicuous, but it is included here for
the sake of convenience. It is a very ornamental tree
fine for mixed plantations and shrubberies. In the country
it might also be used for avenues. Common in rich woods,
and will grow in any moderately good soil.

THE ROSE FAMILY.

Ornamental Cherries, *Cerasus.*—There are several double
flowering cherries of oriental origin. They are exceedingly
beautiful, dwarf trees of an erect or pendulous habit.
Siebold's Chinese cherry (*C. serrulata*) is one of the finest
of them. It grows to a height of about fifteen feet and is
covered with numerous white or pale rose-colored, double
flowers early in spring. The weeping cherry (*C. semperflorens*) has drooping branches and numerous white, axillary

flowers somewhat later in the season. Several species of oriental plums are also sold by nurserymen under the names of flowering and weeping cherries (see *Prunus*). There are a couple of American species of great ornamental value which are commonly grown in gardens. The chokeberry (*C. Virginiana*) is the most common of these. It is a slender tree with shining green leaves and white flowers in pendulous racemes early in the season. The wild black cherry (*C. serotina*) is a handsome tree, with flowers in long drooping racemes, later than the previous species. The wild red cherry (*C. Pennsylvanica*) is another fine, erect growing tree with a dense, rounded crown completely covered in May with pure white flowers. All are fine for shrubberies, and among larger masses of evergreen trees. The common cherry (*C. avium*) is not generally grown for ornament but it may be used with advantage in ornamental gardening. There is a double-flowered variety of great beauty.

Hagberry, *Crasus Padus.*—This small but very ornamental tree, which forms an important feature of European woodland scenery in early summer, has broad, pendulous racemes of pure white flowers. It grows on the outskirts of deciduous woods and sometimes among pine, spruce, and juniper trees, along mountain streams and roads. More valuable than the last two.

There are numerous double-flowering varieties of the peach which also deserve mention. The colors are white, pale rose, and rosy red.

Plum, *Prunus.*—Nearly all species are ornamental shrubs or trees, with numerous white flowers in spring. Of special

14

interest are the doubled-flowered Chinese and Japanese varieties. *P. Sinensis* has numerous single or double flowers,
of a white or rosy-red color, disposed in clusters along the
branches. *Prunus subhirtella* (syn. *Cerasus Japonica pendula* and *C. pendula*) has drooping branches, and small
white or rose-colored, single or double flowers, disposed in
clusters along the branches. This is a very ornamental tree
of a pendulous habit, fine for specimens on choice lawns.
The red-leaved plum (*P. Pissardii*) is a small, erect-growing tree with oval crowns and purplish leaves. The flowers
are insignificant, small, and white. *Prunus Simonii* is another Chinese species of comparatively little ornamental
value.—Cherries and plums will do well in light and gravelly
soil, and they are therefore especially useful where the soil
is thin and poor. In sandy loam most species will thrive
better than in almost any other soil, but moist and low
positions are not suitable.

Thorns and **Hawthorns,** *Crataegus.*—These are among
the most beautiful flowering trees, of neat and compact
habit, with finely cut leaves. The foliage turns into the
most striking colors in autumn,—gold, crimson, and scarlet
together on the same tree. It is chiefly the American
thorns that assume these gorgeous autumn tints.

The hawthorn (*C. Oxyacantha*) is a small tree branching down to the ground, of a fine conical habit, with dense,
dark-colored foliage. The leaves are rather small, obovate,
slightly trifid, or pinnatifid. The flowers are numerous,
white, sweet-scented, corymbose, on short lateral branchlets
along the main branches. The double white thorn is one
of the finest of lawn trees, and so are, also, the various red

or scarlet varieties with single or double flowers. The
hawthorns are occasionally grafted on tall stems for specimen trees, but grown in their natural way they are perhaps
still more effective, with foliage and flowers down to the
ground. The common
type is excellent as a
hedge plant—in fact
it is the best plant
known for this pur-
pose. All the varie-
ties thrive best in a
sandy loam.

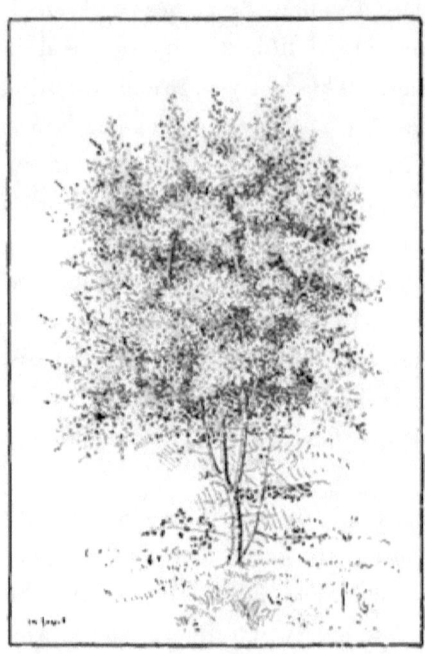

FIG. 104.—NARROW-LEAVED THORN (CRATÆGUS
SPATHULATA).

Scarlet thorn, *C.
coccinea.*—This is one
of the finest of the
American thorns, with
numerous large, white,
corymbose flowers in
May, and clusters of
coral-red fruit in win-
ter. It grows on high
river banks, in thick-
ets, and on the out-
skirts of rich woods, forming a rounded, bushy tree.

Black thorn, *C. tomentosa.*—One of the most beautiful
flowering trees of the Middle States, with large, downy
or woolly leaves, oval or ovate in outline, with a deeply
cut edge. The flowers are very large; in upright corymbs, white, with reddish stamens; followed by large,
scarlet fruit. Habit, dwarf and compact, often with

straight stem and globular crown. Grows in rich woods and thickets.

Cockspur thorn, *C. Crus-galli.*—A small tree with ovate, wedge-shaped, shining green leaves and clusters of large white flowers tinted red, and with reddish stamens. Fruit scarlet, fine in autumn. The leaves of this, as also of the previous species, change into beautiful autumn tints.

Narrow-leaved thorn, *C. spathulata.*—A very small and compact tree, with spiny stem and branches, and small spathulate leaves. Flowers white, small, many in a corymb, followed by small clusters of coral-red fruit. The evergreen thorn (*C. Pyracantha*) is a very slender tree or shrub with small, evergreen leaves and innumerable clusters of beautiful orange-scarlet fruits, persistent throughout the winter. Much used for training on walls, and also as a specimen shrub on a lawn.

Crab-Apples, *Pyrus*: Chinese crab-apple (*P. spectabilis*).—A beautiful, small tree with oval-oblong, serrated leaves and umbels of large, white, blush or rose-colored flowers, which are semi-double or double. Flowers in May.

Japanese crab-apple, *P. floribunda.*—A very small tree or shrub with innumerable rosy-red flowers late in spring. Very beautiful. The variety *atrosanguinea* has much deeper, blood-red flowers. The cherry-like fruit is quite ornamental late in autumn.

Siberian crab-apples (*P. prunifolia* and *P. baccata*) have also very ornamental flowers followed by small, cherry-like fruit. There is a fine double-flowered variety of *P. baccata.*

American crab-apple (*P. coronaria*) is a small, erect tree with stout, horizontal branches down to the ground, forming beautiful thickets in old fields and pastures or growing in the outskirts of rich woods. The flowers are large and sweet-scented, and very numerous in early summer. A very handsome tree to plant in groups on the lawn or mixed in shrubberies. All do best in rich loamy soil.

Mountain Ash, *Pyrus aucuparia.*—This is one of the most ornamental trees of the family, with long, pinnate leaves, slightly hairy and grayish beneath, and erect corymbs of white flowers in spring, followed by showy clusters of scarlet fruit in autumn. Very beautiful in composite groups of trees or several together on a lawn. Also used in some countries for avenues along country roads, with beautiful effect. Grows well on light and comparatively poor ground. The American mountain ash (*P. Americana*) and the elder-leaved mountain ash (*P. sambucifolia*) are also fine ornamental trees.

White Beam, *Pyrus Aria.*—A tree, somewhat larger and more robust than the last mentioned, with simple or slightly pinnatifid, grayish leaves, and large, white flowers in loose corymbs. Requires a deeper and richer soil to develop its full beauty. Habit regular, with fine rounded crowns.

THE DOGWOOD FAMILY.

Flowering Dogwood, *Cornus Florida.*—A bushy and straggling tree common in rocky woods and on river banks. Very showy in spring when in full flower. Extremely beautiful in mixed shrubberies and in groups of three or more on the lawn. There is a variety with red flowers, those of the common one being pure white.

FIG. 105.—FLOWERING DOGWOOD (CORNUS FLORIDA).

THE STORAX FAMILY.

Silver Bell or **Snowdrop Tree,** *Halesia tetraptera.*—This is a broad and bushy tree with black, twisted stems and branches and cherry - like foliage. The beautiful, bellshaped, pure white flowers appear in spring as the leaves unfold. It is then one of our most showy trees, growing along streams, on high rocky banks, leaning over

FIG. 106.—BRANCH OF SILVER BELL TREE (HALESIA TETRAPTERA).

the water in a picturesque manner. Fine for shrubberies and on the outskirts of large masses of trees, or for small groups on the lawn.

THE BIGNONIA FAMILY.

Catalpa or **Indian Bean,** *Catalpa.*—The catalpas are showy, late flowering trees and very valuable on this account. Growth very rapid and strong, forming trees with nicely rounded crowns in a few years. The common catalpa (*C. bignonioides*) has erect, thyrsoid panicles twelve inches, or more long, with white flowers, spotted with yellow and purple, and large, heart-shaped leaves on long stalks. The Japanese catalpa (*C. Koempferii*) has much smaller, creamy-white flowers and glossy, green, heart-shaped leaves. They both flower in July. The variety known as Tea's hybrid flowers very freely. It is of a more spreading habit. The catalpas will grow well in any moderately good soil.

THE FIGWORT FAMILY.

Paulownia, *Paulownia imperialis.*—This very ornamental tree resembles the catalpas in form and habit. The leaves are large and heart-shaped, and the flowers, which appear before the leaves in spring, are collected in very large, terminal panicles. The color is a beautiful violet-

FIG. 107.—PAULOWNIA (PAULOWNIA IMPERIALIS).

blue. A fine lawn tree, tender in the extreme North. It grows well in an open, sandy lawn in a sunny and sheltered position. Perfectly hardy south of New York.

THE OLIVE FAMILY.

Flowering Ash, *Fraxinus Ornus.*—A very handsome tree with pinnate leaves, rounded crowns, and of a graceful habit, with large masses of creamy-white flowers tinged brown late in spring. A fine, showy tree for sheltered positions south of New York. Fine as a specimen on a lawn or by the margin of a lake or river. Perfectly hardy in Europe and growing luxuriantly as far as the fifty-sixth degree north latitude.

IV.

ORNAMENTAL SHRUBS.

AVING considered the flowering trees which are most useful in the hand of the landscape-gardener we have become more familiar with their habit, habitat, and use in gardening. It now remains to make a choice selection of flowering shrubs of a nature that will please and satisfy all. Flowering shrubs are very numerous and, as they are all more or less beautiful, it is a somewhat difficult task to make a selection within the proper limit.

Shrubs should not be used so much by themselves, in separate groups and masses, as in combination with flowering trees and other forms of vegetation, in rounding off and finishing larger masses of trees, in making detached groups and single specimens on the outskirts of such masses. Many too, may be used as an undergrowth in plantations of deciduous trees: especially evergreen shrubs, such as mahonias, kalmias, rhododendrons, holly, and similar forms: others to give a touch of higher color to groups of evergreen trees, and more sparingly in larger masses, if there are secluded lawns hemmed in by coniferous trees only. On

the banks of streams and miniature lakes, shrubs and evergreen trees are often more desirable than larger deciduous
trees, which are apt to make such waters look more insignificant than they really are, while the endeavor should be
to produce quite the opposite result by means of judicious
planting. When planted in groups, too dissimilar forms
must not be brought together in one and the same group;
for while diversity is desirable and necessary, there is a
limit to contrast over which we cannot pass without making
our work disagreeable instead of pleasing.

On bare hillsides and sandy, sterile ground, low tufted
and spreading shrubs may be used instead of grass for covering the surface, such as crowberry, sand myrtle, cross-
leaved heath, and purple heather. They are insignificant
as individuals and effective in large masses only. St. John's-
wort and several plants of the heath family are useful for
covering the ground in shady places.

A failure is often made in growing ericaceous plants,
Vacciniums, Andromedas, and similar forms, simply because
they are grown under too artificial conditions. It is generally supposed that these plants require a peaty soil, but in
reality they are found growing in rich and damp woods
among the common trees, in very ordinary soil, especially
in sandy loam covered with a layer of decayed leaves.
Many grow in swamps in several inches of water, during
the better part of spring and all rainy seasons. A shallow layer of sandy loam mixed with leaf-mould on clay
subsoil, in situations where the ground can be submerged
in water for weeks together, are the most natural conditions for these. Others will grow anywhere in rich

open soil and may be used as an undergrowth in thickets and shrubberies.

Suggestions as to the proper employment of all the different kinds will be found in the descriptions.

THE CROWFOOT FAMILY.

Yellow Root, *Xanthorrhiza apiifolia.*—A low, spreading bush with deeply cut, pinnate leaves and drooping racemes of dull, purplish flowers. It is grown on account of its very ornamental foliage; and useful for covering banks and in shady places in rockeries. Prefers a rich, not necessarily damp soil, and grows to a height of one or two feet.

FIG. 108.—TREE PEONY (PÆONIA MOUTAN)

Tree Peony, *Pæonia Moutan.*—An exceptionally fine plant of an almost globular habit, beautiful, irregular, pinnatifid leaves of a glaucous color, and with single or double flowers, six or more inches across, white, flesh-colored and different shades of rose, purple, or crimson. About three feet high. Suitable for small groups or as single specimen plants on the lawn. Prefers a well-drained sandy loam.

THE BARBERRY FAMILY.

Barberry, *Berberis vulgaris.*—A spiny, erect-growing shrub, four or five feet high, with small obovate-oblong leaves and axillary clusters of yellow flowers followed by bright scarlet fruit. It is sometimes used as a hedge plant, but more commonly in mixed shrubberies. The species known as *B. Darwini* is a broad, spreading bush with very spiny branches and scarlet fruit in winter. A similar and equally useful kind is *B. Thunbergii.* Both are fine in rockeries.

Mahonia, *Berberis aquifolia.*—One of the few evergreen shrubs which are hardy in the North, and very useful on this account. The leaves are leathery, pinnate, with spiny edges. It bears clusters of yellow flowers in spring. Very useful as an undergrowth in shrubberies and in sheltered positions in a rockery. Sometimes used in clumps on the lawn where it is less at home. Naturally a plant of deep, shady woods.

B. repens is a dwarfer and hardier kind, growing into broad masses seldom more than a foot high.

THE ROCK-ROSE FAMILY.

Most of the plants of this family are tender, evergreen shrubs that may be used in the South. Some are very beautiful, with highly-colored flowers and large, glossy foliage.

A few of the rock-roses (*Helianthemum*) will succeed in sunny, sheltered positions in a rockery. The most common are: *H. vulgare*, flowers originally yellow, now much varied in color. A procumbent shrub. *H. polifolium*, with small linear leaves and white flowers. There is also a rose-colored variety.

THE HYPERICUM FAMILY.

Hypericum or **St. John's - Wort.**—Mostly herbaceous plants of moderate ornamental value. *H. Kalmianum* is a low, spreading shrub, with glaucous leaves and bright yellow flowers late in summer. *H. aureum*, a kind found on the banks of mountain rivulets in partial shade. Leaves oblong, glaucous, flowers very large, orange-yellow. Forms a medium-sized shrub of regular habit, flowering in August. *H. calycinum* is a procumbent shrub, a foot high, with ovate leaves and large yellow flowers late in summer. One of the best for covering bare spots under tall shade-trees and also fine in rockeries.

THE TAMARISK FAMILY.

Tamarisk, *Tamarix.*—Graceful shrubs of a cypress-like appearance, with minute, awl-shaped leaves, and very long, arching branches, covered with numerous small, reddish flowers in summer. The most common are *T. Africana* and *T. Gallica*. There is a beautiful vigorous species, *T. articulata*, from China and the Orient, which is equally hardy. Sea-side shrubs, for sandy and exposed shores, in company with sea buckthorn and pine. All grow well in light and sterile soil, in sunny positions.

THE MALLOW FAMILY.

Rose of Sharon, *Hibiscus Syriacus.* —A tall and beautiful shrub of an erect habit and an obovate outline, with broadly ovate, three-lobed leaves, and single or double axillary flowers late in summer. There are numerous varieties, varying in color from pure white to deep crimson and purple. The single white, single purple, and the variety known as *pæoniæflora* are among the best, though many of the double varieties are also beautiful. They are fine in groups of three or more on the lawn in any moderately good soil.

THE RUE FAMILY.

Hop Tree, *Ptelea trifoliata.*—A tall shrub with ornamental trifoliate leaves. Fine in shrubberies.

THE SUMACH FAMILY.

Smoke Tree, *Rhus Cotinus.*—A large shrub with smooth, obovate leaves and large panicles of flowers in early summer. The inflorescence remains after the fall of the flowers throughout the summer, and becomes light and feathery in appearance. The plants, covered with these pale reddish panicles, are very ornamental. Of the common American sumachs few are worth cultivation. They are generally of a coarse and weedy appearance. A variety of the smooth-leaved sumach (*R. glabra laciniata*) with deeply cut leaves is, however, a very beautiful and useful foliage plant. Ordinary, good soil.

THE BUCKTHORN FAMILY.

Buckthorn, *Rhamnus catharticus.* —Thorny shrub useful in screen planting. Leaves ovate. Flowers greenish in axillary clusters. *Rh. Frangula* is a more ornamental shrub, with smooth, obovate leaves and numerous, small whitish flowers.

New Jersey Tea, *Canothus Americanus.*—A small, spreading shrub with oblong-ovate leaves and large clusters of white flowers. Undergrowth in shrubberies and thickets in moderately good soil.

THE ILEX FAMILY.

American Holly, *Ilex opaca.*—This is a small-sized tree or a large shrub, often leafy to the ground. It is one of our few hardy evergreen trees, smaller, but perhaps more beautiful than the European holly. The leaves are oval with slightly spiny and wavy margins; shiny, very dark green. The red fruit is very ornamental in winter. Hollies are most effective when grown in mixed woods or shrubberies among young birch and large flowering trees and shrubs. It may be planted as an undergrowth in deciduous woods, mixed with rose bay, rhododendron, azalea, and mahonia aquifolia. The holly is unfortunately little appreciated and seldom planted, although it is one of the most beautiful of our native trees.

THE SPINDLE-TREE FAMILY.

Spindle-Tree, *Euonymus Europæus.*—Shrub four or five feet high, with ovate-lanceolate leaves and greenish flowers. Ornamental in winter only, when the showy, red fruit is very effective. The American species (*E. atropurpureus* and *E. Americanus*) are also planted occasionally. In woods and thickets as an undergrowth only, or mixed with choicer plants in shrubberies.

The evergreen Japanese species (*E. Japonicus*), which is hardy as far north as New Jersey, is a very ornamental shrub with dark, leathery foliage. The variety *radicans* is useful for covering bare slopes and also in rockeries and on walls.

THE BLADDER-NUT FAMILY.

Bladder-Nut, *Staphylea pinnata.* —A pretty shrub with pinnate leaves and numerous drooping racemes of white flowers. This and the three-leaved bladder-nut are fine in mixed shrubberies.

THE PEA FAMILY.

Dyer's Greenweed, *Genista tinctoria.*—A small, bushy shrub with long terete branches and lanceolate leaves; the whole plant green. Flowers numerous, bright yellow, late in spring. Useful for sea-shores and sandy, sterile soil, for naturalizing in masses on sunny slopes and in rockeries.

Scotch Broom, *Sarothamnus scoparius.*—A taller shrub four to five feet high with angular branches and small trifoliate or simple leaves. Flowers, very showy bright yellow, axillary. A fine plant for shrubberies in sunny positions, or for naturalizing and planting in company with the former.

Purple Cytisus, *Cytisus purpureus.*—A dwarf, bushy shrub with small trifoliate leaves and large axillary purple flowers, very numerous in summer. This is an exceptionally fine plant on the edge of a shrubbery, in sunny positions, or in a rockery.

All the above species do best in a sandy loam.

Furze, *Ulex Europæus.*—This is a dwarf, spiny shrub growing in masses on commons and barren ground in western Europe. Leaves spinate, with minute, hairy leaflets. Flowers yellow, sweet-scented, and very numerous in spring and autumn. The dwarf furze (*U. nanus*) is low and spreading, seldom more than a foot high; very floriferous; flowers yellow all summer. Good for naturalization on sunny hill-sides. Very effective.

False Indigo, *Amorpha fruticosa.*—A tall, graceful shrub with pinnate leaves, slender branches and spicate panicles of deep, purplish-blue flowers from the axils of the upper leaves. For mixed shrubberies, river-banks or rockeries, in moderately rich soil.

Pea Tree, *Caragana arborescens.*—Large shrub with abruptly pinnate leaves and yellow flowers in axillary fascicles. *C. frutescens* is a much dwarfer plant of graceful habit, and the less showy. *C. spinosa* is a very effective and useful hedge plant. All are Siberian plants of great hardiness; fine for shrubberies in sunny positions.

Bladder Senna, *Colutea arborescens*, and *C. cruenta:* the first with axillary racemes of yellow flowers, the second with flowers of a reddish-yellow color; both have pinnate leaves, are upright spreading shrubs with light foliage and of a graceful habit. Fine when planted together in small groups on sunny lawns. Thrive well in ordinary, light soil

Rose Acacia.—See flowering trees.

THE ROSE FAMILY.

Double Flowering Plum, *Prunus triloba.*—A very beautiful shrub of a dwarf and graceful habit, with numerous double, white or rose-colored flowers crowded along the slender branches in early spring. Exceedingly fine in groups of three or more on the lawn, in any moderately light, well-drained soil. One of the showiest plants in spring.

Dwarf Almond, *Amygdalus nana.*—Small shrub, with more or less double, delicately rose-colored flowers in spring before the leaves. Smaller than *Prunus triloba,* equally valuable and useful for the same purpose.

FIG. 109—ROSE ACACIA (ROBINIA HISPIDA).
(SEE PAGE 27.)

Meadow-Sweet, *Spiræa.*—The meadow-sweets are slender and graceful shrubs common in rich woods and meadows. Some of our best summer flowers belong to this genus. The guelder rose-leaved spirea or "seven barks" (*S. Opulifolia*) is the largest and coarsest species. It grows five or six feet high with arching branches, shaggy, yellow

FIG. 110.—THREE-LOBED SPIREA (SPIREA TRILOBATA).

stems and roundish, palmately three-lobed leaves. The white
flowers are produced in corymbs on short, lateral branches.
An American plant of rocky banks and river shores. *S.
ariæfolia* is one of our finest ornamental plants with slender,
graceful branches, roundish, ovate, bluntly lobed leaves and
large compound panicles of beautiful yellowish-white flowers
terminating the branches as late as July. *S. prunifolia*
is a Japanese shrub flowering early in the season, with
plum-like leaves. The cultivated plant has double, pure
white flowers disposed along the branches in great profusion.
One of the best, *S. Cantoniensis (Reevesiana)*, is a small
beautiful species with lanceolate leaves and large terminal
umbels of pure white flowers early in summer. *S. Thunbergii*
is easily distinguished by its slender branches, small linear
leaves, and white axillary flowers. One of the most beautiful of all is *S. trilobata*, a species with roundish, trilobate
leaves and large, close corymbs of pure white flowers early
in the season. *S. Van Houttii* is another very floriferous
kind with pure white flowers in June. More common are:
S. Billardii, with rose-colored flowers in summer; *S. salicifolia* with oblong-lanceolate leaves and terminal panicles of
flesh-colored or white flowers; *S. callosa*, with lanceolate
leaves and dense corymbs of white or rose-colored flowers
along the branches and *S. Bumalda*, with broad terminal
corymbs of rose-colored flowers, a dwarf, upright species.
S. sorbifolia has rather large pinnate leaves and white
flowers in a terminal panicle late in July. *S. ulmifolia* and
S. hypericifolia are also common. The first five mentioned
species are probably the best for general use. Spireas
flower from the earliest spring till late in summer, in suc-

cession as follows: *prunifolia, Thunbergii, Cantonicnsis, trilobata, hypericifolia, ariafolia, ulmifolia, Opulifolia, callosa, salicifolia, sorbifolia.*

Exochorda, *E. grandiflora.*—A large, straggling shrub, with slender, graceful branches, producing an abundance of large, pure white flowers early in May which completely cover the upper part of the plant. Very fine for growing in dense thickets among dark-foliaged plants or near water margins among other shrubs and climbers; or, if well grown, in small groups on a lawn. Ordinary garden soil.

Corchorus, *Kerria japonica.*—A small, bushy plant with smooth branches and thin ovate-lanceolate leaves. The flowers are double, rather large and yellow, disposed in the axils of the leaves. Shrubberies.

White Corchorus, *Rhodotypus kerrioides.*—A very ornamental shrub of graceful habit with ovate-acuminate leaves and large, white, axillary flowers in spring. Small groups on the lawn. Shrubberies.

Cinquefoil, *Potentilla fruticosa.*—A dwarf and very compact plant forming a globular mass two to three feet high. Leaves pinnate, not large. Flowers in loose clusters terminating the young lateral shoots, large, yellow, numerous throughout the summer. A useful plant for rockeries, border of shruberies and for naturalizing in masses on rocky, sunny banks. Thrives best in a good sandy loam.

Flowering Raspberry, *Rubus odoratus.*—A fine, erect shrub, three or four feet high, with palmately lobed, obtuse leaves. Flowers large, rose-colored, in clusters, and produced throughout the summer. A shrub with very ornamental foliage, for shrubberies, or as an undergrowth in woods and thickets. The white-flowered raspberry (*R. Nutkanus*) has larger, pure white flowers, and the Rocky Mountain bramble (*R. deliciosus*), white or rose-colored

flowers resembling a single rose. The wild brambles or blackberries (*R. Occidentalis, R. villosus*) and the dewberry (*R. Canadensis*) as well as many forms of the European bramble (*R. fruticosus*) may be used to produce thickets on stony and rocky banks, or as an undergrowth in certain parts of the shrubbery with the most beautiful effect. The smaller kinds are handsome in rockeries.

FIG. 111. ROSE
BRAMBLE (RUBUS
DELICIOSUS).

All do best in rich, woodland soil.

The Rose, *Rosa.*—The choicer varieties of hybrid and other hardy roses cannot be considered in this treatise: only species that can be utilized in producing landscape effects, such as the sweetbriar and the showy Japanese rose. These are useful both in shrubberies and rockeries and for planting in groups on the lawn. The sweetbriar (*Rosa rubiginosa*) is a tall and graceful shrub with slender, arching branches. Leaves pinnate with roundish, serrate leaflets and solitary, bright pink flowers in June. Plant and flowers both are fragrant. The dog rose (*Rosa canina*) is similar in habit to the last, with smooth leaves, dark and glossy on the upper side. Flowers in clusters pure white, flesh-colored, or of a bright rosy tint, and very numerous. These may be used for forming picturesque thickets in company with the brambles, or in mixed shrubberies or small groups on the lawn. They are both very good hedge plants. The white rose (*R. alba*) is an old and useful hardy shrub, with many double or semi-double varieties, white or red. The yellow rose (*R. lutea*) is a floriferous, compact, rounded shrub, three or four feet high, with bright yellow blossoms in June. *R. multiflora* is a small rose of very slender habit with long, pinnate leaves and terminal panicles of single, white, anemone-like flowers. It is a quick grower, useful in rockeries and on walls and verandas. The recently introduced *crimson rambler* is a double red variety of this species. The Japanese rose (*Rosa rugosa*) is a robust and healthy shrub from five to fifteen feet high, with thickish, bright green foliage and numerous large, single flowers of a bright rose-color. There is also an old white variety and many new single and semi-double forms. The flowers are followed by clusters of showy coral-red hips. This rose is very beautiful in groups on the lawn. It may be used with good effect in the rockery and in mixed shrubberies. These kinds are perfectly healthy and hardy; they do well in any good garden soil.

Cotoneaster, *Cotoneaster Simonsii*.—A small, almost evergreen shrub with leathery, dark green leaves and insignificant white flowers followed by showy fruit. Nice in a rockery in masses.

Juneberry, *Amelanchier Canadensis*.—A slender shrub of woods and thickets, with numerous racemes of showy white flowers and ovate or oblong serrate leaves. There are many forms or sub-species of this, viz.: *Botryapium*, *alnifolia*, and *oblongifolia*, all of equally ornamental value. The European species, *A. vulgaris*, is also a very showy plant. They are excellent for producing fine woodland effects is company with other shrubs and trees of a similar habit. Rich woods and river banks, generally in good soil.

Japanese Quince, *Cydonia Japonica.*—This is a well known, medium-sized shrub of a broad and spreading habit. The branches are stiff and thorny, producing numerous spurs which develop clusters of large scarlet, red, or rose-colored flowers, before the leaves. *C. Maulei* is a smaller shrub with brick-red flowers followed by showy quince-like fruits of a golden-yellow color. May be used together in small groups on the lawn or as specimen plants. Rich, sandy loam.

THE ALLSPICE FAMILY.

Carolina Allspice, *Calycanthus floridus.*—A fragrant shrub with rather large oval or oblong leaves, producing all summer many-petaled axillary flowers of a lurid purple. Several other species are cultivated for the sake of their sweet fragrance. None are showy, but they have rich, healthy foliage, which is very ornamental. All are natives of rich, southern woods.

Japanese Allspice, *Chimonanthus fragrans.*—A slender shrub with sweet-scented flowers in spring, before the leaves appear. Somewhat tender.

THE CURRANT FAMILY.

Red Flowering Currant, *Ribes sanguineum.*—This is one of the showiest of small shrubs in spring. The rosy-red flowers are produced in great profusion in pendulous racemes. Leaves, three- to five-lobed. A broad, roundish shrub, three or four feet high. The golden flowering cur-

rant (*R. aureum*) is also a very attractive plant with golden-yellow flowers in early spring. *R. Gordonianum* is a
hybrid between these two species, with yellow and crimson
flowers and the habit of *R. sanguineum*. The mountain
currant (*R. alpinum*) has smooth, roundish, deeply three or
five-lobed leaves and long racemes of yellow flowers in
spring. The wild black currant (*R. floridum*) is a handsome if not showy plant, with cordate, acutely three-
to five-lobed leaves, and long drooping racemes of
whitish flowers. The foliage of this species changes into
beautiful autumn colors. All the flowering currants are
fine in smaller shrubberies and in groups on the lawn.
They may also be employed with advantage in front of
coniferous trees as a background for rockeries. They thrive
best in a moderately rich soil.

Common Mock Orange, *Philadelphus coronarius.*—This
is without doubt one of the handsomest of all cultivated
shrubs. The branches are erect with opposite, smooth, oblong-ovate leaves. Flowers, in large clusters, milky-white,
large and odoriferous. *P. grandiflorus* is another tall and
graceful species, with recurving branches and ovate-acuminate downy leaves; flowers scentless, pure white, axillary,
and in clusters terminating the lateral branches. Both of
these flower late in spring. Still later, in early summer,
come: *P. inodorus* with much smaller flowers, and *P. latifolius* with ovate, five-nerved leaves and loose clusters of
white, faintly scented flowers. *P. Gordonianus* is the last
to flower. It is a beautiful species with gracefully arching
branches and flowers produced in racemes on the lateral
branches. The mock oranges—that is, the species known

in a native state—grow on rocky river banks, in rich soil, chiefly in mountain regions. In cultivation, they are used with exquisite effects in shrubberies and for small groups on lawns.

Crested Mock Orange, *Deutzia crenata.*—A fine, erect shrub, with ovate, minutely crenate leaves and axillary racemes of white, purple-tinted flowers late in spring. *D. scabra* is a mere form with roughly rugose, more serrate leaves. Flowers similar. *D. gracilis* is a very dwarf and compact shrub, handsomer in front of taller shrubs. It has ovate-lanceolate leaves and numerous crested racemes of snowy white flowers. Use and culture the same as for mock orange.

Hydrangea, *Hydrangea paniculata grandiflora.*—One of our showiest ornamental shrubs, handsome in groups or as single specimens on lawns. Flowers in large, terminal panicles, white, lasting for a long time in summer. Leaves, ovate-oblong, toothed, opposite or in whorls of three. This beautiful shrub will thrive in moderately good soil, in open and sunny positions. It is very fine in front of evergreens or taller shrubs.

THE WITCH HAZEL FAMILY.

Witch Hazel, *Hamamelis Virginica.*—A tall shrub of a spreading habit, with obovate leaves like those of the common hazel and small, yellowish flowers close to the branches late in autumn. It is fine for the borders of streams and lakes, in moist, rich ground and in large shrubberies among trees.

Fothergilla, *Fothergilla alnifolia.*—A small, handsome

shrub with alder-like foliage and white flowers early in spring. Will thrive in moist positions on the shores of rivers or lakes.

THE ARALIA FAMILY.

Angelica Tree, *Aralia spinosa.*—An erect-growing shrub with straight, spiny stems, sometimes twenty feet high, with very large twice- or thrice-pinnate leaves consisting of ovate leaflets. Flowers in terminal umbels in summer. The Chinese angelica tree (*A. Chinensis*) is a somewhat tender plant with white flowers in terminal panicles.

Dimorphanthus Mandchuricus (*Aralia*) is considered a mere variety of the last. It has considerably branched stems, a lighter foliage and very large panicles of white flowers late in summer. This is a perfectly hardy plant fine for specimens on the lawn. Forms broad masses of luxuriant foliage and is exceptionally beautiful in summer when in full flower. The aralias require rich, well-drained soil. The angelica tree may be grown in shady positions, among trees or tall shrubs. All produce a wonderfully rich, sub-tropical effect.

THE DOGWOOD FAMILY.

Red Osier Dogwood, *Cornus sanguinea.*—A shrub of a spreading habit with opposite leaves, bright red branches, and cymes of white flowers in early summer. *C. stolonifera* is of a rambling habit, more spreading, grows into large masses of foliage four or five feet high with smooth, ovate leaves and small cymes of white flowers. These are beautiful in winter on account of their bright red branches.

Fine in shrubberies and woods as an undergrowth or for the formation of broad thicket-like masses of shrubs near water. The numerous other forms may be used in a similar manner. All do well in a moderately good soil.

THE HONEYSUCKLE FAMILY.

Snowberry, *Symphoricarpus racemosus.*—A shrub common in gardens, with erect and slender branches and oval leaves. Flowers, inconspicuous, followed by white berries in autumn. Shrubberies. Ordinary soil.

Honeysuckle, *Lonicera.*—The Tartarian honeysuckle (*L. Tartarica*) is the most showy species of the upright honeysuckles. It is a most beautiful shrub with opposite, oval, cordate leaves and flowers in axillary clusters. The variety known as *grandiflora* is a very attractive form with large, bright rose-colored flowers. There is also a large-flowered variety with white blossoms. These are useful in shrubberies and in groups on the lawn. They grow to a height of five or six feet. Among other desirable kinds are: *L. fragrantissima,* a straggling shrub with fragrant flowers early in spring; *L. caruba,* with creamy-white, sweet-scented flowers; *L. Standishii* and *L. Xylosteum,* bushy, graceful plants with yellow flowers. All will do well in moderately rich soil.

Bush Honeysuckle, *Diervilla* (*Weigelia*).—These are exceedingly showy plants with opposite leaves and axillary or terminal clusters of large, funnel-shaped flowers. *D. grandiflora* has very large, pink flowers and ovate, reticulated leaves. It is of a very bushy habit. There are several beautiful varieties, one with white-variegated leaves. *D. hortensis* is a much smaller shrub, with white or red flowers and ovate, acuminate leaves. There is a fine form of this with variegated leaves, yellow margined in spring, turning into white later on. Under the name of *D. hybrida* many handsome varieties with differently colored flowers are common in gardens. *D. rosea* is a very floriferous kind with numerous white or rose-colored flowers early in summer. This is probably the most desirable species. *D. rosea nana* is a very compact variety, and *nana variegata* a fine spreading shrub with white-margined leaves. The bush honeysuckles make fine specimens for lawns; they are still more effective in groups of three or more. All thrive in a moderately rich soil. Dry and barren ground is not suitable.

Viburnum.—The plants belonging to this genus are known under widely different popular names. They are all more or less ornamental, sometimes very showy, shrubs, producing a wealth of flowers in late spring or early summer.

Snow-Ball Tree or Guelder Rose, *V. Opulus sterilis.*— A well known large shrub with stout, upright branches and three-lobed leaves. Flowers are white and produced in dense balls in summer. The Japanese snow-ball tree (*V. plicatum*) is somewhat smaller in all parts and more compact with fine ovate, plicate leaves and white flowers in globose cymes in May or June. Both are very ornamental for small groups and shrubberies. The wild form of the guelder rose (*V. Opulus*) is also a very desirable plant, growing on river banks and in moist woods. Many of the American viburnums are very ornamental plants, covered with pure white,

cymose flowers in spring or early summer. *V. prunifolium*
is one of the best of these; a large shrub with recurving,

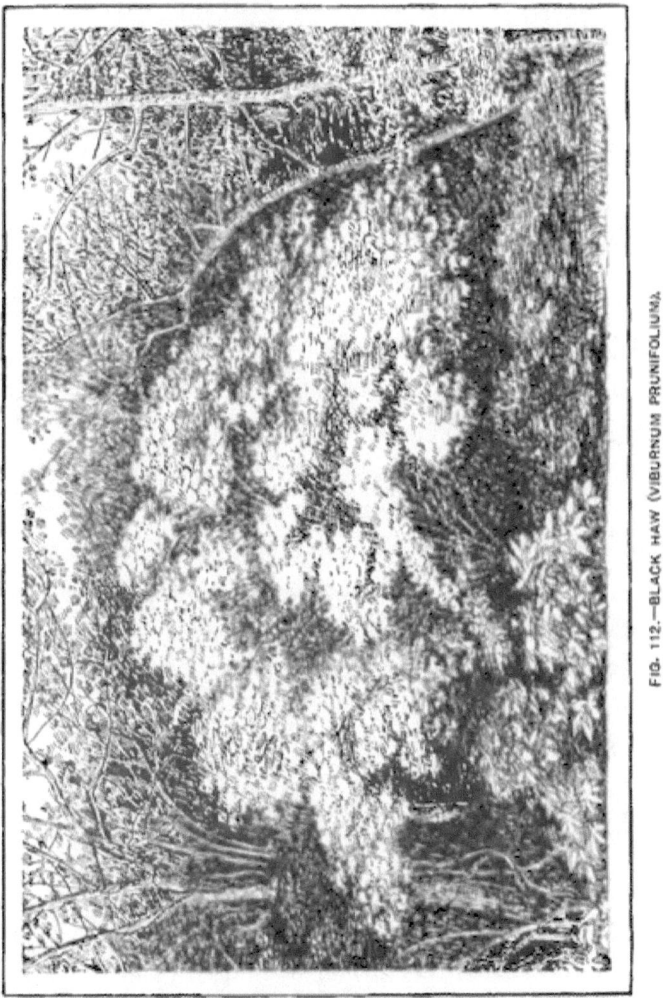

FIG. 112.—BLACK HAW (VIBURNUM PRUNIFOLIUM).

spreading branches, plum-like leaves and numerous clusters
of flowers in spring. *V. molle* flowers at midsummer, has

large cordate leaves and very attractive flowers. *V. pubescens* is a low, spreading shrub with very showy flowers and ovate-oblong, downy leaves. The wayfaring-tree (*V. Lantana*) is a very attractive shrub with large handsome leaves. It is commonly used in shrubberies. The sheepberry (*V. Lentago*) is another desirable and attractive shrub, ten or fifteen feet high, with glossy leaves and broad, flat cymes of flowers. All grow best in comparatively rich soil. They are excellent for shrubberies, and the finer forms are also very desirable for specimens on the lawn.

Elder, *Sambucus nigra.*—A very large shrub or bushy tree with large, pinnate leaves, stout branches, and numerous flat cymes of yellowish-white flowers in summer. The golden-leaved elder (*S. n. aurea*) is a very ornamental foliage-plant with yellow leaves. Very robust and of rapid growth, fine for large shrubberies in rich soil. Canadian elder (*S. Canadensis*) is a much smaller, more spreading plant. A neat and ornamental species is the Hart's elder (*S. racemosa*) with ovate panicles of flowers followed by scarlet fruit in autumn. All are available for large, leafy shrubberies.

THE HEATH FAMILY.

Farkleberry, *Vaccinium arboreum.*— A tall shrub with glossy, oval leaves and numerous white flowers in leafy racemes or from the axils of the leaves. Common in open, rocky woods. The deerberry (*V. stamineum*) is a small bushy shrub a couple of feet high, with oblong-lanceolate or ovate leaves, and numerous axillary, greenish-white flowers with long protruding stamens. These are fine for planting in moist, open shrubberies as an undergrowth. Prefer rich, sandy loam mixed with leaf-soil. They are very attractive when in flower.

Andromeda, or **Lily of the Valley Tree,** *Andromeda floribunda.* — A very handsome plant of rocky woods, growing three or more feet high, leafy to the ground and very broad and spreading, with small, oblong-lanceolate, evergreen leaves and showy white flowers in terminal, nodding racemes growing in the greatest profusion early in summer. *A. speciosa* is an equally valuable shrub with fewer and larger pure white flowers in drooping racemes. *A. Mariana,* or stagger-bush, is another exceedingly pretty species. There is also a hardy Japanese species (*A. Japonica*) of a more erect habit with white flowers. The andromedas should be grown in half-shady positions, in woods or in open shrubberies as an undergrowth, or in prepared beds in suitable places on the lawn. They require a somewhat moist and rich vegetable soil, such as a sandy loam mixed with decayed leaves.

Sorrel Tree, *Oxydendrum arboreum.* — A tall shrub or bushy tree, with oblong-lanceolate leaves and beautiful white flowers in loose panicles late in summer. This is an exceedingly fine plant for shrubberies in rich soil, on the border of groves and other plantations, and on banks of rivers and lakes. The rich foliage turns into fine autumn tints.

All the above forms, when cultivated, should be grown in as natural positions as possible, on shady banks or between trees of light foliage. Grown in artificial positions, in formal beds, they are entirely out of place.

Mountain Laurel, *Kalmia latifolia.* — One of our few

evergreen shrubs, a beautiful plant with large ovate-lanceolate leaves of a leathery texture, and terminal clusters of
very showy white, or rose-colored flowers in late spring or
early summer. It forms a broad, bushy mass of foliage
and flowers, four or five feet high, sometimes more. Grows
in rich woods on high ground, never in swamps or water.
Exceptionally fine for planting among deciduous trees in
groves and thickets as an underbrush.

K. angustifolia is a much smaller plant, growing in
large masses in shady swamps or damp woods. Fine for
naturalizing in similar, or somewhat dryer, positions in
parks and gardens.

Rhododendron or **Rose Bay.**—All rhododendrons are
very ornamental shrubs, chiefly evergreen; growing in
rocky woods and along streams and rivulets in mountain
regions. They are useful for planting in beds and masses
among deciduous trees to produce woodland scenery. Many
creeping vines and tender herbaceous plants find an ideal
home in the shelter of their evergreen foliage. For this
purpose our native species are best, as they are perfectly
hardy and equal any exotic form in size and beauty. *R.
maximum* is a large shrub with broadly lanceolate leaves,
six to ten inches long, and white or rose-colored flowers in
large terminal clusters. *R. Catawbiense* is a much smaller
species of a more compact and spreading habit, with leaves
about half as long as those of the preceding kind. Flowers
of large size, purple, appearing early in summer. *R. Pon-
ticum* is the rhododendron commonly grown in gardens.
It is, in the North, of a dwarf and compact habit, with
dense, dark-green foliage and bell-shaped flowers of various

16

colors late in the spring. There are many beautiful hybrids and varieties, with more or less blotched or spotted flowers, ranging from white to crimson and purple. These are generally planted in prepared beds to form close masses of foliage. A compost of peat and leaf-mold, liberally mixed with the garden soil, that is dug in on the spot, is the simplest and best. All require considerable moisture, and the beds should be soaked occasionally in dry weather.

Azalea, Swamp Honeysuckle.—Our native azaleas are the most gorgeous of all indigenous plants, and deserve universal culture. They should be used liberally in landscape gardening to form large masses of color among deciduous trees in spring. All are deciduous. *A. nudiflora* is the most common in swamps and moist woods. The beautiful rosy-pink flowers develop before the leaves. It is a shrub of a slender, graceful habit, four or five feet high. *A. viscosa* flowers later in summer after the leaves have fully developed. The flowers are almost white, clammy. *A. calendulacea* is a native of rocky woods, growing in rich leaf soil among deciduous trees and mountain laurel. Flowers very showy, flame-colored or yellow. Under cultivation all three thrive in ordinary rich woodland soil.

There is a very attractive evergreen species, *A. amœna* which is quite hardy in New York. It forms compact masses a couple of feet high, and is usually completely covered with red flowers early in spring. *Azalea mollis* is a Japanese species of compact habit, elliptic, softly pubescent leaves, and with large masses of flame-colored flowers in spring. *A. Pontica* is another desirable kind with orange-yellow flowers. A number of varieties and

FIG. 113.—SOFT-LEAVED AZALEA (AZALEA MOLLIS).

hybrids of the last two species, with variously colored flowers, are known in gardens as Ghent azaleas. They are very desirable and beautiful in masses or in beds on the lawn, and should not be grown singly or in too small groups. Ordinary, moderately good sandy loam answers very well for all species, but it is better when mixed with a liberal addition of leaf soil.

White Alder, *Clethra alnifolia.*—This is a fine, hardy, deciduous shrub for growing in moist places, or in moderately rich soil in a shrubbery. The leaves resemble those of the alder. Flowers white, fragrant, in erect terminal racemes in summer.

The following are low, evergreen shrubs or trailing plants, of rich and shady woods or open, barren plains and hillsides:

Purple Heather, *Calluna vulgaris.*—Tufted, spreading shrub, growing in immense masses on sandy heaths or dry hillsides in Northern Europe. Spreads readily from seeds along roads and ditches. The purple flowers which appear in July and August are very numerous, and are disposed in terminal racemes. Foliage is persistent, of a brownish color in summer. Good for naturalizing on sunny hillsides among broom and furze.

Cross-leaved Heath, *Erica tetralix.*—A very small, roundish shrub, as commonly seen, from six to eight inches high. Not spreading. Flowers large, urn-shaped, of a fine rosy color, growing in headlike clusters. Common among purple heather; fine for naturalizing and in rockeries. *E. carnea,* a plant with bright flesh-colored flowers, may be used for the same purpose.

Sand Myrtle, *Leiophyllum buxifolium.*—A dwarf, evergreen plant of pine barrens, with oval leaves, very minute, and white flowers in early summer. Fine for patches in rockeries or naturalized in sandy soil.

Bearberry, *Arctostaphylos Uva-ursi.*—A low, trailing plant with obovate, evergreen leaves forming mats of dark, smooth foliage. The flowers are racemose and white. A nice trailing plant for rockeries and shady hillsides.

The following dwarf, trailing shrubs grow in shady woods among the fallen leaves and are fine for similar positions in thickets and shrubberies: Creeping wintergreen (*Gaultheria procumbens* and *G. Shallon*); trailing arbutus (*Epigæa repens*), a well known spring flowering plant with beautiful white or rosy-red, sweet-scented flowers.

THE VERVAIN FAMILY.

Callicarpa, *Callicarpa pupurea.*—A small, beautiful shrub with hairy, ovate-acuminate leaves, inconspicuous flowers, and numerous small violet berries set in clusters all along the branches in winter. Fine in shrubberies. Moderately good soil.

THE OLIVE FAMILY.

Jasmine, *Jasminum nudiflorum.*—This is a very attractive, rambling shrub with small, ternate leaves and numerous yellow flowers on the bare branch, late in winter. The branches are green, and effective on this account. It may be grown either as a climbing shrub for covering trellises on a wall, or as a specimen among evergreen trees or shrubs, where its masses of bright yellow flowers early in the season show to the best advantage. It will grow in any moderately good garden soil, but should not be planted in too moist or exposed positions. For covering fences it has few equals.

Golden Bells, *Forsythia suspensa.*—A very beautiful shrub covered with bright yellow, bell-shaped, four-petaled flowers on the bare branches in spring. Flowers on very slender peduncles. Branches long, recurving, or hanging with simple and trifoliate leaves. Forms broad, graceful masses five or six feet high and often considerably broader. Also cultivated under the name of *F. Fortunei.*

F. viridissima is a shrub of stouter habit with recurving branches and comparatively large, dark-green, broadly lanceolate leaves and numerous golden-yellow flowers late in spring. These are fine in groups of three or more or as single specimen plants on the lawn. All are excellent for planting in rocky places.

Lilac, *Syringa.*—The lilacs are the most popular of all flowering shrubs. None are more useful in ornamental gardening.

The common lilac (*S. vulgaris*) had originally lilac or pale violet flowers, but is now found in innumerable varieties both single and double. The pure white variety is one of the best of these. Next come: the large-flowered white, *alba grandiflora; Charles X.,* with reddish purple flowers; *cærulea,* of a bright bluish color; *violacea,* deep violet, a fine form; and *grandiflora,* with bright purplish-red flowers in large panicles. They flower in spring.

The Chinese lilac (*S. Chinensis*) is a much lower shrub, about four feet high, with small ovate-lanceolate leaves and compound panicles of bright lilac flowers in June. This is a very neat and beautiful plant.

FIG. 114. CHINESE LILAC (SYRINGA CHINENSIS).

Japanese lilac (*S. Japonica*).—A handsome plant with oblong-ovate, acuminate leaves and large, terminal clusters of creamy-white flowers. Large shrub of a robust habit, flowering late in June.

Persian lilac (*S. Persica*).—This is a small shrub with lanceolate, or sometimes pinnatifid, leaves and loose, terminal clusters of purple-lilac or white flowers in June. Very fine and graceful.

Hungarian lilac (*S. josikaea*) has inferior flowers, late in June, but it is a robust and vigorous shrub, very leafy and ornamental in summer.—The use of lilacs in shrubberies and groups is universal. The smaller kinds are exceptionally fine for specimens on the lawn.

Privet, *Ligustrum.*—The privets are almost evergreen, and have the appearance of evergreen shrubs in summer. They are generally grown in hedges and shrubberies. When growing privet as an ornamental plant on the lawn, no pruning or shearing should be allowed, as it is more attractive when allowed to develop naturally. Privet makes good hedges for divisions in a garden.

The best species and those almost exclusively grown in this country are: common privet (*L. vulgare*), with rather small, broadly lanceolate leaves, and the broad-leaved privet (*L. ovalifolium*), with oval, more or less pointed leaves. Privets flower in summer; the flowers are rather small and collected in terminal racemes. All grow well in almost any soil.

Fringe Tree, *Chionanthus Virginica.*—This is a very large shrub with recurving branches, large oval or obovate

FIG. 115.—FRINGE TREE (CHIONANTHUS VIRGINICA).

leaves, and loose, feathery panicles of pure white flowers appearing early in summer. Fine in shrubberies and on the shores of rivers or lakes, or in small groups on the lawn in moderately rich soil.

THE LAUREL FAMILY.

Spice-Bush, *Lindera Benzoin.*—A fine, spreading shrub with large, beautifully green, obovate-oblong leaves, and numerous small, yellow flowers in lateral clusters on the bare branches in spring. Aromatic-scented shrub, fine for shrubberies in low and rich ground.

THE MEZEREUM FAMILY.

Daphne Mezereum.—An erect-growing shrub a foot or two high with purplish rose-colored, very fragrant flowers early in spring. Leaves lanceolate, glaucous green. It is excellent between trees and shrubs as an undergrowth.

THE OLEASTER FAMILY.

Silver Berry, *Elæagnus argentea.*—Graceful shrub with silvery foliage and small, yellow flowers in July. Fine for shrubberies and seaside gardens. The oleaster (*E. hortensis*) with quite whitish-silvery leaves, and larger, yellow flowers in axillary fascicles is also a common species in gardens, especially the narrow-leaved form *angustifolia.*

Sea Buckthorn, *Hippophæ rhamnoides.*—A spiny shrub with linear-lanceolate leaves of silvery white and yellow flowers in May, followed by showy, orange-colored berries. An excellent seaside plant and very ornamental in its way.

THE SPURGE FAMILY.

Box, *Buxus sempervirens.*—The box is one of the few evergreen shrubs which are hardy in all parts of America. It may be used with excellent effect, either as an under-growth in thickets and shrubberies or in groups on the lawn. It is used in formal gardening for close-cut hedges, for bordering walks and for divisions in kitchen-gardens. When allowed to grow in a free manner it is, however, most attractive. It may be used for covering steep hillsides in company with many coniferous trees. Although of slow growth it attains considerable size in rich ground.

THE OAK FAMILY.

The Hazel, *Corylus avellana.*—Not usually grown for ornament, but useful for hedges between the vegetable garden and the ornamental grounds, or around fields and orchards. There is a purple-leaved variety of considerable ornamental value. The hazel is very useful as a tall under-growth in woods and groves.

V.

CREEPERS AND VINES.

INES and climbing plants are invaluable in modern landscape-gardening, and may be used in many ways to produce strikingly beautiful effects. Most vines and creepers are natives of woods and copses, where they grow to the tallest tree-tops, or hang garlands and wreaths of flowers over the lower shrubs of a thicket. They are often found in rocky woods clinging to the face of a cliff or growing over isolated blocks and stones, according to their nature.

In masses of trees and shrubs similar effects may be produced by means of judicious planting, and, having the advantage of choosing the most beautiful plants, the result should be richer and more varied than it is possible for us to find in the woodland. To introduce strong climbing plants among trees and shrubs might on the other hand result in the destruction of these. Climbers would not be likely to succeed among trees with dense crowns like the beech or of so luxurious a growth as the horse chestnut. Elm, and ivy, locust and Virginian creeper, climbing roses and evergreen trees are beautiful and pleasing associations of these two classes of plants.

In artificial rockeries, many creepers and vines are especially in place, such as periwinkles, silk vines, and ivy. On walls and fences, on the columns and balustrades of verandas, and in similar positions, such exquisite plants as clematis, Boston ivy, and honeysuckle are very useful and attractive. The plants described below are chiefly woody climbers: a few are herbaceous, perennial or annual, and useful for summer effects only. The best are Boston ivy, clematis, ivy, wistarias, climbing roses, and trumpet-flowers.

THE CROWFOOT FAMILY.

Virgin's-Bower, *Clematis.*—Most small flowering kinds are known by this popular name, especially the following: *C. Flammula,* a slender, climbing plant with smooth, pinnate leaves, chiefly oval or oblong, sometimes three-lobed, leaflets, and numerous panicles of white, sweet-scented flowers. A vigorous grower, flowering from the young wood throughout the summer; *C. vitalba,* the traveller's joy of Europe, is a less vigorous grower with cymes of white, almond-scented flowers in July, and finely cut, pinnate leaves. *C. Virginiana* is a common American plant in moist woods and thickets and on river-banks among trees and shrubs. Leaves ternate with cut or lobed segments. Flowers small white, in ample panicles on the summer's growth. All have numerous feathery clusters of fruit later in the season.

Purple Clematis, *Clematis viticella.*—A fine climber with ternate or entire leaves, ovate-cordate in outline; and large blue or purple flowers, with four obovate sepals, produced singly on lateral shoots in summer. *C. Jackmanni* is an excellent garden-form belonging to this type. Flowers large, violet-purple, with four almost orbicular, acute sepals. Leaves ternate with long petioles. A continuous summer bloomer, very free-flowering. There is also a white variety.

Large-flowered Clematis, *Clematis cærulea.*—This is the finest of all the forms, with flowers six inches or more in diameter, consisting of more than six sepals of a blue or

FIG. 116.—LARGE-FLOWERED CLEMATIS CLEMATIS CŒRULEA PATENS).

purplish color, pure white in the beautiful variety known as *patens*. Leaves pinnate with three simple cordate leaflets. This is a slender climber, flowering in spring, with many varieties. *C. florida* is a more tender species valuable as a greenhouse plant.

Clematis of the *Jackmanni* and *cærulea* types may be used with advantage as bedding plants, the branches being tied down to cover the ground. They are among the best

for verandas and on trellises against a wall with a southern
exposure. The small-flowering forms may be used in shrubberies where they must be allowed to grow freely. They
grow best in a rich and moist ground in sunny positions.

THE BARBERRY FAMILY.

Akebia, *Akebia quinata.*—A slender vine or twining
shrub, with pretty, palmately divided leaves consisting of
five oblong leaflets. The flowers are brownish, inconspicuous, but sweet-scented, and the fruit which bursts open on
ripening is bright-colored and attractive. The akebia is
very attractive on rocky banks and also in small rockeries.

THE MOONSEED FAMILY.

Moonseed, *Menispermum Canadense.*—A climbing shrub
with peltate leaves and numerous yellow flowers in pendulous racemes or panicles. Moist ground in woods and
thickets; flowers late in summer. Grown chiefly for the
sake of its handsome foliage.

THE FUMITORY FAMILY.

Mountain Fringe, *Adlumia cirrhosa.*—A delicate and
beautiful biennial climber, growing freely from seeds when
once established. Leaves twice or thrice pinnate with ten-
dril-like petioles. Flowers delicate, flesh-colored, in ample,
leafy panicles throughout the summer. For naturalizing in
shady shrubberies or in hedges where it will grow up
annually.

THE VINE FAMILY.

Wild Vines, *Vitis Labrusca, æstivalis,* and others. These may be used with advantage to cover rocky banks and hill-sides or for growing on tall trees in shrubberies. All have beautiful, more or less five-lobed, leaves and clusters of sweet-scented flowers in spring.

Virginian Creeper, *Ampelopsis quinquefolia.*—This vigorous climber with its handsome five-fingered leaves looks well on tall trees with light foliage or in the crowns of red cedars. May also be used on walls or for covering the ground in shady places under trees with dense foliage. The leaves change into bright autumn tints.

Boston Ivy, *Ampelopsis Veitchii (tricuspidata).*—A slender, Japanese creeper attaching itself to walls or rocks by means of short tendrils. Leaves cordate, tricuspidate, hanging vertically, green in summer, changing into bright scarlet in the fall. A quick-growing and beautiful plant, the best for covering walls. Thrives best in rich sandy loam, and will grow equally well in the full glare of the sun or in partial shade.

THE STAFF-TREE FAMILY.

Staff Tree, *Celastrus scandens.*—A vigorous twining shrub with ovate-oblong, rather thin leaves, and racemes of whitish-green flowers terminating short, lateral branches. Fruits in clusters, bright orange-scarlet in autumn. On columns and fences; ornamental when in fruit.

THE PEA FAMILY.

Wistaria, *Wistaria Sinensis.*—A very large twining shrub of rapid growth. Leaves, long, pinnate; flowers blue, in large pendulous racemes, terminal on lateral shoots developing with the leaves in spring. There are several varieties, one with white flowers. *W. Japonica* has white flowers and another Japanese species, *W. multijuga*, has racemes one or to two feet long, of deep lilac flowers with purple wings.

All the wistarias are fine for growing on verandas or in trees with light foliage, such as the elm or locust. They thrive best in a good sandy loam but will do well in almost any moderately good soil.

Scarlet Runner, *Phaseolus multiflorus.*—An annual twining vine, with trifoliately pinnate leaves, and axillary racemes of bright scarlet flowers in summer. Sown in spring for covering fences or bowers.

THE ROSE FAMILY.

Prairie Rose, *Rosa setigera.*—This is the only perfectly hardy climbing rose. It deserves general cultivation for the great beauty and profusion of its mostly double flowers. There are several varieties of which *Baltimore Belle*, with flowers of a blush-color, and *Queen of the Prairie*, with bright rosy-red flowers, are the best and the most commonly grown. The tall climbing branches are covered with straight prickles and handsome pinnate foliage. Fine for trellises on walls or verandas, in rockeries, or on bare hillsides. Planted among coniferous trees, such as Norway spruce, they will grow to a great height. The delicate foliage in spring and the bright flowers later on contrast beautifully with the dark green of the evergreens. For this purpose they must be allowed a sufficient root-space, and a southern exposure

FIG. 117.- CHINESE WISTARIA (WISTARIA SINENSIS).

257

is the best.   A rich soil is essential to rapid growth, and it is best to prepare special beds or trenches, filled with good loam and plenty of manure, in gardens where the soil is poor.

THE GOURD FAMILY.

Wild Cucumber Vine, *Echinocystus lobata.*—A graceful annual, wild in thickets and damp woods, in sunny positions.

FIG. 118.—PRAIRIE ROSE (ROSA SETIGERA).

A beautiful vine for covering arbors, or on trellises against a wall.   Leaves five-lobed and numerous racemes of white flowers almost covering the plant in summer.   May be grown with good effect on the south side of a shrubbery and will generally remain there when once established.   It has, however, a tendency to become a weed.   A very rapid grower.   Many annual climbers of this family are quite ornamental, with luxuriant foliage and pretty, if not conspicuous, flowers followed by picturesque fruits.

The Bryony (*Bryonia dioica*) is a tuberous-rooted plant of a habit almost similar to the preceding one, with five-lobed leaves and white flowers in summer. It is well worthy of cultivation and may be grown with success in hedge-rows or thickets in a moderately good soil. The slender stems die down annually but the root is hardy.

THE ARALIA FAMILY.

Ivy, *Hedera Helix.*—This is without doubt the best and most useful climber in places where it is hardy. It may be grown with success on northern walls, as it generally suffers more from the sun in winter than from the cold. In Europe, it grows in the extreme North, generally in decidnous or evergreen woods where it finds a slight protection. It is found in innumerable varieties in most European countries, some growing on the trunks of trees in sunny positions, others in deep shade. Where it cannot be grown with success in exposed positions it is useful for covering the ground under large shade-trees or in shrubberies. Some of the smaller varieties are exceptionally beautiful in rockeries. The leaves are generally five-lobed, thick and leathery, evergreen, but differ greatly in size and shape. There are also many beautiful forms with variegated foliage turning more or less reddish in winter or spring. When old, the ivy flowers freely and has then a unique appearance, as it is almost covered with headlike clusters of creamy white flowers. The leaves are not lobed on flowering shoots but entire and of an ovate outline. The best varieties are *Canariensis*, with large, shining-green foliage, also called Irish ivy; *Roegneriana*, with large, broadly cordate leaves;

variegata and *marmorata*, with variegated foliage, and *con-glomerata*, a small and compact kind, fine for rockeries.

Honeysuckle, *Lonicera.*—Woodbine and honeysuckle are general favorites on account of their handsome, sweet-scented flowers and neat, twining habit. They are very useful for porches and verandas, as well as for covering arbors, fences, and enclosures. Some of the smaller kinds are beautiful in rockeries and as climbers among other shrubs in open and sunny positions. All require a moderately rich and moist soil. For planting in thickets and copses or on the banks of a river or lake no twining shrub can be more useful than the evergreen Japanese honeysuckle (*L. Halleana*), which forms dense masses of dark, shining foliage close to the ground, twining here and there among the branches of neighboring shrubs. The flowers are tubular, two-lipped, white, changing into a pale yellow, produced freely throughout the summer. *L. japonica* is another al-most evergreen species with flowers, red on the outside, whitish within. The common honeysuckle (*L. Caprifolium*) is an exceedingly beautiful plant with glaucous, connate leaves and large, terminal clusters of bright orange-yellow or flame-colored flowers in early summer. The woodbine (*L. Periclymenum*) has bright red flowers, ovate obtuse, mostly glaucous leaves, and is similar in habit to the pre-ceding kind. These grow in open woods in Europe, cover-ing rocks, shrubs, and small tree-stems with their delicate flowers. The trumpet honeysuckle (*L. sempervirens*) is an American species with showy, scarlet flowers in spiked whorls, all summer. The Japanese golden-leaved honey-suckle (*L. brachypoda aureo-reticulata*) is a kind commonly grown on arbors and verandas. It has yellow, axillary flowers and foliage reticulated with golden veins.

THE BIGNONIA FAMILY.

Trumpet-Flower, *Tecoma radicans.*— A vigorous climbing shrub with long, pinnate leaves and terminal clusters of orange-scarlet flowers. The Japanese trumpet-flower (*T. grandiflora*) climbs less freely, has narrower leaflets and large bell-shaped flowers with spreading limbs of a scarlet-crimson color. The former is fine on walls, fences, and enclosures, the latter in the rockery, or, if kept low as a specimen plant, on the lawn. Rich and moderately moist ground.

Bignonia, *Bignonia capreolata.*—A very beautiful native climbing shrub growing on fences and trees in open and sunny positions. Leaves pinnate consisting of a single pair of oblong-lanceolate leaflets, and orange-scarlet flowers in axillary clusters. Stem, slender, climbing by means of tendrils. Planted beside trees of light foliage or in hedgerows.

THE CONVOLVULUS FAMILY.

Morning Glory, *Ipomœa purpurea.*—A beautiful annual with funnel-shaped flowers of different colors from white to blue and crimson, freely produced in summer. Grown on fences or in hedgerows and shrubberies. Propagated by means of seeds sown in early spring.

Hedge-Bindweed, *Calystegia sepium.*—A slender, perennial climber, fine for hedgerows or shrubberies. Flowers are mostly pure white, showy; throughout the summer.

THE NIGHTSHADE FAMILY.

Matrimony Vine, *Lycium Barbarum.*—An old-fashioned, somewhat thorny, climbing shrub with obovate or spathulate leaves and axillary clusters of pale purplish flowers. Chinese matrimony vine (*L. Chinense*) is a much more slender plant producing numerous oblong, scarlet berries in pairs from the axils of the leaves. They are neat and ornamental plants for steep banks or rockeries. The more vigorous kinds may be grown on stone enclosures, to cover bare hillsides, or among shrubs and trees on the shores of rivulets or lakes.

THE DOGBANE FAMILY.

Periwinkle, *Vinca minor.*—A dwarf, trailing plant for growing in shrubberies, or for covering bare ground under shade trees, and also in rockeries. Leaves ovate, shining green, opposite. Flowers solitary in the axils of the leaves, beautiful blue or white. The large periwinkle (*V. major*) is very much larger in all its parts, differing but slightly in habit. Leaves sometimes variegated white or reticulated golden-yellow veins. Both grow best in a moderately rich soil. The last one is not hardy in the North.

THE MILKWEED FAMILY.

Silk Vine, *Periploca Graeca.*—This is a slender, rapid-growing twining shrub, with opposite, ovate-acute leaves and inconspicuous flowers. It may be used with advantage for almost any purpose.

THE BIRTHWORT FAMILY.

Pipe Vine, *Aristolochia Sipho.*—This is a very rapid-growing twining vine, with large, cordate leaves and inconspicuous greenish-brown flowers. Grown for the sake of its luxuriant foliage, which gives ample shade for bowers and verandas. May also be planted with excellent effect among shrubs, near the margin of water, and to cover large rocks or trunks of deciduous trees.

THE SMILAX FAMILY.

Greenbriar, *Smilax rotundifolia.*—This handsome climber well deserves cultivation for the sake of its beautiful leaves. In moderately good soil it grows to a considerable height and looks very ornamental, especially in the crowns of evergreen trees. The leaves assume beautiful autumn tints.

VI.

HERBACEOUS PLANTS.

N all temperate countries, the herbaceous flora forms a very important part of the natural scenery. The ground is closely carpeted with grass and flowers, forests and fields vie with each other in variety and color. Along rivulets and streams a hundred forms of the daintiest flowers make their home; and water plants abound in ponds and lakes. Even the rocks and cliffs and dry, sterile sandfields produce a flora as beautiful as it is characteristic.

These plants are just as important factors in landscape gardening as in nature itself; but it is necessary to understand fully their nature and habit in order to use them rightly and with the most pleasing effects. Most herbaceous plants will grow well in light and moderately rich garden soil, whether they are natives of dry and sunny fields or of moist and shady woods. But it is necessary to bear in mind the character and habit of each and every species and use it only in the position for which it is best adapted by nature.

The following selection contains only choice and ornamental plants, and, as it is sufficiently rich in number and va-

riety to be useful for every purpose, the most beautiful results
may be obtained by using these alone in a proper manner.
A great number of species, each represented by small and
insignificant individuals, are not desirable in landscape gardening. Broad masses of one kind are more effective than
an incongruous mixture of a great many contrasting forms.

In a previous chapter the more important classes of herbaceous plants have been treated as to their nature, habit,
habitat, and correct use in ornamental gardening, and suggestions of the same nature will also be given in the
following descriptions:

THE CROWFOOT FAMILY.

Anemones and Windflowers, *Anemone.*—The anemones
are very important woodland- and hillside-plants, generally

FIG. 19.—PASQUE-FLOWER (ANEMONE PULSATILLA), GROWING IN STONY SOIL ON A HILLSIDE.

found in great numbers throughout the north temperate
zone. The pasque-flower (*A. Pulsatilla*) is one of the
earliest flowering plants, with large, nodding flowers of
a pale blue or purple color, springing from a tuft of much

divided leaves; grows on sunny hillsides among the grass, often in sterile soil. *A. patens* and the American pasque-flower (*A. p. Nuttalliana*) are equally desirable plants with purplish, sometimes creamy-white flowers, two inches across These are fine for planting among the grass on a sunny, sloping lawn, in light or moderately good soil. Among species found in woods and forests the best are: the com-mon wind-flower (*A. nemorosa*), a well-known dwarf species

with white flowers, purplish on the outside; and the large wood anemone (*A. sylvestris*) with pure white flowers on slender stalks a foot high or more, and ternate or palmately divided leaves. These are excellent for naturalizing in shrub-beries and thickets or in shady places on the lawn, the larger kind in smaller patches, the smaller to cover the ground uni-formly. A species useful for the same purpose and common in woods in North-ern Europe is the golden wind-flower (*A. ranuncu-*

FIG. 120.—JAPANESE WIND-FLOWER (ANEMONE JAPONICA).

loides), a dwarf but very showy plant flowering in June.

The Japanese wind-flower (*A. Japonica*) is one of the most useful border plants, opening its buds in August or even later. The numerous, rosy-purple flowers are borne on scapes two feet in height or more. The foliage is very ornamental. A white variety (*A. j. alba*), has pure white flowers three inches in diameter, and elegant ternate or palmately divided leaves. These exceptionally beautiful plants may be used in rockeries, in sunny borders of a shrubbery and similar positions, with the most pleasing result. They thrive best in a rich and moist soil. The numerous forms of the garden anemone (*A. hortensis*) and the poppy anemone (*A. coronaria*) are useful in beds and borders in early summer. The flowers of these dwarf tuberous-rooted plants are generally double or semi-double, varying in color from white to scarlet, pale blue and crimson. They must be planted and treated in the same way as bulbs for summer bedding, and do best in moist, sandy loam and half-shady positions. Hence they are excellent for planting in shrubberies or in suitable places in the rockery. The scarlet anemone (*A. fulgens*) is a nearly related form, with flowers of the most vivid scarlet color—a very floriferous kind with ternately divided leaves and of a tufted habit, growing to the height of a foot or more. One of the finest species for rock-gardens is the Apennine anemone (*A. Apennina*), an exceedingly handsome plant with large, bright blue flowers and twice pinnately divided leaves, growing six or eight inches high and producing a quantity of flowers late in the spring. For the same purpose the hepatica (*A. Hepatica*) is equally desirable and easier to obtain. This is a very dwarf plant with three-lobed, leathery leaves, growing in small tufts close to the roots of trees in woods and forests, and producing numerous bright blue flowers early in spring. This is also fine for naturalizing on shady hillsides, in thickets and shrubberies.

Meadow-Rue, *Thalictrum.*—Several of the plants belonging to this genus have exceedingly beautiful foliage and grow to a considerable height; they are chiefly woodland and meadow plants. The rue anemone (*T. anemonoides*) closely resembles the common wind-flower in habit and size. The flowers are similar but of a purer white, appearing in early spring in woods and thickets. The early meadow-rue (*T. dioicum*) is a plant a foot or two high, with glaucous leaves, and greenish-yellow flowers in compound panicles. It grows in rocky woods and may easily be naturalized. The tall meadow-rue (*T. Cornuti*) is the most important one from an ornamental point of view. It grows to a height of six or eight feet, producing immense compound panicles of white flowers, and is found in masses on the borders of rivers or lakes, or in moist ground generally, where it is very effective. This species may be used with good effect in sunny positions in beds and borders or in a low and moist place in the rockery.

Spring Adonis, *Adonis vernalis.*—An early spring flower with finely divided leaves and large yellow flowers. Habit dwarf, tufted. Stems single. Beautiful in rockeries, in open places in the shrubbery, and as a border plant. Should be grown in masses in rich garden soil. The pheasant's eye (*A. æstivalis* and *A. autumnalis*) flowers in summer and autumn, grows about a foot high, has numerous, finely cut leaves and small flowers of an intense scarlet-crimson color. Should be sown early in spring in borders or rockeries.

Crowfoot, Buttercup, *Ranunculus.*—There are numerous

handsome plants of this genus. Most common in gardens
are the so-called bachelor's buttons, double forms of several
species. The garden ranunculus (*R. Asiaticus*) is a very
dwarf plant with double flowers of a more or less intense
yellow, scarlet, or crimson color. It is a tuberous plant
fine for moist places in the rockery or in a border. May be
treated in the same manner as bulbs for spring bedding
where it is not perfectly hardy. The buttercup (*R. acris*)
is of a very variable habit, generally growing a couple of feet
high with rather large, golden-yellow flowers, and palmately
divided leaves consisting of from three to seven segments.
The pretty border plant known as yellow bachelor's button
is a double form of this. The species itself is too weedy for
general use. The white buttercup (*R. aconitifolius*) is a
much more useful and ornamental plant of a close, tufted
habit, with five-parted leaves, and numerous pure white
flowers with yellow stamens. The white bachelor's button
is a double variety of this species and a very fine border
plant. Both may be used with good effect in a rockery.
The heart-leaved ranunculus (*R. amplexicaulis*) is a dwarf
Alpine plant with smooth, heart-shaped, stem-clasping leaves
and pure white flowers. Fine for rockeries in moist places
among boulders and stones. The Parnassia-leaved ranunculus (*R. parnassifolius*) is a still dwarfer plant with
rounded foliage and large white flowers. A beautiful rock-
plant. The marsh crowfoot (*R. Lingua*) is one of the
largest plants of the genus, growing in moist places on the
shores of tarns and lakes. The flowers are bright yellow,
two inches across, on tall scapes from the axils of the
upper leaves. Stem three or more feet high with long

halbert-shaped leaves. A fine plant for naturalizing on the shores of rivers and lakes; grows in masses and is very effective.

The water anemone (*R. aquatilis*) is a charming little water-plant plentiful in ditches and shallow waters generally. Forms nice masses of floating, three-lobed leaves, and numerous pure white flowers with yellow anthers. This is one of the most beautiful water-plants for shallow lakes and ponds.

The lesser celandine (*R. Ficaria*) grows in rich woods and thickets and flowers early in spring. It forms small

tufts of shining, heart-shaped leaves and numerous golden-yellow flowers. Very dwarf in habit, hardy, and easily naturalized in

FIG. 121. LESSER CELANDINE RANUNCULUS FICARIA.

shrubberies.

The Baneberry (*Actæa*) and Bugbane (*Cimicifuga*) are well known plants with ample, thrice ternate leaves and long spikes or racemes of white flowers in spring. They grow from two to eight feet high according to variety and are common in rich woodlands. They are useful for planting in moist places in rockeries or for producing woodland scenery in the shrubbery.

Marsh Marigold, *Caltha palustris.*—A common plant in moist meadows and on the shores of low-land streams growing as single plants and in small groups. The large, bright yellow, cup-shaped flowers appear early in spring and form a feature of the landscape for a considerable time. Planted on the border of a lake or pond in rich masses close to the water's edge this is a very effective plant.

Globe-flower, *Trollius Europeus.*—This is one of our most beautiful garden plants. The plants grow singly among the grass in meadows, and sometimes in rich open woodlands, and, like the preceding kind, form quite a feature of the scenery. The globular, yellow flowers are borne on erect, leafy stems a foot or more high. Leaves on long petioles palmately parted with deeply cut edges, handsome. The Asiatic globe-flower (*T. Asiaticus*) and the American globe-flower (*T. laxus*), the former with orange-yellow flowers, are also fine meadow plants. All are excellent for moist positions in a rockery or on a lawn and especially on a low river shore.

FIG. 122.—CHRISTMAS ROSE (HELLEBORUS NIGER ALTIFOLIUS).

Christmas Rose, *Helleborus niger.*—While the snow is still on the ground the Christmas rose opens its chaste and beautiful flowers, earlier or later in the season, according to the locality where it is grown. The flowers measure several inches across and are slightly suffused with purple in the typical form. The broad-leaved variety, *altifolius*, has very large, pure white flowers. The leaves are large, pedate, of a leathery texture and deep green. A moist and sheltered position in a rockery or under evergreen shrubs is the best. The flowers develop fully only when the buds and foliage are kept moist and cool. Broad masses of this plant early in the season are exceptionally beautiful, especially among evergreen shrubs and trees. Several species of helleborus flower later in the season and are generally known as Lenten roses. Most beautiful among these are *H. Colchicus*, bright purple, *H. Olympicus*, purple, and *H. orientalis* with rose-colored flowers. These flower in March and April and are useful for the same purpose as the Christmas rose. All do best in a rich, sandy loam mixed with plenty of leaf mold and well-decayed manure.

Winter Aconite, *Eranthis hyemalis.*—This is a very attractive, dwarf perennial, flowering in the earliest spring. It grows about six inches high, producing numerous bright yellow flowers on single stems. The winter aconite is desirable for naturalizing in light and rich loamy soil in half-shady positions or in rich, open, rocky woods. It may also be grown in shrubberies and hedgerows with the most beautiful effect.

Fennel Flower, *Nigella Damacena.*—An annual with finely cut leaves and bluish-white flowers surrounded by foliage. A neat, erect-growing herb eight inches or more high, readily increased by seeds; fine in borders or rockeries. Moderately good garden soil.

Columbine, *Aquilegia.*—A family of very ornamental plants of open woodlands and mountain regions, grown in

FIG. 123.—CANADIAN COLUMBINE (AQUILEGIA CANADENSIS) GROWING IN A ROCKY WOOD.

273

beds and borders and especially in rockeries. The common
columbine (*A. vulgaris*) is a well known border plant with
many beautiful varieties, single or double, varying from pure
white to pale blue and purple. It is a very floriferous plant
with fine masses of foliage of biternate leaves. Height about
two feet. The golden columbine (*A. chrysantha*) is an exceptionally fine border plant about as large as the preceding
kind but of a more elegant habit. Flowers are of a pale
yellow on the outside, brighter within.

The following are all rock-plants growing in high mountain regions or in rocky woods: Alpine columbine (*A. alpina*). A very fine plant about a foot high, with biternate
leaves and linear leaflets. Flowers are very large blue or
blue and white, borne on erect stems. Canadian columbine
(*A. Canadensis*). Flowers red and yellow, borne in loose
panicles on leafy stems, about eighteen inches high. Common
in the crevices of rocks on the borders of woods.— Long-
spurred columbine (*A. cærulea*). Flowers large, extremely
beautiful, blue and white. Habit elegant. Leaves biternate, comparatively small, not numerous. One of the best
rock-plants, a native of the Rocky Mountains.—Glandular
columbine (*A. glandulosa*). A very beautiful species seldom a foot high. Flowers large and showy with deep
blue or lilac sepals and pure white petals. Spurs very
much shorter than in the preceding kind.—Siberian columbine (*A. Sibirica*). A species nearly related to the former
but larger and of a denser habit with lilac or white and lilac
flowers. There is also a very handsome, pure white variety.
These are very fine in rockeries but may also be grown
successfully in borders if the soil is not too heavy. They are

most appropriate in the crevices of calcareous rocks in open and sunny positions.

Larkspur, *Delphinium.*—Large perennial, biennial, or annual herbs from one to six feet high, with palmately divided foliage, and racemes or panicles of showy blue, white, or scarlet flowers. Some of the species are very old border plants. All are valuable. The common larkspur (*D. exaltatum*) is most popular as a border plant. It grows to

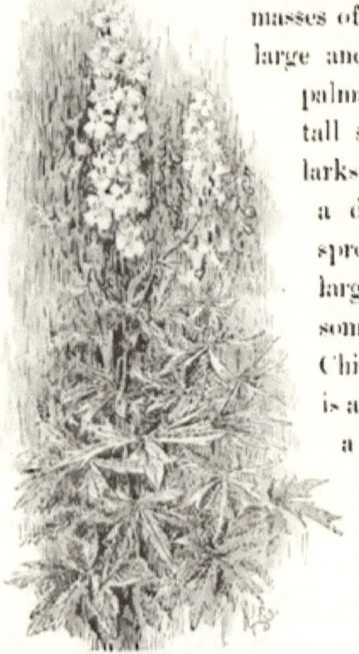

a height of five or six feet, producing masses of blue or white flowers in large and dense racemes. Leaves palmately parted, all along the tall stems. The large-flowered larkspur (*D. grandiflorum*) is of a dwarfer, more elegant and spreading habit. Flowers are large, intensely b l u e and in some varieties w h i t e. The Chinese larkspur (*D. chinense*) is a new variety of this species: a more profuse bloomer with loose panicles of the most intensely blue flowers late in the season. The showy larkspur (*D. formosum*) is also one of the most valuable kinds with sky-blue flowers, earlier than the

FIG. 124. COMMON LARKSPUR—DELPHINIUM EXALTATUM).

preceding kind. Added to these the hybrid larkspur (*D. hybridum*), which in size and habit resembles the common larkspur, brings a profusion of deep blue flowers in July or August. The following are very handsome annuals: field larkspur (*D. consolida*), common in fields, a loose and straggling plant with few-flowered racemes. Flowers blue, white, or pink, showy. Rocket larkspur (*D. Ajacis*), a common garden plant with single or double flowers of many colors. Both are excellent border plants. The red-flowered larkspur (*D. nudicaule*), a dwarf plant with peltate leaves and upright, almost leafless racemes of beautiful scarlet-red flowers, and the dwarf larkspur (*D. tricorne*), a plant seldom a foot high, with five-parted leaves and showy blue flowers; are best grown in rockeries. All the Delphiniums do best in a rich and light sandy loam. The taller forms are fine on the border of shrubberies or in the common border. All are readily increased by means of seeds.

Monkshood, *Aconitum Napellus.*—An elegant but poisonous perennial with dark, pedately lobed leaves, leafy stems three to four feet high, and single racemes of hooded flowers, blue with a metallic lustre. The variegated monkshood (*A. variegatum*) is a still more elegant plant with branched racemes of white and blue flowers. Both flower in June or July; they are among the old standard border plants. The roots are poisonous and must never be left in the hand of a child. Thrive well in any rich garden soil.

Peony, *Paeonia officinalis, albiflora,* and *tenuifolia.*—The various species of peony are our most showy garden plants, valuable for borders, rockeries, and as specimen plants on the lawn. They are of a very graceful habit with beautiful foliage and bright or sometimes delicately colored flowers. The double-flowered forms are special favorites;

they vary in color from pure white to rose and deep crimson. The Chinese peony (*P. albiflora*) flowers in summer; it grows to a height of three feet, with bright green pinnatifid leaves, and, originally, had white, single, fragrant flowers. The varieties now grown are all double, white-or rose-colored. The common peony (*P. officinalis*) has coarser pinnatifid leaves, a more upright habit, and large red flowers, seldom single, mostly semi-double or double, varying from white to deep crimson. The cut-leaved peony (*P. tenuifolia*) has bipinnate leaves with deeply cut divisions. Foliage feathery, light and elegant. Flowers bright crimson, single or double. Most garden varieties are propagated by means of division or grafting, and thrive best in a rich, sandy loam.

THE BERBERIS FAMILY.

Barren Wort, *Epimedium.*—Graceful herbs, with light biternate or pinnate leaves, and terminal racemes of flowers. *E. alpinum* is most common in cultivation; it has biternate leaves on tall stalks, and loose racemes of dull crimson flowers with yellow anthers. *E. macranthum* is a very handsome species with white flowers and tall, graceful biternate leaves with ovate leaflets. Both are exceptionally fine plants for a moist, shady place in the rockery. They thrive in a sandy loam enriched with well-decayed leaf-mold, and increase by means of creeping root-stocks.

Twin-Leaf, *Jeffersonia diphylla.*—A beautiful woodland plant with bilobed leaves and white flowers, singly on slender scapes. Height six or eight inches. Flowers anemone-like with eight petals and yellow stamens. Fine for naturalizing in rich soil in shrubberies, or in a moist, shady position in the rockery. Sandy loam and leaf-mold.

May Apple, *Podophyllum peltatum.*—This is the most important hardy herbaceous plant of the family. The leaves are umbrella-shaped, with from seven to nine lobes.

Stems erect, with two leaves and ending in a single large white flower. Found in scattered masses in rich deciduous woods. The leaves are

FIG. 125.—MAY APPLE (PODOPHYLLUM PELTATUM).

very ornamental with well-marked veins and a glossy surface reflecting the sun. One of the best woodland plants, worth introducing in every garden among shrubs and trees, and also in more secluded lawns. It grows well, especially in sandy loam enriched by decayed leaves.

THE WATER-LILY FAMILY.

Water-Lily, *Nymphæa.*—Well known, beautiful plants in lakes and ponds, with rounded floating leaves and solitary flowers on long fleshy foot-stalks. The white water-lily (*N. alba*) has large, scentless flowers, six inches or more across, milky white. The variety *rosea* has beautiful bright rose-colored flowers of the same size and shape. *N. odorata*, the sweet-scented pond lily, is somewhat smaller, white, with the outer petals tinted green. These are the best and hardiest for naturalizing. The red water-lily is exceptionally fine and hardy, and rivals any tropical species in beauty. In smaller ponds and cisterns many of the tropical water-lilies may be used with success in summer and, where they are not perfectly hardy, they may be stored in their tubs in a frost-free place during the winter months. The Zanzibar water-lily (*N. Zanzibarensis*), a beautiful blue-flowered form, is easy of culture and hardy in many parts of the country. The yellow water-lily (*N. flava*) is a perfectly hardy plant, with bright sulphur yellow flowers, well worthy of cultivation. Many beautiful garden forms have been raised and are commonly grown, such as the bright rosy-red *N. Devoniensis* and the pale rose-colored *N. Sturtevanti*. All water-lilies may be raised from seeds with the greatest of ease, and some will flower

FIG. 126.—WATER PLANTS.

WATER-LILY (NYMPHÆA ODORATA VAR.).   WATER POPPY (LIMNOCHARIS HUMBOLDTII).
WATER ANEMONE (RANUNCULUS AQUATILIS).

in the first season. The *root* of most species is fleshy and tuberous, and may be kept dry in winter without injury. Rarer varieties are best planted in tubs, in a sandy loam enriched with plenty of well-rotted manure, and sunk a foot or even less below the surface. Hardy species may be planted out in specially prepared beds in the bottom of ponds and lakes. Most species flower throughout the summer.

Yellow Pond Lily, *Nuphar.*—These are inferior to the true water-lilies. The leaves are rounded, sometimes held above the surface of the water. Flowers yellow, fleshy, seldom floating. There are two or three species.

Lotus, *Nelumbium speciosum.*—This is the stateliest as well as the most beautiful of all water plants. Leaves borne on slender stalks, two or three feet above the surface

FIG. 197. LOTUS. (NELUMBIUM SPECIOSUM).

of the water, with a rounded blade from one to two feet wide, slightly hollow in the centre. Flowers on tall scapes above the foliage, many-petalled, six to eight inches in diameter, of a delicate pink color, followed by numerous picturesque seed-vessels.

The yellow nelumbium (*N. luteum*) is less showy but still a very desirable plant with bluish-green foliage and large tulip-shaped blossoms of a pale yellow color; sweet-scented. Both are hardy and may be introduced into ponds and lakes. They may be planted in special beds as recommended for water-lilies or in tubs sunk in the bottom. As they increase rapidly, they must be kept in check in small ponds, which would otherwise soon be filled with decaying vegetable matter and the luxuriant growth of the lotus. It is always desirable to keep the greater part of the water surface intact, no matter how beautiful the plants may be.

THE PITCHER-PLANT FAMILY.

Purple Pitcher-Plant, *Sarracenia purpurea.*—A curious plant growing in mossy swamps, with hollow, pitcher-like leaves and unique, deep purple flowers, solitary on slender scapes. May be introduced in moist places in a rockery, and planted in peaty soil. Many of the so-called trumpet-leaves of the South (*S. rubra, flava, and Drummondii*) may be grown with equal success. All are easy-growing weeds and need no special culture.

THE POPPY FAMILY.

Poppy, *Papaver.*—Very showy and ornamental annual or perennial herbs, with more or less cut foliage; natives of fields and roadsides. The oriental poppy (*P. orientalis*) is the most beautiful and useful of all known species. It forms a broad plant with ample, pinnatifid, sharply cut and hairy leaves. Flowers six or eight inches across, deep scarlet, on somewhat leafy stems. The variety *bracteatum* is a still more showy plant with rather large, bright red flowers. The flowers of this species have each petal marked by a black spot. Very fine in the outskirts of shrubberies or as specimen plants on the lawn, or in beds and rockeries. Useful border plants. Thrive well in ordinary garden soil. The following are two very beautiful Alpine poppies which are exceptionally fine plants for rockeries: Mountain poppy (*P. alpinum*), a dwarf perennial six inches high, with small, glaucous, pinnatifid leaves and solitary, rather large and showy yellow flowers on slender scapes: Iceland poppy (*P. nudicaule*), is a somewhat larger and more robust species of a similar habit with orange-yellow or white flowers. These may also be grown on hillsides and slopes of sterile lawns with the most beautiful effect. The following are annuals and flower late in the summer; fine plants for

FIG 126. ORIENTAL POPPY (PAPAVER ORIENTALIS BRACTEATUM).

beds and borders: corn poppy (*P. Rhœas*). Root-leaves almost pinnate, covered with bristly hairs, tufted. Stems single, slightly leafy. Flowers nodding, scarlet, with a black centre; very showy. Most beautiful when grown in irregular groups with ox-eye daisy (*Leucanthemum vulgare*) and cornflower (*Centaurea Cyanus*) in the outskirts of shrubberies or on sterile slopes, in borders, or as a roadside plant. The beautiful double varieties of different colors are fine border plants. *P. Hookerii* is a nearly related species of a more bushy and leafy habit. Flowers varying from rose to scarlet with black or white centre. The opium poppy (*P. somniferum*) is, however, the most varied of all the annual species. There are dwarf and tall, single and double forms, varying from white to deep scarlet and crimson. *P. lævigatum* is another very beautiful annual species, which has deep scarlet flowers with black centres bordered with white. All of these are fine summer flowering kinds, which should be increased by means of seeds sown on the spot early in spring. The border is best for most double varieties.

Mexican Poppy, *Argemone Mexicana.*—A rather showy annual with yellow or white flowers in summer. Leaves sinuate, prickly. The large-flowered Mexican poppy (*A. grandiflora*) is a showy perennial plant well worth growing. Flowers in loose panicles, large, white, with yellow anthers. Leaves pinnatifid, spiny. A robust plant of erect habit two or three feet high. Both will do well in sterile and sandy soil. They are fine for roadsides or rockeries. May also be grown in a border in a sunny position.

Welsh Poppy, *Meconopsis Cambrica.*—A very desirable, erect-growing perennial with pinnate leaves and long racemes of pale yellow flowers on single stems. Fine in rockeries when grown several together. Height one foot.

California Poppy, *Eschscholtzia Californica.*—This is one of the very finest annual plants with glaucous, much divided leaves with linear segments. Flowers solitary on slender, naked scapes, bright yellow, orange or white. In large patches in beds or borders or in the rockery. Will thrive in ordinary, good soil and often in sandy and sterile ground. The seed should be sown in autumn or in early spring.

Blood-Root, *Sanguinaria Canadensis.*—A handsome perennial throwing up a solitary reniform leaf in spring, enclosing the flower bud. Flower pure white, solitary, borne on a slender scape. Beautiful for naturalizing in scattered masses in shrubberies and moist, rich woods. It will grow well in a moist and half-shady position in the rockery.

Plume Poppy, *Bocconia cordata.* This is a stately plant from five to eight feet high, with single stems and rounded, cordate-sinuate leaves. Flowers small, whitish, in ample terminal panicles late in summer. Exceptionally ornamental as specimens on a lawn, fine for rockeries and borders. Thrives well in ordinary garden soil in a sunny position.

THE FUMITORY FAMILY.

Bleeding Heart, *Dicentra spectabilis.*—A well known and popular border plant with much divided, deeply cut leaves and rosy-pink, heart-shaped flowers in nodding racemes. Habit upright. Fine for beds and borders or for large clumps on the lawn. A number of dwarf and delicate woodland flowers belong to this genus; the best are: Dutchman's breeches (*D. cucullaria*), with white, yellow-tipped flowers in short racemes and delicate decompound leaves. Common in rocky woods among decaying leaves. A very pretty species about six inches high is *D. eximia*; flowers are bright purple in short racemes on slender, erect scapes about nine inches high; segments of the foliage broader and more robust than in the preceding forms; *D. formosa,* flowers bright red, in compound ra-

FIG. 129.— DUTCHMAN'S BREECHES (DICENTRA CUCULLARIA) GROWING IN A NATURAL POSITION.

cemes and ample foliage. All flower in spring or early
summer. They are excellent for naturalizing in shrubberies.
Special beds of sandy leaf mold may be prepared for this
purpose. The roots are fleshy and all parts of the plants
are very delicate.

Corydalis.—A genus of exceedingly pretty woodland
flowers nearly resembling the small forms of Dicentra.
C. bracteata is one of the finest. The flowers are large, sulphur yellow, in bracteate racemes on single stems eight or
nine inches high. Leaves biternate, two to each inflorescence.
C. cava has purple flowers and biternate leaves; it grows
about six inches high. *C. nobilis* is a robust, very leafy
and floriferous kind, with pale yellow flowers in bracteate
racemes on leafy stems nine inches high. All thrive best
in shady positions in rich leaf mold. They are fine for
naturalizing in woods and shrubberies and may be treated
in the same manner as Dicentra.

THE MUSTARD FAMILY.

Dames Violet or Rocket, *Hesperis matronalis.* —An old-
fashioned border plant with oblong-lanceolate leaves on
single stems two or three feet high. Flowers large, purple-
lilac or white in loose terminal racemes, sweet-scented. Of
this desirable plant there are several varieties. The night
violet (*H. tristis*) is of a similar habit, slightly smaller, with
reddish or dull purple flowers, which are highly perfumed
at night. Very attractive plants for the border or rockery
or for naturalizing in rich open woods, or on the border
of shrubberies. The first is perennial, the second biennial.
Both can be raised from seeds with the greatest of ease.

FIG. 130.—DAMES VIOLET (HESPERIS MATRONALIS) AS NATURALIZED IN A WOOD.

Moricandia, *Moricandia sonchifolia.*—One of the handsomest plants of the entire family. A graceful, erect annual with beautiful violet-blue or lilac flowers, an inch across, disposed in terminal racemes. Stems erect, mostly simple with ovate leaves. The radical leaves are pinnatisect, more or less lyrate. For the border or rockery, to be sown on the place early in spring.

Virginian Stock, *Malcolmia maritima.*—A pretty annual six or eight inches high. Stems simple, with narrow, spathulate leaves and racemes of white, rose, pinkish-red, violet or purple flowers. A very neat and attractive plant for rockeries or sown on sandy shores. May also be used for beds and borders.

Ten-week Stocks, *Mathiola annua.*—Well known bedding plants with single or double flowers in all colors. The many varieties of summer stocks are also popular plants for beds and borders. All should be raised from seeds in a frame or greenhouse.

Wallflower, *Cheiranthus Cheiri.*—Well known and popular plants for summer bedding, raised in winter, planted out in spring. Varieties of all colors, single or double.

Hedge Mustard, *Erysimum.*— Dwarf annual and perennial plants growing in rocky or sterile, sandy soil. Fine for planting in rockeries or on sandy hillsides and barren, sloping lawns. *E. alpinum* is a spring-flowering plant with numerous sulphur-yellow flowers and lanceolate leaves. *E. pulchellum* forms a tufted mat of small, grayish foliage, covered with sulpher-yellow flowers in spring. *E. Perofskianum* is a pretty annual, flowering in summer and covered with bright orange-red blossoms for a considerable period.

Rock-Cress, *Arabis alpina.*—This is one of the prettiest of all rock-plants early in spring. It forms dense, spreading tufts of small lanceolate, grayish and hairy leaves. Flowers white, very numerous, in short racemes. The variety *albida* has larger flowers and less toothed leaves. Fine among rocks and on bare hillsides. *A. arenosa* is a plant of sandy fields with bright rose-colored flowers. All grow best in a sandy loam but will also thrive in sterile and gravelly soil.

Purple Rock-Cress, *Aubrietia.*—A class of very dwarf, tufted, perennial herbs, with small, grayish foliage and purple flowers in spring. *A. deltoidea* is the typical form. There are many beautiful varieties with larger, differently colored flowers: *A. grandiflora*, violet blue. *Eyrei*, bright purple, *Græca*, reddish-purple, and *Leichtlini*, rose-carmine, are common and ornamental forms. All are excellent for rockeries, bare hillsides, sandy fields, and similar open positions. They thrive best in very light, sandy loam mixed with brick-rubbish.

Whitlow-Grass, *Draba.*—Beautiful dwarf plants of sandy fields and sunny mountain-sides, growing only a few inches high, and forming dense tufts of grayish foliage, covered with white or yellow flowers in early spring. Should be grown in masses only in the same manner as rock-cress. Among the numerous species the following are best for general use: *D. Aizoon* and *Aizoides*, two or three inches high, tufted, leaves almost linear. Flowers very numerous in early spring, bright yellow. *D. Mawei*, very dwarf, tufted with linear leaves and large white flowers. *D. pyrenaica*, flowers white, changing to purple. All may be raised from seeds or by means of division.

Candytuft, *Iberis.*—Some of the candytufts are of a shrubby nature but of a very dwarf habit. A few are pretty garden annuals popular for bedding purposes.

FIG. 131.—CANDYTUFT (IBERIS UMBELLATA).

I. saxatilis is a spreading shrub a few inches high only, with evergreen leaves and white corymbose flowers in spring and summer. *I. sempervirens*, a considerably taller plant with bright green foliage and large racemes of pure white flowers in spring and summer. These are exceedingly fine rock-plants and very floriferous. Among the best annual forms are: *I. umbellata*, a fine plant, with linear-lanceolate leaves, and flat corymbs of white or lilac-purple flowers; about eight inches high. *I. amara* has pure white flowers. *I. coronaria*, the rocket candytuft of gardens, grows about a foot high with leafy stems and lanceolate leaves; flowers white, in several close terminal spikes. All the annuals may be raised with the greatest of ease from seeds sown early in spring. The shrubby species may be increased by means of herbaceous cuttings. All grow best in a moderately rich and light garden soil.

Madwort, *Alyssum.*—Small, charming rock-or maritime-plants with white or yellow blossoms. *A. saxatile* is a tufted perennial, with lanceolate leaves and much branched, flowering stems, with close terminal heads of bright yellow flowers in the very earliest spring. There is a fine form of this with white variegated foliage. *A. alpestris* is an equally beautiful plant. Both are excellent rock-plants, very showy when grown in masses in the crevices of calcareous or sandstone rocks. The pretty little annual known as sweet alyssum (*Koenigia maritima*) is a nearly allied plant common on sea-shores in South Europe.

Meadow Cress, *Cardamine pratensis*.—A handsome and delicate plant growing in moist fields and meadows, and forming an important feature of the scenery in early summer, especially in North Europe. Flowers white or lilac. Beautiful for naturalizing in moist or half-shady lawns where the soil is well worked and rich. It is one of the most dainty plants for this purpose, growing eight or ten inches high. Seeds may be sown in the grass.

Toothwort, *Dentaria*.—Familiar plants of moist meadows and river-sides. Some are very attractive, growing in masses on the water level along mountain streams and rivulets. They may be naturalized in similar positions in the garden or in moist places in rockeries. All require a rich soil and a half-shady position. The best are: *D. digitata*, leaves palmately cut or fingered, flowers large, bright purple: *D. diphylla*, leaves three-fingered, flowers large, white, tinted purple: *D. laciniata*, leaves of three deeply cut leaflets, flowers purple: *D. pinnata*, leaves pinnate, flower large, white or pale purple. Spread by means of fleshy, running root-stocks.

Honesty, *Lunaria biennis*.—An old-fashioned border plant with heart-shaped leaves and large rosy-purple flowers in terminal racemes. Habit erect, slightly branched: flowers in summer. For naturalizing in shrubberies in rich moist ground or in a similar position in the rockery; borders,

The following are maritime plants growing on sandy shores, in the sand or among sea-weeds :

Sea-kale, *Crambe maritima.*—Leaves large, roundish, with a sinuate, wavy edge, smooth and glaucous. Flowers in tall, lax panicles, whitish, sweet scented.

Sea Rocket, *Cakile maritima.*—Leaves oblong, fleshy flowers numerous, large, lilac, corymbose. Plant spreading, forming a broad mass of fleshy leaves and stems, and very attractive in summer and autumn. Both are useful in seaside gardening.

THE MIGNONETTE FAMILY.

Mignonette, *Reseda odorata.*—This well known plant so desirable for the sake of its sweet-scented flowers may be sown in the border early in spring or throughout the summer in favorable locations. It may also be used in the rockery and in open spaces among shrubs.

THE VIOLET FAMILY.

Pansy, *Viola tricolor maxima.*—One of the greatest favorites among garden flowers, with innumerable strains and varieties of all colors. For ordinary use in borders and rockeries, mixed seeds may be sown in autumn or very early in spring. For bedding, only the choicest varieties should be grown and these may be raised in a frame or greenhouse in winter, ready to plant out as soon as the soil can be worked in spring. They should be repricked several times in winter and begin to flower when planted out. A rich and light garden soil is best.

Sweet Violet, *Viola odorata.*—All varieties of this desirable plant may be grown in borders or in moist positions among the grass in a lawn, or in shrubberies. When grown in borders the long runners should be cut off so as to make the individual plant strong and more floriferous than they would otherwise be.

Horned Violet, *Viola cornuta.*—This is one of the finest plants for summer bedding. It forms compact, tufted masses, producing numerous pale-blue or white flowers on leafy stems. Fine for edging and for making a nice undergrowth in beds of summer flowers. Grows well in ordinary garden soil.

The following are attractive wild forms growing on sandy fields, in woodlands and meadows: common blue violet (*V. cucullata*), a large and robust species growing in masses along meadow brooks and rivulets in open woods. It forms quite a feature of the scenery in spring and early summer. Flowers large, blue, on tall scapes six or eight inches high. The leaves are kidney-shaped, borne on tall stalks. Fine for naturalizing in moist lawns or shrubberies, or on the shores of rivers and lakes. Canadian violet

FIG. 132.—VIOLA CUCULLATA.

(*V. Canadensis*) is a tall and leafy form growing a foot high or more; flowers violet-purple, throughout the summer; woodland species. Birdfoot violet (*V. pedata*). An exceedingly pretty and showy plant of dwarf habit growing abundantly in light, sandy soil. Flowers numerous, bright blue, late in spring. This is an excellent plant for rockeries, or mixed with the grass in sandy lawns, or on bare hillsides.

THE HYPERICUM FAMILY.

St. John's Wort.—Numerous species of *Hypericum* are known by this name. All are more or less pretty, tall and branched herbs with opposite leaves and yellow flowers. May be grown on grassy river banks, or naturalized as road-side plants. All thrive best in rich soil.

THE PINK FAMILY.

Carnations and Picotees, *Dianthus caryophyllus.*—Well known garden plants, not hardy in the extreme North. They form tufts of fine glaucous leaves, and produce flowers all summer. There are countless varieties with double flowers of all colors between pure white and deep carmine. Varieties with one-colored or striped flowers are true carnations; those in which the ground color is edged with a narrow band of another color are termed picotees by English gardeners. They are exceptionally fine for bedding, for which purpose young plants should be ready early in spring. As soon as they have done flowering the majority may be discarded, and only a few kept for stock plants. The so-called Marguerite carnation is a pretty variety that may be raised from seed every spring for beds or borders.

Pinks (*Dianthus plumarius*), Garden Pink.—There are numerous large double-flowered varieties of this species now, entirely different in habit and appearance from the type. All are hardy, and fine for borders where the soil is well drained. The species itself forms broad tufts of narrow, glaucous leaves, and bears small, feathery flowers on erect stems. It is a beautiful plant for rockeries.

The Chinese pink (*D. Chinensis*) is a beautiful annual or biennial, one of the most useful for summer display. This species has green lanceolate leaves and single or double flowers, white, rose, pink, and crimson. The best varieties are: *Heddewigi fl. pl., diadematus plenissimus*, and the single *laciniatus*. Should be raised from seeds in a frame or greenhouse, ready to plant out in beds early in summer. They flower continuously and very profusely. Rich and light soil.

Sweet William, *Dianthus barbatus.*—A fine, old-fashioned border plant. Flowers of all colors, except blue and yellow, in flat crowded terminal clusters. Stem about a foot high, with green, broadly lanceolate leaves. May be raised from seeds in winter to be planted out early in spring. It is one of the most attractive plants for small gardens and should be grown in liberal patches in the border. Flowers late in summer. Maiden pink, *Dianthus deltoides*. A slender, graceful herb for naturalizing in lawns and in the borders of shrubberies. Flowers bright rose-colored, leaves lanceolate. Common in grassy fields. Sand pink (*D. arenarius*), a native of sandy fields in Europe, may be used for the same purpose. The mountain

FIG. 133.—MAIDEN PINK (DIANTHUS DELTOIDES).

pink (*D. alpinus*) is a very dwarf and tufted species with rather large, bright rose-colored flowers with crimson centre. It is fine for growing in large masses in rockeries.

Rock Tunica, *Tunica saxifraga.*—This is a small spread-

ing, loosely tufted plant, which may be readily grown in
crevices of rocks, rocky banks, or on the sides of sunny
ravines. The flowers are small, pinkish-white, very numerous. The plant is effective when grown in masses.

Campion, *Lychnis.*—Some of these are very old and
desirable border plants. Scarlet lychnis (*L. Chalce-
donica*) is an erect, tall perennial with ovate-lanceolate
leaves, rough hairy stems, and terminal clusters of small,
intensely scarlet flowers. The red campion (*L. diurna*)
has rosy-purple flowers in terminal panicles. There is also a
double variety. Of more importance are the large-flowered
forms of the Siberian campion (*L. fulgens*), a species with
exceedingly showy, vermilion flowers in loose corymbs.
It grows from six to twelve inches high and has hairy,
ovate-lanceolate leaves. The best forms are: *Haageana*,
bright scarlet; *grandiflora*, with very large scarlet flowers;
Sieboldii, with white flowers. There is a small Alpine
species (*L. alpina*) with pink flowers in terminal heads,
and tufts of linear-lanceolate leaves. It grows in the
crevices of rocks, generally in moist locations and is pretty
in rockeries.

Catchfly, *Silene.*—Very beautiful annual or perennial
plants, growing wild, mostly in sandy or gravelly soil, and
in open woods. *S. Schafta* is a pretty, dwarf species, with
much branched stems, obovate, acute leaves and showy
purple flowers all summer. Fine for rockeries. *S. compacta* is of a more upright habit, grows to the height of a
foot or eighteen inches, with ovate-cordate leaves and ample
corymbs of pink flowers in June or July. The fire pink
(*S. Virginica*) is a showy American plant growing from

215

FIG. 134.—WILD PINK (SILENE PENNSYLVANICA) GROWING NATURALLY IN THE CREVICES OF ROCKS.

one to two feet high. Very beautiful in open woods or shrubberies. The flowers are bright crimson. The following are fine for rockeries: *S. alpestris*, a dwarf, tufted Alpine plant growing six inches high, flowers white; wild pink (*S. Pennsylvanica*), about as high as the preceding kind; flowers pink, very numerous and beautiful; fine for naturalizing in rocky places. The best annuals are the numerous varieties of *S. pendula*, a dwarf trailing plant with, originally, flesh-colored flowers. There are now white, flesh-colored and rosy-red forms, with single or double flowers. The variety *compacta* is especially useful for summer-bedding. For this purpose the seeds must be sown in autumn in a frame or greenhouse to be ready for planting in spring.

Soapwort, *Saponaria officinalis.*—A tall and erect roadside plant with oval and lanceolate leaves and showy white flowers suffused with rose, in ample terminal clusters. May be grown on rocky knolls or high banks of rivulets and lakes. *Saponaria ocymoides* is a very attractive rock plant of a dwarf, trailing habit with numerous light-red flowers all summer. It may be sown very early in spring in the moist soil in the crevices of rocks.

Gypsophila, *Gypsophila paniculata.*—An elegant plant with much-branched stems, linear-lanceolate leaves, and compound panicles of small white flowers. Habit light and airy. A fine plant for growing in rockeries.

Mouse Ear, *Crastium arvense.*—A small, tufted plant, common on sunny banks and road sides. Leaves mostly linear. Flowers numerous, pure white. A conspicuous plant when grown in dense masses in rockeries or among the grass on barren slopes and hillsides. *C. tomentosum* has white, woolly foliage forming dense tufts or mats. *C. Biebersteini* is a plant of a similar habit, but larger in all its parts, much used in carpet-bedding and for edging beds and borders.

Sandwort, *Arenaria.*—Chiefly rock-plants, or plants of sandy fields and seashores. Fine in rockeries, and may also be used to cover barren and sandy soil where grass is not likely to grow. The grass-leaved sandwort (*A. graminifolia*) has white flowers in loose panicles six inches high. Larch-leaved sandwort (*A. laricifolia*) is another pretty species. Other neat forms are *montana* and *Balearica*, the latter, growing only on moist rocks, a very pretty plant. The northern sandwort (*A. Groenlandica*) is common in high mountain regions; it is a closely tufted plant, with white flowers, fine for rockeries.

THE PURSLANE FAMILY.

Showy Purslane, *Portulaca grandiflora.* — A well-known, prostrate, annual herb with fleshy leaves and showy flowers, white, yellow, rosy-purple, scarlet, and crimson. May be sown in autumn or early in spring in sandy places. Also fine for beds in poor soil.

Spring Beauty, *Claytonia Virginica.*—One of our showiest spring flowers, common in rich woods and moist woodland meadows. Flowers white or pale-rose, with deeper veins; leaves linear-lanceolate. Fine for naturalizing in large masses in shrubberies and moist lawns.

THE MALLOW FAMILY.

Malope, *Malope grandiflora.*—A showy annual with rosy-red, purple, or pure white flowers in great profusion in summer. Fine for borders in sandy soil and sunny positions. Seeds should be sown early in spring.

Hollyhock, *Althaea rosea.*—This is an old-fashioned border plant growing from five to eight feet high, with cordate, angular-lobed leaves, and flowers from the axils of the leaves in long, terminal spikes. Color very variable, from white to deep maroon. Flowers double or single. Biennial; should be raised annually from seeds. Flowers the second year, in summer. Requires a good sandy loam and a sunny position in a border or among shrubs.

Lavatera, *Lavatera trimestris.*—A handsome annual with rose-colored or white flowers all summer. Borders.

Musk-Mallow, *Malva moschata.* — A perennial about two feet high with three-parted, musk-scented foliage, and small rose-colored or white flowers.

FIG. 135. HOLLYHOCK (ALTHÆA ROSEA).

Rose Mallow, *Hibiscus Moscheutos.*—A showy, summer flowering perennial of meadows and marshes, growing six or seven feet high with ovate, often three-lobed leaves, and large, rose-colored, crimson or pure white flowers, sometimes with a dark maroon centre. One of the showiest plants of the family; thrives best in rich sandy loam but will grow in almost any soil on high or low ground. It is best as a border plant. There are several other species wild in this country, some with immense flowers; *H. coccineus,* with bright red flowers eight or ten inches across, and *grandiflorus* are the best of these.

Bladder Ketmia, *Hibiscus Trionum.*—A pretty annual one or two feet high forming broad masses of three-parted leaves and showy sulphur-yellow flowers with a maroon eye. Propagated by means of seeds sown in spring in a sunny position.

All plants of this family are excellent border plants flowering throughout the summer. Both annuals and perennials are easily increased by means of seeds.

THE FLAX FAMILY.

FIGURE 136.—BLADDER KETMIA
(HIBISCUS TRIONUM).

Red Flax, *Linum grandiflorum.*—One of the best annual border plants. Flowers large, crimson, abundant in summer. Grown in masses this is an exceptionally attractive plant. Seeds should be sown on the place of flowering, in spring. Rich soil and a sunny position. Perennial flax (*L. perenne*). A tall and slender plant with small, narrow leaves and sky-blue flowers. Fine on river banks or in a rockery.

THE GERANIUM FAMILY.

Wood Sorrel, *Oxalis Acetosella.* —A very small herb with clover-like leaves and numerous red-veined, delicate white flowers. Grows on shady and mossy rocks in moist positions, and is fine for similar places in the rockery. There are several wild species of wood sorrel, some with yellow, others with purple or violet, flowers. Most hardy kinds look well among rocks.

Limnanthes, *Limnanthus Douglasi.* —A dwarf, spreading annual with pinnate leaves and handsome white flowers with a yellow centre. Showy in masses in moist positions among rocks. Propagated from seeds in spring.

Cranesbill, *Geranium.* —Two or three of the wild species of Europe are very ornamental and floriferous plants. The meadow cranesbill (*G. pratense*) forms a bushy plant two—three feet high, with rounded, seven-parted leaves and pretty, large, violet-blue flowers in loose corymbs. The blood-red cranesbill (*G. sanguineum*) is a spreading herb with five- or seven-parted leaves. Flowers on axillary peduncles, large crimson. This is the finest hardy plant of the genus. The wood cranesbill (*G. sylvaticum*) is almost similar in habit to the preceding kinds. The flowers are purple with conspicuous crimson veins. All these are fine for rockeries in open woods and shrubberies, or on grassy banks of rivers and lakes, in sunny or half-shady positions. All thrive best in rich soil. The silvery cranesbill (*G. argenteum*) is a neat little Alpine plant with almost pel-

FIGURE 137. COMMON CRANESBILL (GERANIUM MACULATUM).

tate, much-divided leaves of silky, silvery appearance and large, pale-red flowers. Grows three or four inches high only. Sunny positions in rockeries.

Storksbill, *Erodium.*—There are several very neat rock plants of this genus all much dwarfer than the geraniums. The best are *E. macradenum* with pale lilac or purple flowers and pinnate leaves; *E. Manescavi,* also with pinnate leaves and bright purplish flowers in umbels; *E. alpinum* with pinnatifid leaves and purple flowers in large umbels. All do best in sunny positions in rich and light soil.

Indian Cress, *Tropœolum majus.*—A rapid growing climber with rounded, peltate leaves on long petioles and showy, axillary flowers, yellow, scarlet, crimson, or deep carmine. The dwarf varieties known under the name of *nanum* are best for beds and borders. All are very desirable plants for sunny positions. They look well in a border near the house, in rockeries, vases and window-boxes. Raised from seed in spring.

Touch-me-not, *Impatiens fulva* and *flava.*—Tall straggling annuals with succulent stems and small leaves. Flowers on slender, thread-like peduncles, yellow or of a tawny orange color. The seed-pods are sensitive and open suddenly when touched. Fine for naturalizing on grassy banks and river shores in moist and rich ground.

THE RUE FAMILY.

Rue, *Ruta graveolens.*—Old-fashioned border plant of no ornamental value. Leaves strongly scented, decompound, glaucous green. Flowers yellowish. Habit bushy. For borders in moderately good soil.

Fraxinella or Gas Plant, *Dictamnus Fraxinella.*—This is a very ornamental plant about three feet high. Leaves pinnate. Stems upright with terminal racemes of large rosy purple or white flowers. Fine for borders or on the outskirts of shrubberies; also for specimen plants on the lawn. Strongly scented.

THE MILKWORT FAMILY.

Common Milkwort, *Polygala.*—A very pretty plant of grassy fields and roadsides, growing six or eight inches high. Stems simple, with small linear-lanceolate leaves and one-sided racemes of blue, lilac, purple, or pure white flowers. An excellent species for mixing in lawns or for naturalizing on grassy banks. Fringed polygala or babes in the wood (*P. paucifolia*) is a dwarf woodland plant two or three inches high. Flowers large, fringed, rosy red. Fine for naturalizing in light soil in shrubberies.

THE PEA FAMILY.

Lupine, *Lupinus.*—The lupines are all showy, annual or perennial plants growing in sandy ground or in open woods. The many-leaved lupine (*L. polyphyllus*) is the most common species. It grows about three feet high and forms a broad mass of rounded, fingered leaves. The stems are simple and terminate in a very long cylindrical raceme of blue, purple, or white flowers. Very fine border plant. Wild lupine (*L. perennis*) is a handsome spreading perennial about a foot high. Leaves fingered; flowers very showy, blue, late in spring. Fine for naturalizing in masses on bare hillsides or in sandy lawns. It is also a nice plant for rockeries. The annual forms are very attractive plants for summer bedding. They vary in color from white to deep purple. The best are: *nanus*, blue or white; *luteus*, dwarf yellow; *mutabilis*, flowers large, sweet-scented, violet-purple with the standard yellow in the centre; *hybridus*, in many colors, one rosy-purple. All these should be sown early in spring, in the place where they are to flower. Light, sandy loam.

Clover, *Trifolium*.—Several kinds of clover are useful for lawn-grass mixtures. The white clover is the most useful for this purpose, but for sandy soil the trailing, yellow-flowering kinds, such as the hop trefoil and the sand clover, are also very useful, while in large, pasture-like lawns in extensive grounds the common red clover may be used and allowed to bloom.

Sainfoin, *Onobrychis sativa*.—An agricultural plant, also useful for ornament on grassy banks. It grows one or two feet high with bright green, pinnate leaves and loose racemes of rosy-pink flowers in summer.

Coronilla, *Coronilla varia*.—A very ornamental, spreading plant with long, pinnate leaves and numerous umbels of white and rosy-purple flowers all summer. Fine for naturalizing in sandy soil, on rocky banks, or barren slopes. Inclined to spread rapidly by means of underground shoots.

Cherokee Bean, *Erythrina herbacea*.— An exceedingly fine and showy plant with leafy, erect stems, trifoliate leaves, and long, terminal racemes of scarlet flowers in summer. Grows best in sandy soil in open and sunny positions. Fine for the border, in the outskirts of shrubberies, or in beds and rockeries. The root must be protected in winter in the far North.

Everlasting Pea, *Lathyrus latifolius.*—A climbing herb with winged stems, and pinnate leaves of two leaflets, ending in a tendril. Flowers large, rose-colored, in axillary racemes, very numerous in summer. Other desirable kinds are: *grandiflorus, rotundifolius,* and *sylvestris.* All are fine border plants, and may also be utilized to produce charming effects in thickets and shrubberies. There is a very floriferous species, *L. pratensis,* with bright yellow flowers, growing in meadows and on grassy banks. It is well worth growing in similar positions in large grounds.

The Sweet Pea, *Lathyrus odoratus,* is a well-known annual vine with sweet-scented flowers of many colors. There are also very desirable dwarf varieties. A very useful border plant, propagated by seeds early in spring. Should be sown where it is intended to flower. This useful annual may also be planted in hedge-rows or for covering fences in light and sunny positions.

Thermopsis, *Thermopsis fabacea.*—A rather large, erect-growing plant resembling the lupine. Leaves trifoliate, hairy. Racemes of bright yellow flowers, terminal.

Bird's-foot Trefoil, *Lotus corniculatus.*—A very pretty dwarf plant with trifoliate leaves and loose clusters of bright yellow or sometimes reddish-yellow flowers all summer. One of the best for mixing in lawns on sunny slopes or among the grass on river-banks. It will grow equally well in any soil.

THE ROSE FAMILY.

Meadow-Sweet, *Spiræa Ulmaria.*—One of the most attractive riverside plants of Europe. It forms broad masses of rather rough, pinnate foliage. The yellowish, or creamy-white flowers are borne in ample compound cymes on leafy stems about two feet high. A fine plant for growing on high river-banks or in the rockery. The dropwort (*S. filipendula*) is a smaller plant with tufted, pinnately cleft leaves. The stems are nearly leafless, one or two feet high. Flowers white or slightly rose-colored, in compound terminal cymes. Fine for masses in rockeries in sunny positions; the most delicate and beautiful of all the smaller forms. Queen of the Prairie (*S. lobata*). An American meadow plant of great beauty. Leaves pinnately parted with a deeply cut terminal leaflet. Flowers of the color of peach blossoms, in large panicled cymes on stems from two to eight feet high. Moist places in a rockery; shores of rivers and lakes. *S. palmata*, a Japanese species, is equally desirable. It has palmate leaves and corymbose panicles of bright crimson-colored flowers.

Goat's-Beard (*S. Aruncus*).—This is a very tall and robust plant with ample pinnately-compound leaves and numerous whitish spicate flowers in compound panicles. Fine for the same purpose as the previous kinds. It may also be planted in shrubberies and as a specimen plant on the lawn.

Bowman's Root, *Gillenia trifoliata.*—A tall and slender perennial with trifoliate leaves and loose panicles of white or pale rose-colored flowers. This, as well as all the meadow-sweets, requires rich soil.

Waldsteinia, *Waldsteinia fragarioides.*—An insignificant plant grown in rockeries. Leaves three-fingered. Flowers rather pretty, yellow. On grassy or rocky banks.

FIG. 133.—GOAT'S-BEARD (SPIRÆA ARUNCUS).

Water Avens, *Geum rivale.*—A very floriferous riverside plant of grassy, sunny banks. Flowers nodding. Stamens and pistils large, petals purplish. The numerous wild hybrids of this and *G. ursinum* are well worth growing even in choice rockeries. They flower all summer and some are quite showy, with large yellow or reddish-yellow flowers. They grow beautifully along roads and stone fences in Northern Europe; seldom cultivated. *Geum coccineum* is a dwarf plant with lyrate-pinnatifid leaves and large crimson-purple flowers. The mountain avens (*G. montanum*) is another dwarf and very desirable kind of a similar habit, with erect yellow flowers. Both are beautiful plants for rockeries.

Cinquefoil, *Potentilla.*—Few of these are of any real ornamental value. Some are neat rock plants, and deserve

cultivation on this account. Among the best are: *nitida*, very dwarf, with small ternate leaves forming dense mats, and numerous white or pale rose-colored

FIG. 139.—SHINING CINQUEFOIL (POTENTILLA NITIDA). flowers on short peduncles; *nivalis*, leaves five- to seven-fingered, flowers white, in small terminal clusters; *Nepalensis*, somewhat taller than the last, leaves three- or five-fingered; flowers in summer, rose-colored; *Russeliana*, an erect, spreading plant with ternate leaves and scarlet-crimson flowers two inches across; *Hopwoodiana*, of a similar habit with yellow flowers edged with bright rose. All the cinquefoils are useful in rockeries only.

THE SAXIFRAGE FAMILY.

Grass of Parnassus, *Parnassia palustris.*—A very handsome plant of wet peat bogs and highland meadows. Stems simple, with one or two sessile leaves and large, solitary, white flowers; root leaves cordate, on long stalks; height six or eight inches. Grows in scattered masses among the grass, never in dense masses. Very fine for moist places in a rockery or in moist lawns. *P. Caroliniana* is an American plant about twice as tall as the preceding one. Stems simple, one-leaved, bearing one solitary large white flower with greenish veins. Root leaves orbicular or reniform. Banks of meadow-brooks. Flowers in July.

Alum Root, *Heuchera.*—Most of the species of this genus are of no importance as ornamental plants. The Mexican alum root (*H. sanguinea*) is, however, an exceedingly beautiful plant with tufted, heart-shaped or rounded, slightly lobed leaves and leafless peduncles bearing a panicle of bright red flowers. A fine plant for moist places in rockeries. Grows best in a mixture of sandy loam and leaf mold.

Saxifrage, *Saxifraga.*—Very handsome plants growing in alpine meadows or in the crevices of rocks in high mountain regions. The following are true rock plants and should be planted or sown in the crevices of rocks well filled with a compost of rich, sandy loam, leaf mold, and old mortar or brick rubbish. If grown in very dry positions, an occasional soaking will be very beneficial, especially in places where there is no dew: *S. aizoides*, leaves linear-oblong, in crowded masses; flowers golden-yellow, half an inch in diameter, very numerous in summer. Height two or three inches. *S. Burseriana*, leaves sharply three-angled in rosettes; plant

FIG. 140.—BURSER'S SAXIFRAGE (SAXIFRAGA BURSERIANA).

densely tufted with large, creamy white flowers. *S. casia*, leaves linear-oblong, grayish; flowers milky white, in small panicles. Height one to three inches. *S. Camposii*, leaves spathulate or three angled with a deeply lobed apex; flowers in loose corymbs, large, white. Height three or four inches. *S. Cotyledon*, leaves linear-spathulate in rosettes, forming neat masses of foliage. Flowers small, white, in ample compound panicles from one to two feet high; one of the finest. *S. hypnoides*, the Dovedale moss of England, leaves wedge-shaped, deeply cleft at the apex, forming dense, green mats; flowers white, bell-shaped, nearly an inch wide. *S. longi-folia*, leaves six inches, linear-oblong, disposed in beautiful dense rosettes; flowers white, in tall pyramidal panicles a foot high. *S. nivalis*, leaves spathulate, flowers white, small, in capitate cymes; scapes simple, erect. *S. oppositifolia*, leaves opposite, rounded, imbricated; flowers bright purple, on short, leafy shoots in spring. *S. Rocheliana*, leaves very short and broad, pointed, forming small rosettes, flowering shoots, leafy, with several small white flowers. Most of these flower in summer. The following species grow in moist and rich soil, some on the shores of rivulets, others in meadows: *S. crassifolia*, leaves large, fleshy, obovate, six or more inches long; root and stem fleshy; flowers rosy-red or flesh-colored, disposed in a tall thyrsoid panicle. Handsome in moist places in rockeries or in borders. *S. Fortunei*, leaves cordate, rounded, slightly lobed, borne on tall petioles; flowers white in ample, loose panicles. Probably tender in the far North. *S. granulata*, the fair maids of France or meadow saxifrage of England; leaves reniform, slightly lobed; stems simple, leafy, bearing several large white flowers with greenish veins. Forms quite a feature in moist fields and meadows and along roadsides. Grows abundantly among the grass and flowers in June. This species is fine for sowing or planting on lawns, or naturalized on moist banks. *S. peltata*, a large growing riverside plant with peltate leaves on long stalks and tall scapes bearing a large corymbose raceme of white or pinkish flowers in spring.

False Mitrewort, Diadem Flower, *Tiarella cordifolia.*— A handsome ornamental plant of rocky woods growing in moist places along rivulets; leaves heart-shaped, slightly lobed, on slender petioles; flowers pure white, in loose racemes on slender scapes sometimes a foot high. A beautiful subject for moist places in rockeries or for naturalizing in shrubberies. One of the prettiest plants of the family.

Mitrewort, *Mitella diphylla.*—A delicate plant with heart-shaped, lobed leaves on long petioles, and slender scapes bearing a loose raceme of white flowers. For woodland scenery, planted in a compost of leaf mold and sandy loam. Moist places in a shady rockery.

Golden Saxifrage, *Chrysosplenium.*—Several species of a dwarf habit with rounded leaves close to the ground, and numerous greenish-yellow flowers. Fine for moist or boggy places in a rockery. In masses only.

THE STONE-CROP FAMILY.

House-leek, *Sempervivum tectorum.*—An interesting plant with dense rosettes of fleshy leaves. Flowers in autumn or winter, purplish. There are several other hardy species differing slightly but of a similar habit, such as *calcaratum* and *soboliferum*. All are excellent rock plants and may also be used in carpet bedding for edging.

Stone Crop, *Sedum.*—Next to the saxifrage these are the most numerous and important of rock-plants: *S. acre,* stems slender, creeping; leaves scale-like, fleshy; flowers numerous, yellow, in forked cymes throughout the summer. *S. Aizoon*, leaves alternate scattered, oblong-lanceolate, toothed; stems erect, a foot high, bearing loose panicled cymes of bright yellow flowers. *S. album*, leaves linear-oblong; stems reddish, erect, bearing loose cymes of numerous white flowers in summer. *S. Anglicum*, leaves small, crowded; flowers white or pale rose; plant forming dense mats of green foliage. *S. caruleum*, annual or biennial; leaves oblong, small glaucous green; flowers pale blue in many-flowered cymes, in summer. *S. glaucum*, leaves evergreen, glaucous, linear, and much crowded; flowers white or reddish in umbellate cymes, on stems three or four inches high. *S. pulchellum*, leaves terate, evergreen; flowers rosy-purple in loose cymes, on scapes five or six inches high. Summer.

The following are field- or meadow-plants: *S. Telephium*, stem erect, a foot high or more; leaves oblong-ovate, alternate, somewhat fleshy; flowers white or pink in flat terminal cymes. *S. spectabile*, as tall as the preceding species; leaves ovate or spathulate; flowers pink in large and broad cymes. *S. Maximowiczii*, leaves oblong-lanceolate; stems erect, as tall as in *spectabile*; flowers yellow, forming flat, spreading cymes, in July; foliage reddish-green. These may be naturalized on high, grassy banks or grown in moist places in rockeries.

THE EVENING PRIMROSE FAMILY.

Willow Herb, *Epilobium angustifolium.*—A tall, erect herb with willow-like leaves and long racemes of crimson flowers; quite showy, growing five or six feet high and forming large masses on the outskirts of woods or along stone enclosures in fields. Useful in wild gardening in scattered masses or sparingly in rockeries. *E. rosmarinifolium* is another dwarfer and very attractive species.

Zauschneria Californica.—A fine ornamental plant, very bushy and branching, with ovate-lanceolate leaves. Flowers two inches long, tubular, bright scarlet, produced singly or in pairs from the axils of the upper leaves, in late summer and autumn. Probably tender in the far North. A useful plant for a moist place in a rockery.

Evening Primrose, *Œnothera.*—A number of very showy plants of easy culture belong to this genus. Many are inclined to run wild and become weeds in lawns and cultivated fields, and had better be excluded from choice gardens. Of the perennial species the following are the the best: *Œ. Missouriensis,* stems fleshy, prostate; leaves crowded, broadly lanceolate, entire; flowers very large, axillary, pale sulphur-yellow. *Œ. eximia,* leaves lanceolate, pubescent; flowers axillary, four inches across, white; a low and very handsome species. *Œ. Fraserii,* leaves oblong-lanceolate, glaucous; flowers axillary, bright yellow. Grow best in sunny positions in light sandy, loam. Rockeries, borders, or bare hillsides.

There are many annual forms with innumerable garden varieties grown under the name of Godetia. The flowers vary in color from white to rose and deep crimson. Some of the best are: *White pearl,* dwarf, white; *bijou,* white with crimson; *Duchess of Albany,* white, satiny; *the bride,* white and red. All are useful border plants, propagated from seeds.

THE LOOSESTRIFE FAMILY.

Purple Loosestrife, *Lythrum Salicaria.*—A handsome waterside plant growing three or four feet high with simple, erect stems, willow-like leaves, and long terminal spikes of reddish-purple flowers. For growing on the margins of rivers and lakes in large grounds.

THE CACTUS FAMILY.

Prickly Pear, *Opuntia vulgaris.*—A unique and picturesque plant with fleshy, jointed stems bearing handsome yellow flowers in summer. Common in rocky and sandy soil. *B. Rafinesquii* is another species, larger and more spiny. *O. Missouriensis* is a species with short tubercled joints and large yellow flowers. All these are very desirable rock plants interesting at all seasons and especially so when covered with flowers. They thrive best in a sandy loam in warm and sunny positions.

Several other plants of the cactus family are perfectly hardy and make very interesting objects in a rockery. None are common in cultivation but many can easily be obtained from the West. The hardiest are: *Echinocactus longihamata,* a dwarfish, almost globular plant, ribbed and spiny, with yellow flowers. *Mamillaria longimamma,* with long fleshy tubercles and yellow flowers; *M. pusilla,* small, almost globular, flowers minute, pinkish. *M. vivipara,* globular, from one to five inches high with comparatively large purplish flowers. Plant in a compost of sandy loam and old mortar.

THE PARSLEY FAMILY.

Sea Holly, *Eryngium maritimum.* —A rather ornamental thistle-like plant with pale, glaucous leaves, cordate, long petioled with wavy and spiny edges. Stem leaves palmately lobed; flowers pale blue in small heads. Common on the seashore, useful in seaside-gardening. It is also very desirable in rockeries. *E. amethystinum,* stems erect, one or two feet high, with lanceolate leaves; root leaves pinnatifid, spiny; flowers of a beautiful amethyst color, in globose heads. Grows best in sandy loam, otherwise useful for the same purpose as the preceding one.

Sweet Cicely, *Myrrhis odorata.*—A very desirable plant with finely decompound leaves, and leafy, flowering stems bearing ample compound umbels of white flowers. Forms a large leafy mass two or three feet high. The leaves are sweet-scented. Suitable for naturalizing on grassy banks and even as a foliage plant in moist places of the rockery or in old orchards.

Giant Fennel, *Ferula communis.*—One of the most effective, hardy, foliage plants forming a mass of beautifully green, feathery leaves four or five feet high; flowers yellow, umbellate, forming an inflorescence eight feet high. It is handsome as a specimen on the lawn or in the background of rockeries. Prefers a rich sandy loam.

Cow Parsnip, *Heracleum giganteum.*—A coarse and very large foliage plant eight or ten feet high; leaves pinnatifid, several feet long; flowers white, umbellate. In large grounds on the margins of streams and lakes.

THE DOGWOOD FAMILY.

Dwarf Cornel, *Cornus Canadensis.*—A small but very ornamental woodland flower forming quite a feature of the scenery in moist and rich woods. Stem a few inches high, bearing only a single whorl of ovate or oval leaves; flowers in terminal heads surrounded by four large, showy, pure white involucral leaves. Very desirable for planting in shrubberies and thickets to form woodland scenery. May also be grown in moist places in a rockery.

THE MADDER FAMILY.

Madder, *Rubia.*—Several species may be employed among the grass on the margins of streams and lakes with good effect. Most are weedy and insignificant as individuals.

Bedstraw, *Galium verum.* —A slender, graceful plant effective when grown in masses on grassy banks or in openings of woods and thickets. Leaves whorled, flowers numerous, bright yellow in terminal, leafy panicles. Height about a foot.

Woodruff, *Asperula odorata.*—A small herb, with lanceolate whorled leaves and terminal corymbs of white flowers in summer. Very attractive in shady woods, forming loose, graceful masses of leaves and flowers about eight inches high. May be naturalized with ease. Not showy.

Partridge-Berry, *Mitchella repens.*—A minute evergreen creeping plant of rich woods. Leaves ovate, small bright green; flowers very pretty white or tinted rose followed by scarlet berries in winter. In woodland scenery to form close mats on the ground, planted in a rich leaf-soil.

Bluet, *Houstonia cærulea.*—A slender plant three or

four inches high, growing in large scattered masses in pastures and moist grassy fields, and sometimes in small patches
in open woods or on sandy shores. Leaves minute, spathulate; flowers bright blue, purple, or white on slender
peduncles. Very attractive for naturalizing in moist lawns,
in glades, and in open spaces among shrubs. Flowers in
spring and summer.

THE VALERIAN FAMILY.

Valerian, *Valeriana officinalis.*—This plant, which is
not showy but very attractive, may be grown with good
results on grassy banks of streams and lakes. Leaves pinnate, pretty; stems simple, erect, two to three feet high;
flowers whitish-pink, in broad paniculate corymbs, sweet-
scented. Marsh valerian (*V. dioica*), is a much smaller
species growing in shallow running water on the margins
of streams and brooks. Both are readily naturalized and
are excellent for wild gardening.

Spurred Valerian, *Centranthus ruber.*—A rather pretty
annual border plant a foot or two high, with ovate-lanceolate
leaves and red or white flowers in panicled cymes.

THE TEASEL FAMILY.

Mourning Bride, *Scabiosa atropurpurea.*—A garden annual sometimes used for summer-bedding. Stem slender,
slightly branched, about two feet high; root-leaves obovate
or spathulate, toothed, stem leaves pinnately-parted. Flowers
black-purple, crimson, or white in large button-like heads on
long and slender peduncles. Propagated from seeds in
spring and often grown in borders.

Pincushion Flower, *S. Columbaria.*—A graceful peren-

nial about two feet high. Leaves of the root entire, stem-
leaves pinnatifid; flowers rosy-lilac in large heads.
Flowers in early summer; a handsome plant of
grassy hillsides and meadows. Fine for naturalizing on grassy banks or margins of water.

Blue Bonnets, *S. Succica.*—A plant common
in meadows and on grassy banks in Europe, very
handsome, with almost globular heads of deep
blue, purple, or white flowers; leaves obovate or
oblong; stem leaves small, lanceolate, toothed.
Grows a foot high and flowers during a long
period in summer.

FIG 141.—BLUE
BONNETS
(SCABIOSA
SUCCICA).

THE COMPOSITE FAMILY.

Marianna Thistle, *Silybum marianum.*—A dwarf and
ornamental plant with foliage close to the ground. Leaves
oblong, sinuately lobed with spiny teeth, pale green blotched
with white; flowers purple, insignificant. For use in seaside gardening on sandy shores.

Cornflower, *Centaurea Cyanus.*—A handsome annual a
couple of feet high with narrow, linear-lanceolate leaves and
heads of bright blue flowers in summer. There are several
varieties with lilac, rose-colored, or white flowers all inferior
to this type. In beds with Paris daisies and scarlet poppies,
or in borders. Moderately good soil. Sweet sultan, *C.
moschata.*—Annual with lyrate leaves and purplish flowers.
A yellow-flowered species with sweet-scented flowers (*C.
suaveolens*) is frequently grown under the name of sweet
sultan. Both may be grown with good effect among rocks
or on sunny, barren slopes. *C. montana* is a perennial plant

with large, blue flower-heads. It is a handsome species for rocky banks.

Tansy, *Tanacetum vulgare.*—A coarse but rather ornamental plant, effective in masses on grassy banks or roadsides. Stem simple, three or four feet high, with pinnate, deeply cut leaves of a feathery appearance. Flower-heads button-like, golden-yellow in large corymbs, numerous in summer and very lasting. Prefers sunny positions and a light, loamy soil.

Abrotanum, *Artemisia Abrotanum.*—A somewhat shrubby plant three or four feet high, with pinnately divided leaves of a grayish color, very strongly scented and cultivated for this reason. Flowers inconspicuous. Borders or shrubberies in rich soil.

Golden Immortelle, *Helichrysum arenarium.*—Common on sandy shores in Northern Europe. Stem five or six inches high, with lanceolate, whitish, downy leaves, and corymbs of small golden yellow flower-heads. Forms tufted masses, very effective when in flower. Excellent for seaside gardening or for naturalizing in barren and sandy lawns. May also be grown in rockeries with good effect. *H. bracteatum* is a familiar annual border plant; grows about a foot high and has large globular heads of yellow, deep crimson, rose-colored or white flowers. Propagated by seeds in spring.

Button-Snakeroot or **Blazing Star,** *Liatris.*—Rough but rather showy plants with erect stems and almost grass-like leaves. Flowers in spiked heads. The best are: *L. squarosa*, heads bright purple, height two feet; *pychnostachia*, pale purple, fine for dry soil; *spicata*, purple, a foot high; for margins of streams and lakes or in borders.

Trumpet Weed, *Eupatorium purpureum.*—One of our largest and most effective perennials, growing in scattered masses on moist banks and in low grassy fields, flowering late in the season. Leaves long, lanceolate, in whorls of three or more. The very numerous purplish heads are collected in compound corymbs sometimes a foot and a half across. Height from three to twelve feet. Fine for naturalizing on margins of water or in open glades in low ground. *E. ageratoides* is a smaller, more spreading plant with numerous white heads of flowers in compound corymbs. Useful for the same purpose as the preceding one.

Mist Flower, *Conoclinium coelestinum.*—This is a very handsome native plant forming broad and dense masses of leaves and flowers, late in summer and autumn. Leaves triangular-ovate, coarsely toothed. Flowers blue or purple, sometimes white, in small heads forming dense corymbs much like those of Ageratum. Grows in open woods or among Eupatorium in open fields. Fine for naturalizing in scattered masses on grassy banks or hillsides.

Golden Senecio, *Senecio aureus.*—A graceful plant with simple stems about two feet high, and very varied, mostly heart-shaped, petioled leaves; root leaves lyrate. Flower-heads with golden-yellow rays, in flat corymbs. For river shores, margins of water, or moist places in rockeries. The purple ragwort (*S. elegans*) is an elegant annual used for summer bedding. Flowers purple and white with yellow disk, in many shades, single or double, somewhat like the common cineraria. Propagated by seeds indoors.

Arnica, *Arnica montana.*—A very handsome plant of highland meadows and grassy fields, chiefly in Northern

Europe. Leaves lanceolate, mostly tufted at the root. Flowers on almost leafless scapes seldom a foot high. Heads large, golden-yellow or orange, several together. Fine for rockeries or on high banks. Will grow well in light or gravelly soil. Flowers in summer.

Leopard's Bane, *Doronicum Caucasicum.* — A very pretty spring-flowering plant, fine for rockeries. Leaves on long petioles, cordate. Stems mostly simple, with a few large heads of bright yellow flowers. Desirable for growing in sunny positions.

Goldenrod, *Solidago.*—There are many showy species of goldenrod, but as they are so common all over the country there is little need of their cultivation. The most beautiful are: *S. Canadense,* with ample panicles on stems several feet high; *S. lanceolata,* a bushy, branching plant with flat corymbs of small yellow heads; *S. serotina* flowers in pyramidal panicles on stems two or three feet high; *S. speciosa,* with large flower-heads in thyrsoid panicles, stems from three to six feet high; *S. cirga-aurea,* somewhat branched, heads racemose.

Chinese Aster, *Callistephus Chinensis.*—Favorite border or bedding plants, of which there are many strains, some tall, others very dwarf, some bushy, others slender, bearing only a few large heads of flowers. All cultivated kinds are double; some unite two colors in one head, white and blue, white and purple or lilac, and so on; others are one-colored, white, pale rose, purple-crimson, and purplish-blue. They should be raised in boxes or pots in a cool frame and planted out late in spring. They require frequent waterings in dry summers in order to prevent them from flowering prematurely. As a rule China-asters do best in high altitudes, or in countries where the summer is cool and pleasant.

Aster, *Aster.*—These, like the goldenrods, are common hillside- and field-plants, flowering late in the season; they

are as yet too common to be cultivated, and the glorious panorama they spread out before us could not be excelled in the garden. It is to be hoped it will always be so. There

FIG.—142. ALPINE ASTER (ASTER ALPINUS).

are however many exotic kinds of great beauty that may be grown together with the most attractive of the native species. Some are dwarf and entirely different from any American species. The best are: *A. alpinus,* leaves lanceolate-spathulate forming tufts close to the ground; flowering stems, single, a few inches high, bearing a single large head with purple ray-florets and yellow disk. A pretty plant for rockeries. *A. Amellus,* leaves broadly lanceolate, stems two feet high, simple at the base, branched above and bearing large solitary heads of purple flowers. A very floriferous and showy kind, fine for borders. *A. Bessarabicus,* a larger and showier variety of the last.—The following are exceedingly fine American species: *A. grandiflorus,*

FIG.—143. TURBINATE ASTER (ASTER TURBINELLUS).

height two feet, leaves small linear, rigid stem branching at the top, bearing numerous large purple heads. *A. Nova-Anglia,* most common species, leaves linear-lanceolate, heads large, purple, height six feet. *A. Nova-Belgia,* leaves lanceolate, stem clasping or nearly so; stem branching, four feet high, flower-heads pale blue. *A. spectabilis*, height two feet; leaves lanceolate, nearly amplexicaul, heads beautiful blue. *A. turbinellus*, leaves small, lanceolate, stem slender, graceful, two or three feet high, heads mauve. Besides these the little white flowering *A. ericoides* is sometimes grown.

Fleabane, *Erigeron*.—Generally inferior to the asters as ornamental plants. *E. alpinum* is a neat and attractive rock-plant with bluish flowers. *E. aurantiacus*, showy; leaves oblong, flower-heads large, of a bright orange-color. Height seldom a foot. *E. speciosum*, a pretty American plant a foot high, with oblong leaves and large heads of lilac flowers; disk yellow. In rockeries or borders. Ordinary, garden soil.

Swan-River Daisy, *Brachychome iberidifolia*.—A very handsome annual cultivated in beds and borders. It forms a nice and compact bushy plant about a foot high and equally broad, covered all summer with innumerable deep blue flower-heads; leaves pinnately parted, small. Raised from seeds. Sown on the spot in early spring.

Daisy, *Bellis perennis*.—The true European daisy is a very small plant with mats of obovate-spathulate leaves close to the ground, and simple leafless scapes four or five inches high, bearing one solitary head of white flowers suffused with rose. The double white or pink varieties are the most desirable for edging beds and borders. They are very floriferous and should be grown in every garden. They may also be naturalized in lawns, but the single form should be excluded as it spreads and becomes a weed. Increased by means of seeds or division.

Yarrow or Sneeze-wort, *Achillea.*—The double sneeze-worts (*A. Ptarmica plenissima* and *A. serrata plena*) are very fine and floriferous subjects for a border; they grow one or two feet high, with single stems, narrow lanceolate leaves, and heads in terminal corymbs. The variety known as *the pearl* is the best. Few other plants of this family deserve consideration. The following are attractive in rockeries: *A. Clavenna*, leaves all radical, crowded, bipinnatifid; flower-heads corymbose, pretty, white; height from six to ten inches. *A. tomentosa*, leaves bipinnatifid, finely divided, woolly; flower-heads bright yellow, corymbose.

Yellow Chamomile, *Anthemis tinctoria.*—A desirable summer flowering plant about a foot high forming broad masses; leaves bipinnatifid; stems slender, bearing numerous golden-yellow heads of flowers. In rockeries or borders. Ordinary, garden soil.

Double white Chamomile, *Matricaria inodora fl. pleno.* —A pretty spreading, much-branched annual border-plant with doubly pinnate leaves and very double heads of pure white flowers. Floriferous and ornamental. Flowers in summer. Propagated by means of seeds.

Fever-few, *Pyrethrum parthenifolium.*—A fine annual with double white flowers and pinnate, much-divided leaves. The variety *aureum* is generally used for summer-bedding in mosaic-groups. Raised from seeds in a greenhouse or frame, or by means of cuttings. *P. roseum* is a perennial with simple, erect stems, feathery, doubly pinnate leaves and large showy heads of mostly rosy-purple flowers with many varieties. Must be grown in a moist and rich ground to develop fully. Very handsome.

Great Oxeye Daisy, *Pyrethrum uliginosum.*—This is a tall and graceful plant about three feet high, with lanceolate, coarsely dentate leaves, and heads of large white ray-florets and yellow disk. Fine for margins of streams and lakes in rich ground.

Gaillardia, *Gaillardia aristata.*—A very floriferous plant about a foot high, with lanceolate leaves and large yellow flower-heads. The variety *grandiflora* is the most common in gardens: it has the lower half of the ray-florets of a reddish color. *G. pulchella* is a very showy annual of a similar habit but with bright crimson ray-florets tipped with yellow. Both are excellent for dry ground in sunny positions where they flower all summer.

Marigold, *Calendula officinalis.*—A compact, floriferous annual with oblong-obovate leaves and bright yellow heads of flowers, single or double, all summer.

FIG. 144.—
GAILLARDIA.

Compass-Plant, *Silphium laciniatum.*—A rather coarse perennial, with pinnatifid leaves and tall leafy flowering stems bearing a few large heads of yellow flowers.

Dahlia, *Dahlia variabilis.*—Well known border plant with fleshy roots and pinnate leaves. Flowers double or single, of all colors. There are some dwarf and small flowering varieties. The cactus dahlia (*D. Juarezii*) is one of the most desirable kinds, with bright scarlet-crimson flowers similar in shape to some kinds of cactus. Planted in beds or borders in spring. Roots stored in winter.

Thickweed, *Coreopsis.*—Exceedingly showy and floriferous annual or perennial plants for sunny positions in borders or naturalized in gravelly soil. *C. tinctoria* is an annual a couple of feet high, branched and spreading, leaves bipinnatifid; heads numerous, ray-florets deep crimson on the lower half, the rest yellow. *C. Drummondii*, resembling the last, ray-florets yellow with a dark spot at the base. *C. lanceolata* is a perennial; leaves lanceolate, flowers pure yellow; very desirable. Flowers all summer.

Sunflower, *Helianthus.*—All the species are very large and coarse but showy plants. The common annual species hardly deserves culture except for economic use. The most desirable are *H. decapetalus*, a tall plant common on sunny shores of rivers; heads three inches across, showy, bright yellow. *H. angustifolius*, leaves linear, a medium-sized or small species about three or four feet high; ray-florets bright yellow, disk purple. *H. Maximilianus*, leaves long, linear-lanceolate; stems six feet, more or less; flower-heads very numerous golden, yellow. A most desirable species. All are perennial. On the margins of water; in borders or shrubberies.

Oxeye, *Heliopsis lævis.*—A kind of sunflower on a smaller scale, leaves ovate; flower-heads terminal on numerous lateral branches; *H. Pitcherianus*, a recently introduced kind, is of a very spreading and branching habit, about three feet high, with numerous heads of golden-yellow flowers late in summer. A beautiful and very floriferous kind. Fine in borders; ordinary soil.

Cone-flower, *Rudbeckia.*—A genus of very attractive perennial plants flowering all summer. *R. speciosa* has coarsely toothed, lanceolate leaves and terminal heads of yellow flowers; disk conical; habit branching, height less than two feet. *R. hirta*, the popular yellow daisy, is a very showy plant of sandy fields and barren hillsides; stem simple, erect, about a foot high; leaves oblong-lanceolate; ray-florets orange-yellow, disk brown. *R. fulgida*, flowers smaller than in the preceding species; the plant is twice as tall; same color. All the Rudbeckias are very handsome plants for use in wild gardening, for natural groups in sandy and gravelly soil, in rockeries and borders.

Purple Cone-flower, *Echinacea purpurea.*—A simple, erect plant, one or two feet high, with ovate-lanceolate leaves, heads several inches across, ray-florets rosy-purple, disk conical or columnar, brown. Fine in borders or for planting in sunny positions on the margin of water. Flowers in summer.

Sanvitalia, *Sanvitalia procumbens.*—A dwarf, trailing plant growing a few inches high only, and covered in summer with numerous small yellow flower-heads with a purple disk; leaves ovate. Fine for covering the ground in groups of taller plants such as eucalyptus or silk oak, or on sunny banks to cover the ground. Increased by means of seeds annually.

Zinnia, *Zinnia elegans.*—One of the most popular late-flowering annuals with single or double flowers of the most intense and brilliant colors. Used in beds or borders with good effect. Seeds may be sown in flat boxes in a greenhouse or frame and the plants should be kept ready to take the place of spring- or early summer-flowers.

French Marigold, *Tagetes patula.*— A very floriferous, strongly scented annual with pinnate leaves, and mostly double flowers of rich and effective colors, chiefly pale yellow, deep yellow, and brown. The African marigold (*T. erecta*) is considerably larger in all parts, growing as high as two feet. It is also more varied in coloring. *T. signata pumila* is a dwarf and floriferous kind with numerous bright yellow flowers all summer. The marigolds are easily raised by means of seeds sown in the open border.

THE LOBELIA FAMILY.

Cardinal Flower, *Lobelia cardinalis.*—A very showy American plant growing in moist places along streams and rivulets, and flowering in June or July. The stems are simple, a foot or eighteen inches high, with oblong-lanceolate leaves, and long terminal racemes of bright scarlet flowers. Grows in small tufts on grassy banks close to the water. The Mexican cardinal flower (*L. fulgens*) is a more robust plant with broader leaves tinted red; petals wider than in the preceding kind and of a still deeper scarlet. These are suitable for moist places in a rockery, along a rill of water, or by the side of a stream or lake. Thrive well in a rich, sandy loam.

THE BELLFLOWER FAMILY.

Venus's Looking-Glass, *Specularia Speculum.*—A pretty annual with numerous blue flowers all summer. Sown in beds or borders early in spring.

Bellflower, *Campanula.*—There are many very attractive summer-flowering plants belonging to this genus, some of which are tall, robust-growing subjects, excellent for borders; others are dwarf, tufted, and compact Alpine plants, with slender, delicate stems and pretty blue or white flowers. The best are: The Canterbury bell (*C. medium*), stems erect, branching, two or three feet high, with ovate-lanceolate, crenate leaves; flowers in leafy panicles, large, bell-shaped, blue-purple, or white. One of the best; flowers in July. Clustered bell-flower. (*C. glomerata*), stems simple, one or two feet high; leaves ovate, upper ones somewhat stem-clasping; flowers in close heads, violet-blue, pale blue, or white, flowering all summer. A desirable plant for naturalizing in glades and open woods, or on grassy banks. Pale

FIG. 145.—PALE BELL-FLOWER (CAMPANULA LACTIFLORA).

bell-flower (*C. lactiflora*), stems two or more feet high, branched; leaves ovate-lanceolate, sessile; flowers in loose racemes, pale blue or white. Nice border plant, forming large tufts and flowering all summer. Chimney bell-flower (*C. pyramidalis*), stem almost simple, forming many flowering branches at the top, about four feet high; leaves ovate or sometimes cordate, petiolate; flowers in pyramidal racemes, very numerous, deep blue or white, flowering in June or July. Border plant. Peach-leaved bell-flower (*C. persicifolia*), stem simple, one foot high or more; root leaves like the leaves of the peach, stem leaves few, linear-lanceolate; flowers very large, racemose, deep blue to pure white, sometimes semi-double or double. Excellent border plant; fine for naturalizing in grassy and half-shady positions. Carpatian bell-flower (*C. carpatica*), a very graceful plant, with slender branched stems about a foot high and more or less cordate leaves on long stalks; flowers in loose racemes, cup-shaped, deep blue or, in one variety, white. This is a very fine plant for borders or rockeries, flowering in summer for several months. It forms broad masses of leaves and flowers. There are a few very dwarf varieties of this spe-

cies fine for rock-gardens, such as *turbinata*, leaves all radical, ovate, on long stalks; flowers solitary, erect, on slender stalks six inches high, color purple; *pelriformis*, taller, with loosely racemose flowers

FIG. 146.—DWARF CARPATIAN BELL-FLOWER (CAMPANULA CARPATICA TURBINATA PALLIDA).

of a bright lilac color, two inches across. The following are chiefly dwarf and trailing plants, inhabitants of alpine meadows or stony banks of mountain streams: *C. cæspitosa*, stems short, tufted; leaves ovate, crowded; flowers terminal, blue or white, numerous. On rocky shores of rivulets or in moist ground near a stream in a rockery. *C. garganica*, stems trailing, leaves reniform or heart-shaped, downy; flowers at the end of the shoots, axillary, blue, or sometimes white. Charming rock plants for growing in a compost of leaf soil, sand and brick rubbish, or old mortar. Protected in winter by a covering of leaves. *C. pusilla*, very dwarf; leaves tufted; flowers on slender leafy stems, pendulous, almost cylindrical, blue. Neat in moist places in rockeries. *C. Rainerii*, dwarf, two or three inches; leaves ovate, hairy; flowers mostly solitary, erect. *C. Waldsteiniana*, dwarf; leaves small, cordate; stems four or five inches high, bearing one or more erect, violet-blue flowers. All these are suitable for rockeries, but enjoy half shade and moisture and a light, well-drained soil. The common harebell (*C. rotundifolia*) is one of the prettiest of all bell-flowers. The stems are nearly always simple, but it often forms rich tufted masses; flowers solitary, drooping, blue or white. Grows in rocky, open woodlands, and is especially desirable for naturalizing in lawns and grassy openings among trees and shrubs. Another fine species for naturalizing is *C. rapunculoides*.

Chinese Bell-flower, *Platycodon grandiflorum.*—This is the largest flowering species of the family; stems somewhat branching; leaves ovate-lanceolate, large and handsome; flowers blue, several inches across, solitary or in small clusters at the top of the branches. Height about two feet; flowers late in summer. There is a white variety. *P. Mariesii* is a dwarf and very floriferous form. Both are very fine plants for borders and rockeries; the best bell-flowers for small gardens.

THE PYROLA FAMILY.

Wintergreen, *Pyrola.*—A genus of several small evergreen woodland flowers. They grow in partial shade in leaf soil, chiefly in sandy ground, and are excellent for planting in thickets and shrubberies among other woodland flowers. Most common are: *P. chlorantha*, flowers greenish-white, scented, borne in umbels on simple scapes

a few inches high; leaves reniform or rounded on slender
stalks. *P. rotundifolia*, taller and showier, with petiolate,
shining green leaves; flowers rather large, ten to twenty
in terminal racemes on slender scapes, pure white, fragrant.
The pipsissewa (*Chimaphila umbellata*) is an equally desirable plant; leaves cuneate-lanceolate in a whorl on the
middle of the slender stem; flowers umbellate, white,
waxy, with violet anthers. Where they are rare and can
be obtained only in a limited number these may be used for
moist, half-shady positions in a rockery or for small patches
among choice evergreen shrubs.

THE LEADWORT FAMILY.

Thrift or Sea Pink, *Armeria vulgaris.*—A very handsome seaside plant covering acres of sandy shores, with
tufts of small, linear, bright green leaves and rosy-red
flowers. The flowers are borne on scapes five or six inches
high in close heads. There is a pretty white variety. *A.
Laucheana* has bright pink flowers. Excellent for seaside
gardening or for naturalizing on sandy ground or here and
there in lawns. It is also fine in rockeries or for edging
beds or borders. *A. Cephalotes* is a larger growing species
with a scape a foot high bearing a head of crimson flowers;
leaves lanceolate, tufted. *A. plantaginea*, leaves lanceolate
with several longitudinal nerves; flowers rose-colored, on
scapes eight inches high. These two are best for rockeries
in a light, sandy soil. All require a sunny position.

Sea Lavender, *Statice.*—A genus of plants common in
the Steppes of Eastern Europe, in salt marshes and on sea-
shores. They have small flowers in immense panicles,
which look very elegant and feathery. Nice for rockeries

and open sandy ground. The best are: *S. Tartarica*, leaves all radical, more or less spade-like, six inches long; flowers crimson, in small spikes collected in ample panicles a foot or more wide. *S. data*, leaves radical obovate, blunt, in crowded tufts; flowers blue in spikelets forming oblique panicles. Flowering stems many, forming a dense mass of flowers in summer. *S. Limonium*, common sea-lavender, American species with lavender-colored flowers all summer.

Leadwort, *Plumbago Larpente (Ceratostigma).*—A very showy trailing or procumbent plant, with obovate leaves, and heads of violet or bright blue flowers late in summer. Exceptionally fine for rockeries; will grow on high and dry ground almost anywhere. May be planted to cover barren slopes or in similar positions.

THE PRIMROSE FAMILY.

Common Primrose, *Primula vulgaris.*—A small but handsome European plant common in open grassy woods and on moist hillsides, chiefly in the Northern countries. Leaves wrinkled and veiny, spade-like; flowers on short axillary peduncles, very numerous in early spring, pale sulphur-yellow or in cultivated varieties white or more or less deep yellow, single or double. Fine for naturalizing in moist, grassy woods or for rockeries. Thrives best in a moist, sandy loam.

Cowslip (*P. veris*).—This is another very attractive spring flower growing abundantly in meadows and moist, open woodlands; the yellow flowers are borne in many-flowered umbels on scapes six or eight inches tall; leaves similar to those of the primrose. Fine for planting in similar positions in parks or gardens.

The Oxlip (*P. elatior*) resembles the cowslip in habit, the flowers are, however, larger and of many different colors, from yellow and white to deep crimson. It is a very desirable border plant with tufted leaves, and numerous showy flowers in spring. Will grow in sunny positions in any moderately good garden soil. It is essentially a plant for small gardens. Also cultivated under the name of polyanthus.

Bird's-eye Primrose (*P. farinosa*).—A pretty little plant of woodland meadows and grassy fields, with small spade-like leaves and many-flowered umbels of rosy-purple flowers with yellow eyes, borne on slender scapes about six inches high. It covers acres of ground in many places in Northern Europe and makes quite a feature of the scenery about midsummer. For moist places in rockeries or among low grass in lawns or shrubberies.

Auricula (*P. Auricula*).—A beautiful alpine plant of a dwarf and compact habit, much used for summer bedding in half-shady positions. It is also a very desirable plant for a rockery. Flowers pale yellow, darker around the centre, fragrant. There are many garden varieties with white, yellow, rose-colored or lilac flowers. Leaves generally powdered, grayish, obovate. The scape is only a few inches high bearing a many-flowered umbel. Should be wintered in a cool frame where it is not fully hardy. Rich and moist loam. Of the numerous other species of *Primula*, few have been tried in American gardens and some are probably tender. All deserve cultivation; many are exceedingly beautiful rock-plants.

Fairy Primrose, *Androsace*.—A genus of very dwarf and tufted primrose-like plants, mostly alpine. Exceedingly pretty, of delicate colors and very floriferous. Probably none have been tried in American gardens. The following are most likely to succeed: *A. alpina*, two or three inches high, with very crowded, tongue-shaped leaves in rosettes. Flowers numerous, from the axils of the leaves, rosy-purple. On moist, mossy rocks near water, rooting in crevices. *A. carnea*, leaves awl-shaped, forming tufts or cushions three inches high; flowers rose-colored, umbellate on short peduncles. In crevices of rocks. Pretty. *A. Laggeri*, leaves small, awl-shaped, flowers terminal, rose-colored, very numerous in spring. In crevices of moist and shady rocks. *A. lanuginosa*, foliage covered with silken hairs; flower rose, with a yellow eye, umbellate, on scapes five or six inches high. Summer. In the crevices of sunny rocks. A very beautiful species.

Shooting Star, *Dodecatheon Meadia.*—A well-known, beautiful woodland plant growing in half-shady positions in rich soil. Leaves six inches or more, oblong or spade-like, in rosettes. Scape commonly a foot high, bearing an umbel of pretty large, rosy-purple or white flowers in early summer. *D. integrifolium* is a smaller, not less desirable species. There are also some well-marked varieties of the common shooting star. For planting in moist and half-shady positions in a rockery or in patches in grassy shrubberies or thickets.

FIG. 147. SHOOTING STAR (DODECATHEON MEADIA).

Alp Violet, *Cyclamen Europeum.*—A charming floriferous plant of high, rich, diciduous woods in central Europe. Flowers solitary on single scapes, bright rose-colored, fragrant, appearing with the heart-shaped, petioled leaves in August or September and forming quite a feature of the scenery. The stem is globular and tuberous, half buried in the ground. Hardy in the partial shade of trees and evergreen shrubs. One of the most desirable plants for woodland

FIG. 148. ALP VIOLET (CYCLAMEN EUROPEUM).

scenery late in summer. Should be planted in open woods or thickets in a sandy loam made light and rich by the addition of leaf mold. There are several other species, probably not quite hardy. The finest are: *C. Græcum*, white; *C. Neapolitanicum*, white and pink; *C. repandum*, with ivy-like leaves, rosy-red.

Loosestrife, *Lysimachia vulgaris.*—This is a robust perennial two or three feet high, with single stems and whorled ovate-lanceolate leaves, rather hairy or downy. Flowers showy, bright yellow, in large terminal panicles. A fine plant for riversides and margins of water generally or in grassy woods. The moneywort (*L. nummularia*) is a small trailer growing in moist meadows or on grassy banks; leaves opposite, rounded; flowers large yellow, axillary. Often used in vases and window-boxes. Fine in damp places in a rockery, or on moist banks.

Water Violet, *Hottonia palustris.* — A handsome water plant with simple leafy stems one or two feet high; leaves pectinate, feathery; flowers white or lilac with a yellow eye, in whorls forming a long terminal raceme. Flowers in June. Pretty in shallow water or in bogs.

FIG. 149. WATER VIOLET (HOTTONIA PALUSTRIS).

THE BLADDERWORT FAMILY.

Bladderwort, *Utricularia.* — A genus of very handsome water plants common in pools and ditches and nice for growing in cisterns and small artificial waters. The following are common: *U. vulgaris,* leaves pinnate, divided into thread-like segments. The stems floating by means of bladders formed on the leaves; flowers several in a raceme, inflated, yellow. *U. purpurea,* flowers three or four in a raceme, violet-purple.

THE BIGNONIA FAMILY.

Dwarf Trumpet Flower, *Incarvillea Olga.* — A very ornamental perennial three or four feet high, has pinnate, opposite leaves with pinnatifid segments. Stems very leafy, ending in a loose raceme of a few large, rose-colored, trumpet-like flowers rather late in summer. This is a very desirable border plant, when well grown forming a bushy specimen with very handsome foliage and flowers. It seems to thrive best in a rich, sandy loam and a sunny position.

THE FIGWORT FAMILY.

Salpiglossis, *Salpiglossis sinuata.*—A very pretty annual known in gardens under the name of *variabilis*. The stem is slender and graceful, two feet high, more or less, according to variety; leaves, lower ones pinnatifid or sinuate, stem leaves ovate or lanceolate, entire. Flowers at the end of the lateral branches large and showy, of all colors, from pale yellow to deep crimson. Propagated from seeds sown in a border in spring.

Mullein, *Verbascum.*—These are chiefly coarse weeds of dry and barren fields and roadsides. None deserve cultivation in this country with the possible exception of *V. Phœniceum*, a tall and rather graceful plant with long racemes of violet or red flowers, a weed in gravelly soil.

Dwarf Mullein, *Ramondia pyrenaica.*—This exquisite alpine plant grows in the crevices of moist, mossy rocks near running water in half-shady positions. It is of a very dwarf and compact habit, with coarsely dentate and hairy, ovate, rosulate leaves, and axillary scapes bearing several purple, purplish-blue or whitish-blue flowers in great profusion. It grows best in moderate shade near the margin of a rocky stream, in crevices.

Speedwell, *Veronica.*—Few of these are of any importance as ornamental plants. The best are: *V. longifolia,* a very handsome plant with opposite, ovate leaves and long racemes of lilac flowers late in summer. The Japanese variety *subsessilis* is a much superior plant of a very compact habit growing a foot high, with very long terminal, cylindrical racemes of bright blue flowers. This variety deserves general cultivation in borders or rockeries. The germander speedwell or angel's eyes (*V. chamadrys*) is a small and slender herb of grassy fields and meadows. It is one of the prettiest wild flowers in Europe, with bright green leaves and terminal racemes of large sky-blue flowers all summer. Deserves to be naturalized in grassy woods and thickets or in moist lawns.

Toad-Flax, *Linaria vulgaris.*—A showy but weedy plant that may be used to produce good effects on very poor soil. It had better be excluded from choice gardens as it spreads too readily. Flowers bright yellow, in long terminal racemes; leaves linear or nearly so, alternate, crowded on the stems which are mostly simple. Height one or two feet; flowers all summer. *L. macrocana* is a pretty annual less than a foot high, with linear leaves and numerous racemes of deep lilac flowers. Well worth growing in a border. The following two species are very desirable alpine plants of neat habit; they are very fine for rockeries: *L. alpina*, stem slender, forming tufted masses of small, linear leaves; flowers in head-like racemes in summer and autumn, bright bluish-purple with a yellow centre. *L. cymbalaria*, leaves on slender, trailing stems, reniform; flowers mostly axillary, lilac. Both are perennials, but may be treated as annuals. They look well in crevices of rocks in half-shady positions.

Snapdragon, *Antirrhinum majus.*—This perennial is often grown as an annual for summer bedding. There are many beautiful varieties of which some are quite dwarf and compact, forming dense masses of deep green foliage; leaves oblong or lanceolate, opposite; flowers large, in terminal racemes, varying in color from pure white to bright crimson and purple. It may be propagated annually from seeds sown in a frame or greenhouse. It forms nice beds and is also very desirable in borders and rockeries.

Foxglove, *Digitalis purpurea.*—A very showy plant with simple, erect stems from three to five feet high, lanceolate or oblong wrinkled leaves and a long dense raceme of thimble-like flowers varying in color from purple to pale rose and pure white, the corolla being more or less spotted inside. A desirable biennial or perennial plant for sunny positions, easily raised from seeds. Large-flowered foxglove (*D. ambigua*) is less tall and has larger, creamy-white flowers veined with brown. Both flower in summer, sometimes quite late. Thrive in any moderately good soil. They are fine in borders and shrubberies.

FIG. 150. FOXGLOVE (DIGITALIS PURPUREA).

Monkey-Flower, *Mimulus cardinalis.*—A handsome riverside plant of an erect, branching habit, with opposite, ovate, stem-clasping leaves and very showy axillary flowers of a bright orange-scarlet color. Flowers freely in summer and is desirable both in borders and for planting on the margins of water or in moist places in a rockery. Height two feet. More common is the winged monkey-flower (*M. alatus*), with winged, erect stems, lanceolate, stalked leaves, and attractive blue flowers in early summer. Fine for naturalizing on moist, grassy shores. Both are perennial but may be propagated freely by means of seeds. Musk (*M. moschatus*) is a small trailing plant with numerous yellow flowers all summer. It is fine for rockeries, window boxes, and vases, and may be raised annually from seeds.

Shell Flower, *Pentstemon barbatus.*—One of our most beautiful native plants, of an erect but slender and graceful habit, with bright flowers late in summer. Stem three or four feet high with smooth, lanceolate leaves; flowers bright scarlet, tubular, with a bearded lip, collected in loose racemes or panicles. One of the best plants for a border or for moist places on the shores of rivulets or lakes or in open places in shrubberies. Thrives best in a well-drained but moist and rich soil. The variety *Torreyii* is larger with deeper colored flowers. The hybrid pentstemons of European gardens may be grown with success in the South; they are extremely beautiful and floriferous plants with flowers of many colors

FIG. 151.—BEARDED PENTSTEMON (PENTSTEMON BARBATUS TORREYII).

and of a more compact habit than the shell flower. They must be grown in a well-drained, sandy soil, in beds that should be covered with leaves in winter.

There are several showy and perfectly hardy American species that may be grown in shrubberies or borders in light, well-drained soil. The best are: *P. Cobæa,* flowers two inches long, purple or sometimes white. Height one or two feet. *P. grandiflorus,* as tall as the preceding species; flowers showy, lilac-purple. *P. Hartwegii,* a Southern species, somewhat tender; may be wintered in a frame and planted out in beds in summer. Flowers very beautiful scarlet-crimson, panicled. Height two feet.

THE ACANTHUS FAMILY.

Acanthe, *Acanthus mollis.*—An old-fashioned plant with pretty, large, heart-shaped, lobed leaves, forming a fine mass of foliage. Flowers insignificant, in whorls collected in long, erect spikes. For sheltered positions in shrubberies only, in good sandy loam protected with a covering of leaves in winter.

THE MINT FAMILY.

Lavender, *Lavandula vera.*—A small, sweet-scented shrub used for edging borders and walks in kitchen gardens. Forms a bushy, grayish shrub one or two feet high with linear-lanceolate leaves and numerous slender spikes of pale blue flowers. Increased by means of seeds. When planted for edging it should be trimmed into a low, close hedge for which purpose it is very desirable.

Peppermint, *Mentha piperita.*—Cultivated on account of its fragrant leaves; spreads readily by means of running underground shoots. May be naturalized on moist, grassy banks.

Hyssop, *Hyssopis officinalis.*—A bushy plant one or two feet high with linear-lanceolate leaves and numerous blue flowers in crowded terminal spikes in summer. Very sweet-scented. Used in the same way as lavender.

Wild Thyme, *Thymus Serpyllum.*—A creeping, tufted herb forming mats of small green leaves; flowers rosy-purple or flesh-colored, very numerous. *Th. Chamædrys* is an almost similar species. Both grow in poor, gravelly soil in open and sunny positions, and are quite showy when grown in large masses and covered with flowers. Fine for dry rockeries or when naturalized in sunny, barren lawns. Propagated by means of seeds or division. Stem somewhat woody.

Sage, *Salvia officinalis.*—A very sweet-scented herb with oblong-lanceolate, hoary leaves in tufted masses; flowers blue in spiked whorls. Grown in borders for its fragrant leaves. The meadow sage (*S. pratensis*) is a fine hardy plant growing about two feet high, with ovate leaves three or more inches long; flowers in whorls collected in long bracteate spikes; blue, purple, bright rose, or sometimes two-colored; bracts colored. Habit graceful, slender. Fine for naturalizing on moist, grassy banks, or on the border of thickets or shrubberies. Flowers all summer. *S. bicolor* is a handsome plant for a border or rockery; flowers blue and white dotted with yellow, whorled in long racemes; root-leaves pinnatifid or palmately lobed; stem-leaves ovate or lanceolate. Hardy biennial, easily raised from seeds for summer flowering. The following are tender perennials that may be raised and treated as annuals in the North; *S. splendens*, stem almost simple, three or four feet high, terminated by a long whorled raceme of bright scarlet bracts and flowers; leaves bright green, ovate or ovate-lanceolate sometimes heart-shaped at the base. An exceedingly showy, bushy plant, forming masses of the most intense color. Exceptionally fine for summer-bedding. *S. coccinea*, about half as large as the preceding kind; flowers scarlet-red in loose, distant whorls, racemose. *S. fulgens*, flowers two inches long, scarlet, in six-flowered whorls collected in long racemes. Stem branching, two or three feet high. *S. patens*; leaves petiolate, deltoid or cordate; stem slender, terminating in a few-flowered raceme; flowers intense blue, very handsome. These may be propagated annually from seed in a frame or greenhouse for summer bedding, or stored in a cool place in winter. They are easy of culture, will do well in ordinary garden soil in sunny positions, and are ideal bedding plants for American gardens.

Rosemary, *Rosmarinus officinalis.*—A sweet-scented, somewhat tender herb of old cottage gardens.

Bee Balm, *Monarda didyma.*—A beautiful native riverside plant of the greatest ornamental value, growing about two feet high, with ovate-lanceolate leaves and numerous heads of bright red flowers. Exceptionally fine for planting by the margin of water or in moist places in a rockery.

Wild bergamot (*M. fistulosa*) is of a nearly similar habit, but a native of rocky woods, generally growing in partial shade in rich soil. Flowers rose-colored in large heads. For planting in thickets and shrubberies in dense masses; very effective. Both flower in June or July.

Hedge Nettle, *Stachys.*—Most of these are insignificant weeds; a few are very showy, but tender. *S. lanata* is a procumbent plant with hairy, silvery-gray leaves of an oblong outline; flowers inconspicuous. Nice for rockeries or in carpet bedding. *S. coccinea* is a small bushy perennial almost as showy as the scarlet sage but not so large. May be treated in the same way and used for summer bedding or in rockeries.

THE BORAGE FAMILY.

Lungwort, *Pulmonaria officinalis.*—An attractive, small spring-flowering plant common in open, grassy woods in Europe. Leaves of the root ovate-heart-shaped, of the stem ovate-oblong; stems simple about a foot high ending in a small cyme of red and violet flowers. The following are also very desirable: *P. angustifolia*, blue cowslip; leaves narrower, downy; flowers in twin racemes, pink, changing into a bright blue; habit and size like the first. *P. saccharata*, leaves spotted white; flowers erect, pink. *P. mollis*, a nice little rock plant, spreading, eight to nine inches high; flowers numerous, large, blue; leaves ovate-lanceolate. All but the last are

FIG. 157.—BLUE COWSLIP (PULMONARIA ANGUSTIFOLIA).

woodland plants; they may be grown in shrubberies among other flowers, or in rockeries in light and rich soil.

Virginian Cowslip, *Mertensia Virginica.*—A pretty, rare American plant scattered in low woods in alluvial soil. Very ornamental, with stems a couple of feet high, smooth, almost glaucous, leaves obovate; radical ones petioled.

Flowers handsome, in terminal clusters, pale blue or lilac, in early summer. Nice for moist and half-shady positions in rocky woods and shrubberies.

Golden Drop, *Onosma stellulatum.*—Somewhat like the preceding species, but with narrower linear-lanceolate or spatulate leaves; stem only six or eight inches high; flowers in curved racemes, tubular, bright yellow or white. A neat plant for rockeries, flowering in summer. The variety *tauricum* is larger with pure yellow flowers.

Arnebia, *A. echioides.*—A fine spreading plant for shady rockeries. Stem ascending, eight or nine inches high with oblong, ciliated leaves and terminal spikes of very showy yellow flowers; corolla marked with five large, black spots in the angles of the segments. *A. Griffithii,* smaller, with bright yellow flowers. May be treated as an annual. Both are very desirable. Thrive well in a rich, sandy soil.

Hairy Puccoon, *Lithospermum hirtum.*—A pretty perennial about a foot high with linear-lanceolate leaves and showy, orange-yellow flowers in terminal cymes. *L. Gastoni,* a European mountain plant, has bright sky-blue flowers in summer. Both are fine rock plants.

Forget-me-not, *Myosotis palustris.*—A very beautiful plant of the old world, growing in or near water on the margin of clear running streams or brooks, in sunny positions. Leaves mostly tufted at the root, oblong, bright green; flowering stems about eight inches high with a long, slightly curving raceme of sky-blue, yellow-eyed flowers. Grows in large masses and is very effective when flowering in summer. Very desirable, but should be grown under quite natural conditions in order to retain its freshness and beauty; planted on the water level or even in shallow water on the margin of a stream it will prove to be one of the most attractive of plants. *M. dissitiflora* is a nice floriferous border plant with looser racemes, and flowers earlier in spring.

Alkanet, *Anchusa tinctoria.*—A low, diffuse herb with deep blue flowers in twin racemes, flowering in early summer. Pretty in a rockery. A more desirable plant is *A. Italica,* which grows to the height of three feet, forming a broad mass. Flowers in panicled racemes bright bluish-purple. Border. *A. myosotidiflora;* root-leaves reniform or cordate, quite large, stem-leaves ovate; flowers deep blue in panicled racemes. Rockery.

Navelwort, *Omphalodes verna.*—A dwarf tufted plant with ovate leaves; flowers intensely blue, white-eyed, in loose axillary racemes early in spring; very useful for edging beds or borders. *O. Lucilia* is one of the finest plants in the order; the flowers are about half an inch across, lilac-blue, and appear in summer. A very beautiful plant for shrubberies, in rich soil and half-shady positions.

Hound's Tongue, *Cynoglossum linifolium.*—An annual with pretty white flowers in summer. Raised from seeds sown in a border in spring. Also nice in beds and rockeries.

Comfrey, *Symphytum officinale.*—A plant with rather large, oblong-lanceolate root-leaves and white or yellowish flowers in curved racemes. Very floriferous, but not showy. *S. asperrimum* has more showy, blue-purple flowers. Both are best adapted to planting on grassy shores of rivulets or lakes in half-shady positions. Flower throughout summer.

THE WATER-LEAF FAMILY.

Blue Eyes, *Nemophila insignis.*—A very beautiful annual with pinnate leaves, deeply cut leaflets, slender stems, and numerous sky-blue flowers in summer. The flowers measure an inch across. When sown in beds it forms dense masses of leaves and flowers about eight inches high. *N. atomaria,* white with numerous purplish-blue dots. *N. maculata,* flowers large, white, with a deep violet blotch on each lobe. *N. discoidalis,* chocolate-brown with white border. All are charming summer flowers of the easiest culture. To be sown in a bed or border early in spring.

FIG. 153.—SPOT-TED NEMOPHILA (NEMOPHILA MAC-ULATA).

THE POLEMONIUM FAMILY.

Phlox.—Very beautiful annual and perennial herbs of an erect or trailing habit, flowering in spring, summer, and autumn. The best spring-flowering kinds are: *P. subulata,* the moss pink; leaves awl-shaped; stems procumbent, forming

FIG. 154 MOSS PINK (PHLOX SUBULATA).

dense mats of foliage; flowers very numerous, pink or rosy-purple, sometimes white, in small clusters. Fine for dry ground, for naturalizing on barren hillsides. *P. amana,* stems ascending, from six inches to a foot high, forming spreading masses; leaves lanceolate; flowers corymbose, purple, pink, or white. Rockeries or barren ground. *P. reptans,* stemless, spreading by runners forming rosettes of obovate leaves; flowering stems nearly bare, with a large corymb of purple or violet flowers. Common in moist woods in the South. *P. divaricata*, very beautiful, larger than the last named; leaves broadly lanceolate; flowers large, pale blue, lilac, or white, in loose corymbs on peduncles six or eight inches high. A beautiful woodland plant. The last two are fine for naturalizing in woods and thickets. The following are tall, autumn-flowering perennials: *P. paniculata*, from two to four feet high, with ovate-lanceolate leaves and large terminal panicles of highly colored flowers. The numerous garden varieties raised from this species and *P. maculata*, a similar but dwarfer species, vary in height, in the size of the inflorescence, and in color, which ranges from the purest white to the most intense crimson and purple tints. They are generally grown as border plants but may also be used sparingly to produce beautiful effects in wild gardening and in shrubberies. Thrive best in sunny positions and in a light but rich soil.

Phlox Drummondi is a valuable annual having flowers of all colors except blue and yellow. It is very floriferous, and useful for summer bedding. Seeds may be sown either in a frame or in the open ground.

Jacob's Ladder, *Polemonium cæruleum.*—An old-fashioned border plant with long, narrow, pinnate leaves forming a dense mass of foliage, and blue flowers in a long panicle. Flowers in early summer. May be grown

FIG. 155—PHLOX (PHLOX DRUMMONDI).

in borders or rockeries or naturalized on grassy banks. *P. reptans* forms a tufted mass of pinnate leaves; flowers large, nodding, corymbose. A desirable woodland plant for shady rockeries and shrubberies.

THE CONVOLVULUS FAMILY.

Tricolored Bindweed, *C. tricolor.* —An annual trailing plant useful for beds or rockeries. Leaves obovate, almost sessile, hairy; stem branching, ascending; flowers large, axillary, sky-blue, with white centre and yellow throat. Raised from seeds sown on the place in spring. Field bindweed (*C. arvensis*) is a perennial vine growing in barren and sandy soil, and therefore useful in dry situations. Leaves ovate or slightly hastate. Flowers axillary, delicate rose with white centre, very numerous all summer. May be used in vases and window-boxes or to trail among rocks.

THE POTATO FAMILY.

Solanum.—Many of the annual species have very ornamental foliage, usually broad, sinuate, prickly leaves, forming handsome masses. They are used in foliage-groups and may easily be raised from seeds. Some of our own weeds like the horse nettle (*S. Carolinense*) may be used for this purpose with good effect. A few others are *S. laciniatum, S. robustum, S. marginatum,* and *S. Warscrviczii.*

Ground Cherry, *Physalis Alkekengi.* —A straggling weed from Southern Europe, one or two feet high, with triangular leaves and greenish flowers of which the calix develops to inclose the fruit, and assumes a bright red color in late summer. Propagated by means of seeds.

Petunia, *Petunia nyctaginiflora.*—Annual, or cultivated as such, with ascending stems and oblong or spatulate, hairy leaves; flowers originally white, now found in all colors. *P. riolacea;* leaves smaller, ovate-lanceolate, rosy-red or violet. The original species is seldom met; the hybrid forms sold under the name of *P. hybrida* are the most common, and are much used for summer bedding. The finest strains of these are *grandiflora,* found in the following colors: white, white and rose, rose-crimson, carmine, violet, and often two-colored; *grandiflora flore pleno,* the double varieties of the above; *superbissima,* fine outline, wide throat, and brilliant colors. All are propagated by means of seeds sown in the open ground or in a cool frame or greenhouse.

Tobacco, *Nicotiana.*—The only species generally grown for ornament is the very handsome and desirable *N. affinis.* As an annual, it may be propagated with ease. The leaves are comparatively small, six inches long, ovate, stem-leaves smaller; stems two or three feet high, simple, bearing a loose panicle of creamy white flowers with a terete tube three inches long and a flat limb as much across. Forms very nice beds in summer. The ground between the plants may be covered with some low, constant-flowering species such as pansies or bedding violets, or even verbenas.

THE GENTIAN FAMILY.

Gentian, *Gentiana.*—These are very attractive plants, but sometimes difficult to cultivate. They do best when introduced under natural conditions and left undisturbed afterwards. Some of the rarest and choicest of all herbaceous plants belong to this genus. Most common are:

23

fringed gentian (*G. crinita*), a very beautiful American
plant of moist ground on the outskirts of thickets and
woods. Stem erect, eight inches or a foot high with
broadly lanceolate leaves; flowers erect, solitary, terminating the branches; corolla intensely blue, tubular with four
fringed lobes; flowering late in the season. Annual or biennial. Seeds to be collected and sown in a moist lawn or
on a grassy bank. *G. angustifolia* is a perennial, from half
a foot to a foot high, with linear leaves and sky-blue flowers. In moist sandy soil. *G. Andrewsii*, erect, with
simple stems or branches, flowers blue, closed. *G. Pneu-
monanthe*: a European species of moist, peaty soil.
Leaves almost linear, stems simple, eight inches or a foot

high, bearing axillary and terminal clusters
of deep blue flowers. The following are fine
for moist places in rockeries: *G. acaulis*, a very
handsome plant growing on the borders of
alpine rivulets. Leaves all radical or nearly
so, broadly ovate, crowded; flowers erect, campanulate, solitary, on short stems; corolla two
inches long and nearly as broad, deep blue with
five yellow bands down the throat. Flowering
in spring. *G. verna*, the smallest of all the species, as large as or slightly larger than the
common bluet. Stems much branched, forming tufted masses three inches high; leaves
small, ovate; flowers numerous, erect, corolla

FIG. 156.
BLUE WIND-
FLOWER (GEN-
TIANA PNEUMO-
NANTHE).

azure blue. Flowers in spring. This one may be grown
among the grass in moist sandy lawns; cannot be grown in
a dry place.

Water-Trefoil, *Menyanthes trifoliata.* —A very beautiful water plant with trifoliate leaves, somewhat fleshy, as is the creeping and rooting stem; flowers handsome, white tinged with bright rose, in a dense raceme on scapes about a foot high. May be grown as a water plant in open and sunny positions or in boggy ground on the margins of a stream. Flowers in spring.

THE LOGANIA FAMILY.

Indian Pink, *Spigelia Marylandica.* —A showy native plant growing a foot high, more or less; with simple stem and smooth, sessile, ovate-lanceolate leaves. Flowers in terminal clusters, large, of a delicate rosy-red with yellow throat and deep lanceolate lobes. In woods or sometimes on railroad embankments in moist ground; very beautiful in masses when flowering. May be grown in moist places, in rockeries, or on the margins of water.

THE DOGBANE FAMILY.

Dogbane, *Apocynum androsœmifolium.* —A very loose and spreading plant growing several feet high; leaves ovate, smooth; flowers urn-like, small, white or tinted rose in terminal cymes. Common on the margins of woods and thickets. Will grow in any soil.

Amsonia, *A. Tabernamontana.* —A modest and attractive plant with simple, leafy stems growing eighteen inches or two feet high, with willow-like leaves and terminal clusters of pale blue flowers in summer. Fine for a rockery or for borders of shrubberies.

THE MILKWEED FAMILY.

Silkweed, *Asclepias.*—Mostly showy, sometimes coarse and weedy, American plants with opposite or whorled leaves and white, purple, or orange-yellow flowers. The most desirable are: The butterfly weed (*A. tuberosa*), a plant of dry hills and sandy fields with simple stems, narrow oblong leaves, and large compound corymbs of bright orange-colored flowers in summer. Fine for rockeries or naturalized in barren soil. *A. rubra,* leaves ovate-lanceolate, flowers umbellate, reddish purple: on river banks or in moist, sandy ground. *A. incarnata,* stem branching, two feet high or more; leaves lanceolate; flowers rosy-purple, umbellate, collected into a large flat corymb. A handsome plant of low ground. *A. quadrifolia,* stem about a foot high, smooth, with several whorls of ovate or ovate-lanceolate leaves, four in a whorl; flowers of a delicate rosy-red or white. A very attractive plant of rocky woods suitable for similar places in the garden or park.

THE BIRTHWORT FAMILY.

Birthwort, *Aristolochia clematitis.*—A bushy and ornamental foliage-plant, with deep green, cordate leaves, and small, axillary, greenish-yellow flowers in summer. Height about two feet. As a foliage-plant in rockeries or on the margins of water.

THE FOUR-O'CLOCK FAMILY.

Four-o'Clock, *Mirabilis Jalapa.*—Generally grown as an annual in old gardens. A bushy, leafy, and showy plant with white, yellow, rose-colored, or crimson flowers in summer. Stems branching, two feet high or more; leaves broadly ovate or heart-shaped. Very floriferous; ornamental in beds or borders.

Sand Vervain, *Abronia umbellata*.—A slender, trailing plant grown as an annual in rockeries or for filling vases and window-boxes; leaves ovate-lanceolate, flowers umbellate, rosy-purple. May be grown for beds in sandy ground and can be sown on the place.

THE AMARANTH FAMILY.

Amaranth, *Amaranthus*.—Many of these are coarse and weedy in appearance though rather showy. They fit in in no natural scenery that can be produced in a garden and are out of place except in a border. The following are the most common: *A. caudatus*, prince's feather, tall with red flowers in drooping panicles. *A. melancholicus ruber*, or love-lies-bleeding, almost similar, entirely red. Sown in the open ground early in spring.

Cockscomb, *Closia cristata*.—Annual, with erect, close, pyramidal panicles of white, yellow, rosy-red or crimson flowers. There are many varieties of which some are dwarf, with an inflorescence widely differing from that of the original form. Often grown in beds and borders and raised annually from seeds.

THE BUCKWHEAT FAMILY.

Japanese Knot-weed, *Polygonum cuspidatum*.—A tall and graceful perennial growing five or six feet high, more or less. Stems slender and very leafy, producing ample, feathery panicles of white flowers in the axils of the upper leaves; leaves large, oval-oblong, sometimes heart-shaped, stalked. Forms a nice mass of foliage and flowers and is particularly attractive on the margins of water or as a background in moist places of a rockery. It may also be grown as a specimen on the lawn. This species is better in every particular than the much larger *P. Sachaliense* which, although very ornamental, is apt to spread and become a weed. Both thrive best in a rich and moist soil and in half-shady positions.

Rhubarb, *Rheum palmatum.*—This is a handsome foliage plant with large, palmately lobed leaves, and tall, leafy panicles of creamy-white flowers. It forms a nice specimen on the lawn, in or out of flower. Even the common rhubarb may be employed for ornamental purposes, as very few foliage plants are more attractive. Rhubarbs should be grown in well worked and fertile soil in order to develop as large leaves as possible.

THE SPURGE FAMILY.

Flowering Spurge, *Euphorbia corollata.*—A branching, slender and graceful plant about two feet high, very light and airy in appearance. Leaves ovate or linear on the upper branches, few; alternate below, opposite above; the five bracts around the greenish flowers, white, petal-like, forming numerous corolla-like involucres. Floriferous and ornamental, flowering late in the season. Will thrive well in rockeries in dry and gravelly soil in sunny and exposed positions.

Palma-Christi, *Ricinus communis.*—This well-known plant may be used for foliage groups with good effect. The

large, handsome leaves are very ornamental in young plants.
It will grow to the height of six or eight feet when treated
as an annual and should be used only as such. The seeds
are sown in a greenhouse or frame early in spring. The
young plants grow rapidly. Thrives best in a rich and well
worked garden soil.

THE ARUM FAMILY.

Cuckoo-Pint, *Arum maculatum.*—A very ornamental
plant nine inches high, forming handsome masses of foliage.
Leaves sagitate or hastate, bright green with black-purple
spots. Flowers whitish, spotted. Nice in moist places in
a rockery or wood or on the margin of a stream. The
evergreen *Arum italicum* is also useful for covering the
ground beneath trees and shrubs in moist places.

Arrow-Leaf, *Peltandra Virginica.*—A common waterside plant from one to two feet high. Leaves large, hastate, pale green, forming nice masses of foliage; flowers
insignificant. In very shallow water or in moist places in
a rockery.

Wild Calla, *Calla palustris.*—Very attractive; leaves
ovate or heart-shaped, erect, bright green. Spotless white
and showy, spadix yellow. Height six or eight inches. A
handsome plant for very shallow water; may be grown in
tubs for cisterns and small ponds.

THE WATER-PLANTAIN FAMILY.

Water Plantain, *Alisma Plantago.*—Leaves all radical,
ovate or heart-shaped, on long petioles. Flowers small,
white, in a large panicle two feet high. In shallow water,

naturalized. Desirable. The floating water-plantain (*A. natans*) is a very handsome plant of ponds and stagnant water; flowers showy, white, solitary from the axils of the long-stalked, small, elliptical leaves.

Arrow-Head, *Sagittaria sagittifolia.*—A handsome plant

for shallow water, growing less than two feet high. Leaves hastate, all radical. Flowers in a small raceme as tall as the leaves, half an inch across; petals three, pure white, stamens yellow. Fine in cisterns or small ponds, planted in tubs.

Water Poppy, *Limnocharis Humboldtii.* — The showiest of the more common plants of the family, tender in the North but may be used anywhere for summer display. Leaves rounded, bright green, floating. Flowers solitary, large, with three sulphur-yellow petals. The plant flowers con-

FIG. 157.—ARROW-HEAD (SAGITTARIA SAGITTI-FOLIA).

stantly in summer. It may be planted in shallow pans in rich soil and sunk a few inches below the surface of the water. Stored in a greenhouse in winter.

THE PONTEDERIA FAMILY.

Water Hyacinth, *Eichornia crassipes.*—A floating plant with swollen leaf-stalks, rounded leaves in rosettes, and erect racemes of blue flowers in summer. Racemes of flowers resembling hyacinths. May be grown and treated in the same manner as water poppy, but needs no soil. Pickerel-weed (*Pontederia cordata*) is of a similar habit but has smaller flowers. It is perfectly hardy.

A very interesting water plant belonging to another family is the water hawthorn (*Aponogeton distachion*). It has small flowers disposed in forked spikes, white, as are the rather fleshy bracts; sweet-scented. Leaves oblong-lanceolate, bright green. Planted and treated as water poppy.

THE ORCHIS FAMILY.

Orchis.—A genus of very showy meadow or woodland plants with a few more or less broadly lanceolate leaves in a rosette disposed around a leafy, flowering stem bearing a raceme of white, yellow, or purple flowers in spring or summer. It includes some of our rarest flowers, which are sometimes difficult to cultivate. The secret of success lies in selecting quite natural positions and in transferring the plants without the least disturbance to the roots. The roots are sometimes tuberous, always brittle and tender. The best species for cultivation are: *O. maculata*, leaves lanceolate, spotted black, flowers purple in a short spike on stems a foot high. *O. mascula*, leaves spotted brown, flowers of richer purple in a long and loose spike, spring flowering. *O. foliosa*, leaves numerous, oblong, smooth and green; flowers purple, in spikes eight or nine inches long, three inches in diameter on stems eighteen inches high or more; very showy. *O. spectabilis*, American species; leaves two, oblong-obovate; flowers pink and white in bracted racemes five or six inches high. All are fine in woodland scenery. Beds of rich, well decayed leaf mold and sandy loam a foot deep should be prepared for these in a half-shady position. Plant in August or September and water thoroughly.

Purple Fringed Orchis, *Habenaria fimbriata.*—A tall meadow plant two or three feet high; root-leaves oval,

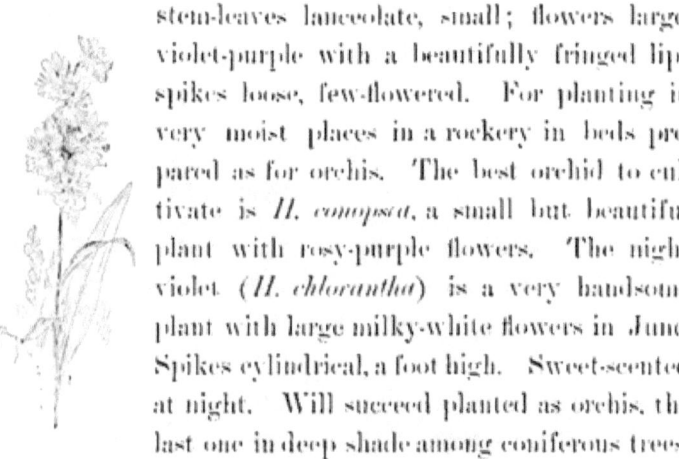

stem-leaves lanceolate, small; flowers large, violet-purple with a beautifully fringed lip; spikes loose, few-flowered. For planting in very moist places in a rockery in beds prepared as for orchis. The best orchid to cultivate is *H. conopsea,* a small but beautiful plant with rosy-purple flowers. The night violet (*H. chlorantha*) is a very handsome plant with large milky-white flowers in June. Spikes cylindrical, a foot high. Sweet-scented at night. Will succeed planted as orchis, the last one in deep shade among coniferous trees.

FIG. 158.—FRINGED ORCHIS (HABENARIA FIMBRIATA).

Rattlesnake Plantain, *Goodyera pubescens.*—Leaves in large tufts a couple of inches high, ovate, beautifully veined with silvery white. Spikes of white flowers in June, six or eight inches tall. Planted in sandy loam in shady shrubberies or among *H. chlorantha.*

Moccasin Flower, *Cypripedium.*— The showiest of all wild orchids, with large plaited leaves and mostly solitary flowers in spring or summer. Will succeed planted and treated as orchis among evergreen shrubs such as rose bay and mountain laurel. The

FIG 159. MOCCASIN FLOWER (CYPRIPEDIUM PUBESCENS).

best are *C. acaule,* leaves in pairs, large, oblong; flowers on a slender scape eight inches high or more, large, with purplish sepals and rosy-purple lip. *C. spectabile*, fully two feet high, leafy; leaves oblong, downy; flowers white with a rosy-tinted lip. *C. pubescens*, a foot high or more, leafy; flowers yellow; leaves ovate or oblong-lanceolate. All do best in rather moist ground in half-shady positions. Very showy when seen in masses.

THE AMARYLLIS FAMILY.

Star-Grass, *Hypoxis erecta*.—A modest little plant of grassy fields, especially on the outskirts of woods. Leaves long and narrow ; flowers yellow, half an inch across, several on a slender scape six inches high, more or less. For naturalizing on lawns. Very desirable.

Daffodils, Narcissi, *Narcissus*.—Some of the most attractive spring- and summer-flowering bulbs belong to this genus. All are white or yellow with linear leaves and simple scapes bearing one or more flowers. The *daffodils* proper have a large crown in addition to the six segments of the perianth, as long as, or even longer than these. In the *Bulbocodium* section the crown is much larger and more conspicuous than the narrow segments of the perianth, while in true *narcissi* the crown is very small as compared to the segments. Daffodils are exceedingly beautiful subjects for naturalizing in grassy thickets

FIG. 160.—PEERLESS NARCIS-SUS (NARCISSUS INCOM-PARABILIS).

and shrubberies or in moist ground along streams and lakes. Once established they spread rapidly and need no attention. They thrive best in a good rich loam and need no prepared beds.

The smaller species of the Bulbocodium section grow best in open positions in gravelly soil. They are fine for planting in barren lawns or in rockeries. The poet's narcissus may be grown on the margin of a stream among the grass, in half-shady positions, or in rockeries on the border of a small rill of water. The best daffodils are: *N. pseudonarcissus*, the Lenten lily. Leaves flat, erect, glaucous, several to a scape; flowers solitary, bright sulphur-yellow. The perianth is white in the variety *princeps*, pale yellow

FIG. 161.—POET'S NARCISSUS (NARCISSUS POETICUS).

in *bicolor*, while the crown is bright yellow; *major* has very large flowers, *minor* unusually small ones and grows only about six inches high. *N. incomparabilis*, peerless narcissus; larger than the preceding species but with a shorter crown; flowers on simple scapes about a foot high, solitary, two inches and a half wide, with a deep yellow crown and somewhat paler perianth. In *aurantius* the crown is orange-yellow. *N. odorus* is similar in color and habit but bears two or three flowers on a scape.

The best species of the Bulbocodium section are: *N. Bulbocodium*, a dwarf species with few grass-like leaves and yellow trumpet-like flowers on slender scapes five or six inches high. *N. monophyllus*, leaves one to a scape; flowers large, nearly white. *N. nivalis* is a very small variety three or four inches high; flowers yellow.

Species with small crowns are: *N. poeticus*, perhaps the most beautiful of all narcissi, with snowy white flowers late in spring; crown very short with a curled edge, saffron-yellow bordered with scarlet. Grown in masses this is very effective; flowers fragrant. *N. Tazetta*, or polyanthus narcissus, bears from four to eight flowers in an umbel on tall, slender scapes; perianth white, crown rich yellow, very fragrant. Most of the species are fine border plants and are sometimes used for edging walks in kitchen gardens.

Snowdrop, *Galanthus nivalis.*—A well-known flower of early spring, growing four or five inches high; perianth of three white, conspicuous segments, and the three inner ones smaller with green spots at the apex. There are several very handsome varieties with larger flowers.

FIG. 162.—SNOWDROPS (GALANTHUS NIVALIS).

G. Elwesii is a stronger species with larger flowers. All are fine for naturalizing in shrubberies and half-shady lawns. They thrive well in ordinary garden soil.

Snowflake, *Leucoium vernum.*—This differs from the snowdrop in having all the segments of the perianth equally large. The flowers are white and appear late in spring. Very desirable for rockeries and borders.

Peruvian Lily, *Alstræmeria aurantiaca.*—A very beautiful plant with highly-colored flowers late in summer. Should be planted in a warm, sheltered position in light and rich soil and must be covered in winter in the North. Flowers of a rich orange color, ten to fifteen in an umbel on leafy stems three feet high; stem-leaves linear, elliptical, radical; lower ones larger and broader.

Tuberose, *Polianthes tuberosa.*—A tall, bulbous plant with simple stems two or three feet high with linear-lanceolate leaves and long spikes of white fragrant flowers, mostly double. May be planted out in the border for the sake of the flowers which are useful for cutting.

THE IRIS FAMILY.

Flower de Luce or **Flag,** *Iris.*—This is a genus of extremely fine, often bulbous- or tuberous-rooted plants, with

FIG. 163. GERMAN IRIS (IRIS GERMANICA).

linear or sword-shaped leaves and highly colored flowers. Some, like the yellow flag and the Japanese iris, are very beautiful in low ground on the margin of a stream or lake, others are fine border plants. The following are among the most useful: German iris (*I. Germanica*), leaves rather broad, sword-like; flowers several inches wide; were originally bright purple and yellow with brownish veins but are now found in a number of varieties. Height about two feet. Florentine iris (*I. Florentina*) is of a similar habit but has almost pure white and fragrant flowers. *I. sambucina* is much taller than the preceding kind; the outer segments of the flowers are violet-blue with darker veins, the inner ones yellowish-brown. *I. variegata*, smaller than the German iris but of a similar habit. The inner segments of the flower are of a bright claret color, the outer and erect ones bright yellow with brownish veins. *I. hybrida* is another very desirable kind, with the outer segments white, veined and tipped with lilac-purple, inner ones white. These are the most desirable border plants of the genus. They may also be used in beds and rockeries with good effect. *I. pumila* is a very dwarf, spring-flowering species suitable for rockeries only; the flowers are deep blue or violet-purple on very short peduncles six or eight inches from the ground; leaves very short and broad, sword-like.

The following are best adapted for naturalizing on the shores of ponds and streams in rather moist and rich soil. Yellow flag (*I. pseudacorus*), leaves narrow, sword-shaped, glaucous green; flowers bright yellow, large and clustered; flowering stems two or three feet high. A very showy and desirable plant flowering in spring or early summer. *I. lævigata*, Japanese iris, stem slender, two feet high or less, leaves narrow, sword-shaped, small in comparison with the flowers, which measure five or six inches across and are of many rich and beautiful colors, mostly shades of blue and purple. This is one of the finest of all flags. American water-flag (*I. versicolor*) is a common but very handsome plant growing in or near shallow water. It grows about two feet high and forms large masses of leaves. Flowers purple-claret or purplish-blue veined with deep blue and white. *I. Siberica* is of a tufted habit with very narrow leaves; flowers bright lilac-blue in great profusion in summer.

These are only a few of the numerous species all of which are ornamental.

Chinese Panther Lily, *Pardanthus Chinensis.*—An elegant plant with sword-like, plaited leaves. Flowers bright orange-yellow, spotted crimson, in branched panicles on leafy stems three or four feet high. Fine for naturalizing in open woods where it spreads freely and flowers profusely late in summer. Will grow in almost any light and gravelly soil.

Blue-eyed Grass, *Sisyrinchium Bermudiana.*—Common in grassy fields and fine for naturalizing in moist lawns. Stems slender, winged ; leaves long and narrow, ensiform. Flowers all summer, blue, in small umbels on scapes about eight inches high. Not showy but attractive.

Tiger Flower, *Tigridia pavonia.*—Flowers very large and showy, orange-yellow or white : centre profusely blotched with crimson. Leaves sword-like, plaited, few in number. For summer display only, planted out in a border or rockery in light and rich soil. Treated like gladiolus.

Corn Flag, *Gladiolus.*—This is a genus of very beautiful plants, mostly tender. They are, however, largely grown in borders for the richly colored flowers which appear late in summer or autumn. The following are the most common : *G. communis,* flowers bright rose or white, rather few in a onesided spike. Flowers in summer ; height two feet or less. *G. Colvillei,* a beautiful hybrid form about a foot high ; flowers red with deeper markings ; variety *alba,* pure white. *G. cardinalis,* stems three or four feet high ; flowers large, scarlet, in loose, branched spikes. *G. Gandavensis,* as tall as the preceding, a garden hybrid with crimson flowers marked with yellow. There are many varieties of this gladiolus with white, scarlet, rosy-red and orange-colored flowers; the most common in cultivation. *G. psittacinus*, as large as the preceding, with one-sided spikes of scarlet flowers spotted yellow with green tube. All are bulbous-rooted plants and must be taken up after flowering and kept in a cool, frost-free place in winter. They increase rapidly by means of offsets and are of extremely easy culture. Require rich and moist ground.

Crocus.—The many varieties of *Crocus vernus*, as also those of *C. aureus*, are exceedingly showy and floriferous spring flowers either for bedding or naturalized in the grass. They vary in color from pure white to deep violet in the first named species; the varieties of *aureus* are of different shades of yellow. There are also several rare species suitable for rockeries. Many species flower in autumn, such as the common *C. sativus* with its fragrant, violet flowers; *C. speciosus*, bright lilac; *C. nudiflorus*, bright purple, of which last species the leaves appear in spring and die down before the time of flowering. When planted in a lawn there should be a sufficient number to make an attractive display in spring or autumn. Bulbs taken from beds may be used for this purpose and may be planted, by means of a dibbler, about two inches deep.

THE LILY FAMILY.

Meadow Saffron, *Colchicum autumnale*.—This species resembles a large-flowered crocus in appearance. The flowers, which appear late in the season after the leaves have died down, are of a bright purple color, open, erect, with a very long tube. The leaves are large, lanceolate, and appear in spring. There are several varieties with white, violet, purple, and double flowers. Besides this, which is the common species, there are several other very desirable kinds. *C. speciosum* is the largest of these; flowers crimson or purple with a white throat; leaves a couple of inches wide and a foot long. *C. alpinum*, a small species with rosy-red flowers, and *C. montanum*, a spring-flowering kind with lilac flowers, are nice plants for a rockery. The others delight in a rich and moist soil, may be naturalized on a lawn or in low places in a rockery or open woods. The corms which are quite large should be planted twice as deep as crocus.

Wake Robin, *Trillium.*—Dwarf, tuberous-rooted woodland plants flowering in early spring. Leaves three in a

FIG. 164.—WHITE WOOD LILY (TRILLIUM GRANDIFLORUM).

whorl about the middle of the stem; flowers solitary, erect or nodding. The best are: *T. grandiflorum*, stem a foot high or more; leaves sessile, rhombic-ovate, four inches long, more or less; flowers three inches across, pure white, changing into a faint rose-color. Very fine. *T. erectum*, purple birthwort; smaller than the preceding kind; flowers dark dull purple. *T. nivale*, stem three to four inches high, leaves ovate-obtuse; flowers pure white, two inches across. A fine early-flowering species of moist ground. *T. erythrocarpum*, painted wood lily; stem a foot high; leaves large, ovate; flowers smaller, white, striped inside with pink. All grow in rather moist ground in shady positions and prefer a rich vegetable soil. Very handsome for

FIG. 165.—FALSE SOLOMON'S SEAL (SMILACINA RACEMOSA), GROWING IN A ROCKY RAVINE.

374

woodland scenery ; may be planted and treated as *Orchis* in woods and shrubberies.

Mariposa Lily, *Calochortus Gunnisoni.*—Most of the mariposa lilies are too tender for general use. *Gunnisoni* is the only perfectly hardy species. It is a dwarf but showy plant, with flowers two or three inches wide ; petals three, lilac with yellow base marked with a purplish bar ; leaves few, sword-shaped. Bulbous. For sunny positions in a rockery in moderately moist, sandy loam.

Bellwort, *Uvularia grandiflora.*—Stems tall, erect, with oblong, smooth leaves ; flowers an inch and a half long, yellow, one or more from the axils of the upper leaves. *U. flava* has brighter yellow flowers. For naturalizing in rich soil in open woods or shrubberies.

Lily of the Valley, *Convallaria majalis ;* radical leaves one or two, elliptic-oblong, glaucous green, erect ; flowers pure white, urn-shaped, disposed in a one-sided raceme six or eight inches high. Fragrant woodland flower. Thrives best planted in prepared beds of sandy loam and leaf mold in half-shady positions in a shrubbery or wood. Early summer.

Twin Leaf, *Smilacina bifolia.*—A small, very common woodland plant with racemes of minute white flowers and two heart-shaped stem-leaves. Attractive, naturalized among lily of the valley, in the same bed or in the common soil.

False Solomon's Seal, *Smilacina racemosa.*—A tall and graceful plant two feet high, with oblong or ovate-lanceolate leaves ; flowers small but numerous in a compound raceme or panicle. A very effective plant when seen in masses. Rich moist ground in rocky woods ; fine for similar positions in a rockery or in woods and shrubberies.

Solomon's Seal, *Polygonatum multiflorum.*—A graceful plant with recurving, leafy stems two or three feet high, with oblong, stem-clasping leaves, alternate, in two rows; flowers on slender pedicels, several in a bunch in the axils of the leaves, long cylindrical, milky white. Flowers early in summer. *P. officinale* is considerably smaller but equally desirable. The American *P. giganteum* sometimes grows to a height of five or six feet with axillary peduncles of from two to eight flowers. All are fine for naturalizing in thickets and shrubberies. They thrive best in rich vegetable soil and may be treated in the same way as *Orchis.* May also be used with fine effect in moist places in a rockery.

Lily, *Lilium.*—Lilies are without exception the most beautiful of all bulbous-rooted plants. The flowers are large and showy, while the habit is graceful and elegant. Many are exceedingly fine border plants, while others may be grown in rockeries or naturalized in woods or on moist lawns to produce the most charming effects. The best are: White lily (*L. candidum*), stems simple with numerous lanceolate leaves; flowers many in a thyrsoid raceme, pearly white, inclined; summer. Bulb-bearing lily (*L. bulbiferum*), stems three or more feet high; leaves lanceolate, scattered, very numerous; flowers large, erect, reddish-orange with a few dark spots inside, disposed in large umbels; one of the best for naturalizing in rich woodland soil in half-shady positions; spreads rapidly. Orange lily (*L. croceum*), similar in habit to the preceding kind, but more elegant; leaves linear, scattered, slightly woolly, as is the slender terete stem; flowers rich orange-yellow, erect in a large umbel. Tiger lily (*L. tigrinum*), stem three feet high or more; leaves lanceolate, scattered; flowers orange-red, spotted with black, segments of the peri-anth recurved; one of the most popular and showy lilies with flowers in broad, loose panicles. Panther lily (*L. pardalinum*), tall and slender, from four to seven feet high, with several crowded whorls of large, lanceolate leaves, and a long ra-ceme of bright orange-colored, purple-spot-ted, nodding flowers; segments of perianth rolled back. Scarlet lily (*L. tenuifolium*)

FIG. 165. PANTHER LILY (LILIUM PARDALINUM).

is one of the smallest but not least elegant species, growing about a foot high, with very leafy stems bearing one or two bright scarlet flowers; leaves linear, very numerous. Grown in patches in rockeries or on the margins of shrubberies, it forms a glowing mass of flowers in July.

Turk's-cap lily (*L. Martagon*), stems three or four feet high with distant whorls of oblong-lanceolate leaves; flowers in a long panicle violet-purple, sometimes pure white, small, nodding; segments of the perianth rolled back. A woodland plant growing in deep shade; fine for naturalizing; flowers late in summer. Canada lily (*L. Canadense*), stem two or three feet high; leaves lanceolate whorled; flowers bright yellow or pale scarlet, spotted, four or five on a stem, nodding on long peduncles; segments of the perianth turned back at the tip. A charming plant of moist fields and meadows. Thrives in any soil; exceptionally fine for naturalizing in lawns. The numerous other species, less important from a landscape-gardener's point of view, all deserve cultivation. All the above thrive in a rich sandy loam and are perfectly hardy.

Crown Imperial, *Fritillaria imperialis.* — A showy, spring-flowering plant three or four feet high, with numerous closely whorled or scattered leaves; flowers several in a whorl near the top of the stem, bell-shaped, large, crimson or orange-yellow. May easily be established in open woods in small patches here and there. A fine border plant. Thrives best in partial shade in this country.

Checker lily (*F. Meleagris*), an exceptionally fine plant of moist meadows in Northern Europe. Stems a foot high with a few scattered, linear leaves and a solitary, nodding flower checkered dark and light purple, or sometimes white and only faintly tessellated. Beautiful in spring or early summer; fine for naturalizing in moist, sandy lawns or in a rockery. Another attractive species is *F. pallidiflora* of Siberia, with stems nine inches high bearing several bell-shaped, pale yellow flowers. *F. pallida* is an American species with deep yellow flowers.

FIG. 167.— CHECKER LILY (FRITILLARIA MELEAGRIS).

Tulip, *Tulipa.*—The tulips are beautiful plants for spring-bedding, or planted permanently in a border. Some of the species may be naturalized in shrubberies and woods; others are exceptionally fine for rockeries. When left undisturbed for years in the same position, they are far more attractive than if they are taken up and planted annually. The flowers of the common tulip (*T. Gesneriana*) are more or less bell-shaped, erect, and of bright and gorgeous colors; two colors are frequently seen in one flower, as white and crimson or yellow and scarlet. There are single and double varieties; for all landscape-work the single ones are best. The colors range from white, pale sulphur-yellow and yellow, to bright scarlet and dazzling crimson or carmine shades. The fragrant tulip (*T. suaveolens*) is another of the parent forms of our garden varieties

which are earlier than the Gesnerianas; flowers large, erect, red and yellow; leaves broadly lanceolate or oblong; much dwarfer than the preceding species. The wood tulip (*T. sylvestris*) is a beautiful plant of deciduous woods in Europe; flowers sweet-scented, bright yellow; leaves very long, linear-lanceolate; scape almost leafless, a foot high or more. Fine for naturalizing; the bulbs should be planted in irregular patches in a grassy copse or wood; they will soon spread in a rich and light soil and cannot be excelled in beauty; flower in late spring. *Tulipa Greigi* is one of the showiest of all tulips. The flowers measure three or four inches across; the color is of an intense crimson, each segment having a black, yellow-edged blotch extending

FIG. 168. — WOOD TULIP (TULIPA SYLVESTRIS).

over half its length: leaves broadly lanceolate, flat with numerous linear, blackish spots. This is a fine plant for a sunny position in a rockery.

Dog's-tooth Violet, *Erythronium dens-canis*—Woodland plants with simple scapes from four to six inches high bearing solitary nodding flowers, white or rosy-red: leaves oblong, pale green, blotched with brown-purple. *E. Americanum* has pale yellow flowers. *E. grandiflorum* is a large-flowered species having one or more flowers to a scape, and *E. albidum* is a very pretty plant with white flowers. All are fine subjects for naturalizing in scattered masses in woods, copses, and shrubberies.

Star of Bethlehem, *Ornithogalum umbellatum.*—Flowers white, greenish on the outside, large star-like, disposed in many-flowered umbels: leaves weak, grass-like. A summer-flowering plant; may be naturalized in sandy lawns or planted in a rockery. Yellow star of Bethlehem (*Gagea lutea*) is a dwarf bulbous plant with bright yellow blossoms flowering in early spring: it is fine for naturalizing in shrubberies.

Golden Garlic, *Allium Moly.*—A showy, summer-flowering plant with broad, lanceolate, tufted leaves, and masses of bright yellow flowers disposed in crowded umbels. Height about a foot. Naturalized on the borders of shrubberies or on grassy banks.

Asphodel, *Asphodelus albus.*—A beautiful riverside or shore plant of Southern Europe, growing a foot high with linear, keeled leaves in large crowded tufts, and naked stems bearing a spike-like raceme of white flowers. *A. Villarsii* is a dwarfer, equally desirable kind. Both are fine for planting on grassy banks of streams and lakes, or in a somewhat moist position in a rockery.

Quamash, *Camassia esculenta.*—Leaves narrow, almost grass-like, tufted ; flowers large, blue, in loose racemes a foot high. The wild hyacinth of western woods is *C. Fraseri,* a smaller species with whitish-blue flowers. Both are fine for planting in shrubberies.

Cape Hyacinth, *Galtonia candicans.*—A tall, bulbous plant with long racemes of milky-white flowers. Perianth campanulate, drooping ; scape stout, two or three feet high ; leaves lanceolate, half as long as the inflorescence. Often used in summer-bedding ; lasting and effective.

Squill, *Scilla.*—There are several dwarf and floriferous plants of this genus which are fine for naturalizing in shady lawns or for patches in rockeries. Some may be used with the nicest effect in covering the ground in shrubberies and

woods. The most useful are : *S. bifolia,* leaves two to a scape, opposite ; flowers blue or sometimes rosy-red or white from three to eight in a raceme ; scape four inches high or more. Beautiful for planting in lawns in rich and light soil ; flowers early in spring. *S. Sibirica,* dwarfer than *bifolia,* leaves shorter and broader ; scapes several from a bulb, four inches high more

FIG. 169.—WILD HYA-CINTH (SCILLA NUTANS).

or less, bearing one or more intensely blue flowers very early in spring. *S. amœna,* larger than the preceding kinds ; flowers in loose racemes pale blue. All useful for the same purpose. The bluebell, or wild hyacinth of England (*S. nutans*), a beautiful woodland plant, resembles a hyacinth and is much larger than any of the preceding forms. It grows a foot high or more; flowers many in a long raceme, bell-shaped, blue, rosy-red, or white; leaves very long, several from a bulb. One of the best plants for naturalizing in woods and shrubberies. Flowers late in spring or early summer.

Glory of the Snow, *Chionodoxa Luciliæ.*—Not less attractive and perhaps more beautiful than the common squills; leaves several from a bulb, long and narrow; flowers nearly an inch across, bright blue, with a white centre, five or six in a spike six inches high. Thrives best in a sandy loam in open and sunny positions, as in a lawn. May also be used in a rockery.

Grape Hyacinth, *Muscari botryoides.*—Like a small hyacinth in habit but with globular flowers in a dense cylindrical or oval raceme; leaves linear, flowers blue or white in one variety. Height from six to ten inches. *M. racemosum* is another common species; flowers blue tipped with white, oval, in a dense raceme; leaves linear, fleshy. Height six inches or less. *M. Comosum* is higher; flowers violet, on short pedicels in a longer and looser raceme. *M. moschatum* is grown for its sweet-scented but insignificant flowers. These may be grown in a border or rockery or naturalized in shrubberies. They are easy to establish, and take care of themselves.

Hyacinth, *Hyacinthus orientalis.*—The common hyacinth is only used for spring bedding, for which purpose the single varieties are best. They are planted in autumn six inches apart, in well-prepared beds. Varieties that flower simultaneously should always be grown together.

Mixed bulbs are apt to flower at different times, thus spoiling the effect of an otherwise fine group. The colors are very varied, but the lighter tints of blue, purple, rosy-red, salmon, and white are preferable to others for our purpose.

St. Bernard's Lily, *Anthericum Liliago.*—A very handsome summer-flowering plant growing about eighteen inches high, with tufts of narrow, grass-like leaves, and rather large white flowers in few-flowered spikes. St. Bruno's lily (*A. Liliastrum*) is a somewhat larger plant with flowers two inches long: perianth milky-white, fragrant. Flowers earlier than the preceding kind. Beautiful border plants, and may also be used on grassy banks of rivulets and lakes or in a moderately moist position in a rockery. There is a taller-growing species with branching, flowering stems (*A. ramosum*) growing to the height of two feet: leaves grass-like, tufted; a rapid grower, and best for naturalization.

Plantain Lily, *Funkia.*—A genus of very ornamental plants with more or less cordate leaves forming bold masses of foliage. The flowers are generally borne in one-sided, nodding racemes. The following are common in cultivation: *F. Fortunii*, leaves ovate-heart-shaped on long stalks; flowers funnel-shaped, lilac; *F. ovata*, leaves ovate, six or eight inches long; flowers lilac or white, in a long, loose, nodding raceme. The variety *marginata* has white-margined leaves and is a very ornamental foliage plant. *F. grandiflora* has very large pure-white flowers, ten to fifteen on a scape two feet high. Leaves ovate-cordate, long-petioled, with a blade eight inches long. A very beautiful late-flowering plant. *F. sub-cordata*, leaves ovate-cordate, on long stalks; flowers pure white, four inches long, many in a rather short, nodding raceme, above or among the leaves. These are all extremely beautiful for massing on rocky shores or in rockeries in deep and rich soil. All are perfectly hardy; they flower all summer.

Day Lily, *Hemerocallis.*—Two species nearly alike in habit: *flava,* with pure yellow, and *fulva,* with tawny or reddish-yellow flowers. Leaves long and narrow, keeled, forming very large tufts of foliage. Flowers freely produced in summer in small corymbs disposed in loose panicles. *H. minor* is a much smaller species, less tufted; flowers bright yellow, slightly green outside, on scapes eight inches high; leaves narrow, keeled, grass-like; fine for good deep soil in rockeries. The larger forms are excellent waterside plants, and are also commonly grown in borders. Both do well in ordinary garden soil.

Flame Flower, *Kniphofia aloides* (*Tritoma uvaria*).—A very showy plant in late summer and autumn, forming tufts of stiff grassy leaves of a dark shining green. Scape three or four feet high, bearing a crowded, cylindrical spike of bright coral-red flowers which change into orange and greenish-yellow. Excellent for dry soil in open and sunny positions; very desirable as a lawn plant. It will thrive in almost any soil.

Adam's Needle, *Yucca filamentosa.*—This desirable plant, with several handsome varieties, is very useful for planting in rockeries and dry, gravelly soil on high knolls and in other exposed and sunny situations. The leaves are evergreen, stiff and leathery, short sword-like, with thread-like fibres on the margin, from thirty to forty or more, in a dense rosette close to the ground. Flowers white, bell-shaped, more or less open, drooping, disposed in a crowded panicle rising several feet above the ground. Of the several varieties, the following are most beautiful: *Maxima*, flowers larger than in the type, of a purer white; *orchioides*,

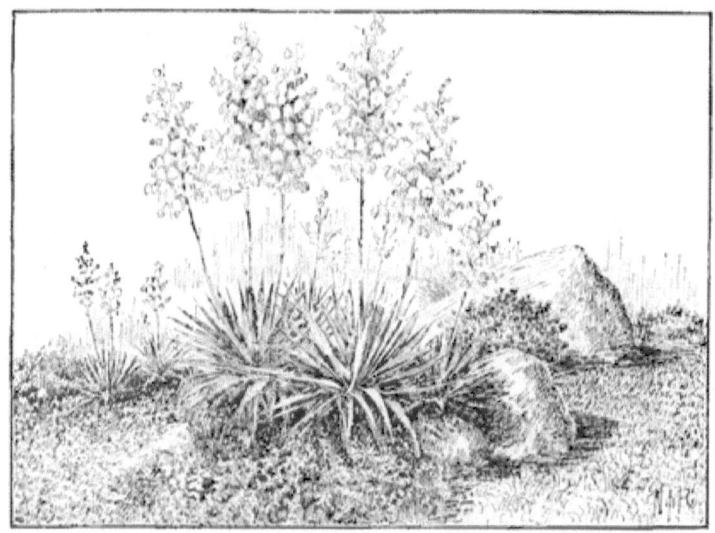

FIG. 170.—ADAM'S NEEDLE (YUCCA FILAMENTOSA).

a small, large-flowering variety, with flowers disposed in a simple raceme two feet high or less; *flaccida*, leaves shorter, with more fibres on the margin, panicles looser and more regular, flowers less open. The *yuccas* will thrive in any soil not too moist, and are among the most useful plants in the hand of a landscape-gardener.

THE SPIDERWORT FAMILY.

Day-Flower, *Commelina Virginica.*—A very attractive little plant with bright sky-blue flowers; petals two, conspicuous; leaves oblong-lanceolate; stem reclining, rooting at the swollen nodes. Fine for rockeries or in moist, light, or sandy soil in sunny positions, but must be seen in masses to be appreciated.

Spiderwort, *Tradescantia Virginica.* — A somewhat weedy plant with rather showy, violet-blue flowers. Stems erect, two feet high, more or less; leaves linear-lanceolate, keeled; flowers crowded in a terminal umbel and in clusters from the axils of the upper leaves. For planting on moist grassy banks. Sometimes planted in borders.

GRASSES.

Variegated Orchard Grass, *Dactylis glomerata variegata.* — A tufted grass; pale green, striped with white and faint red lines. Much used for edging beds and borders.

Zebra Grass, *Eulalia zebrina.* — Very ornamental, growing about four feet high. The bright green leaves have bars of yellow. The original type of this variety is *E. japonica,* of the same size and habit, with deep green foliage. Flowers pale purple, in large feathery panicles. There is a form of this having a white stripe down the centre of the leaves. All are fine for specimens on a lawn, especially near water.

Erianthus, *Erianthus Ravenna.* — Grows to a height of five or six feet, forming large masses of foliage.

Pampas Grass, *Gynerium argenteum.* — A very fine and stately grass with linear, arching leaves six feet long, rigid and glaucous, forming very large masses of foliage in a suitable position. The feathery and silky panicle of flowers is silvery white, sometimes more than a foot long, and grows to a height of ten or twelve feet. The plant, with masses of these silky plumes, is very ornamental. Cultivated as a lawn plant, but requires protection in winter in the Northern States.

The various grasses employed in lawn-making cannot be described here. The list in the chapter on lawns must suffice.

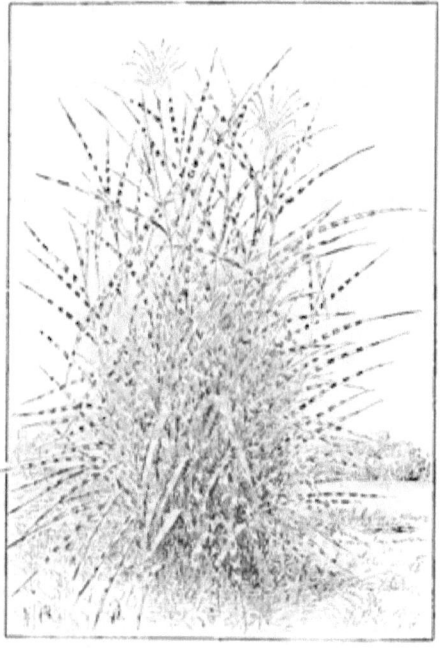

FIG. 171.—ZEBRA GRASS (EULALIA JAPONICA ZEBRINA).

FERNS.

Ferns are nearly always associated with rocks and water, and delight in the shade of deciduous woods. They are seldom found in the full glare of the sun and are then

often covered with a white or yellow farinaceous matter.
The favorite haunts of the majority of the more delicate
kinds are crevices of moist and shady rocks, where they
grow into tufts of lace-like foliage. Some of the stronger
and more robust kinds form quite a feature of woodland
scenery. They are most abundant in marshy ground or on
the shores of slow, shallow brooks. The delicate beauty of
the mostly tender green foliage well compensates for the
lack of flowers. In gardening, the favorite use of ferns is
for the embellishment of rockeries, and species of all kinds
are generally brought together there. While this is a very
sensible practice and satisfactory from all points of view, it
must still be remembered that there is a much wider scope
for their use in natural or artificial scenery. Woods and
shrubberies especially offer ideal places for growing a great
variety of our most beautiful ferns, but even in the open
lawns naturally formed groups of such species as the eagle
fern are perfectly in keeping with their nature and habit.

All ferns deserve cultivation, and the following list is
only an enumeration of some of the best :

Common Polypody, *Polypodium vulgare.*—A handsome
evergreen of mossy rocks, especially in shady positions,
but sometimes in the full glare of the sun. Frond simple
pinnatifid, six or eight inches long, with a short stalk, dark
green. Best for planting in crevices of rocks where there
will be a constant supply of moisture; in such places it
will form large masses of leaves. Several varieties of this
fern are grown in European gardens, such as *elegantissimum*,
a form with bright green, finely divided and feathery leaves
twice as large as those of the type; *cristatum*, apex of the

leaf branched and cristed; *Cambricum*, pinnæ with finely
and deeply cut edges. These have developed from plants
growing in rich soil and should not be planted on rocks.

Beech Fern (*P. Phegopteris*).—A very tender and delicate plant. Leaves six inches long, triangular, pinnate,
with the lower pair of pinnæ long and deeply pinnatifid.
Color pale green. Common in shade at the roots of
trees mostly in rich soil. Fine for shady places. Oak
Fern (*P. Dryopteris*), a similar form with more divided
fronds.

Maidenhair Fern, *Adiantum pedatum*.—The most beautiful of American ferns, grows in rich, shady woods, frequently among the débris of eroded rocks. Leaves pedate,
pinnules very numerous. Height one or two feet, forming
masses of very light and elegant foliage. Fine for shady
positions in a rockery or among trees and shrubs; thrives
best in a sandy loam mixed with leaf-mold. *A. Capillus-
Veneris* may be grown in moist and shady rockeries planted
in deep fissures.

Eagle Fern, *Pteris aquilina*.—A large, robust-growing
fern common in barren fields and light, open woods.
Fronds almost triangular, lower pinnæ stalked and pinnate,
upper ones pinnately parted or pinnatifid; blade from a
foot to three feet long, more than half as broad; leaf-stalk
slender, one foot high, brown. This is an elegant species
for naturalizing.

Lomaria.—Of this genus there are a few beautiful
evergreen species, smaller or more slender than the common
polypody. They are exceptionally fine plants for rockeries.
L. alpina has fronds from four to eight inches long by

three-quarters of an inch wide, pinnate with closely set, oblong pinnae. Should be planted in a shady position below evergreens and covered in winter. *L. spicant* is a perfectly hardy kind. The fronds are sometimes a foot long, but more often shorter, linear in outline, with closely set, narrow pinnae. There are a number of very beautiful varieties, some with divided or crested fronds. They are among the most desirable hardy evergreen ferns.

Spleenwort, *Asplenium.*— Of this genus there are several small ferns with very delicate foliage, mostly natives of rocky woods. Others are quite large with ample masses of very attractive foliage. The best of the smaller kinds are: *A. Adiantum-nigrum,* fronds three-angled, twice pinnate, from six to twelve inches long, leaf-stalk six inches long or more. Of this handsome species there are many desirable forms. *A. ebeneum,* fronds delicate, a foot long or more, linear-lanceolate, pinnate. A slender plant, frequently growing in dry and exposed places, forming small tufts in crevices of rocks. *A. Trichomanes,* fronds very slender, pinnate with rounded pinnae growing in large tufts in fissures of moist and shady rocks; there is a handsome crested form of this. *A. Ruta muraria,* seldom more than three inches high; fronds twice pinnate, pinnae wedge-shaped. Will grow on the surface of moderately moist rocks even in exposed positions. The most common as well as the most ornamental of the larger species is the lady fern (*A. Filix-femina*). It grows several feet high; the fronds are erect or arching, lower ones spreading, forming leafy rosettes of twice-pinnate fronds of a delicate green in summer. There are many more or less divided or crested varieties of this species. It is fine for massing in woods and shrubberies or in a shady corner of the rockery. Thrives best in rich soil.

Shield-Fern, *Aspidium.*—Many of the shield-ferns resemble the spleenworts in form and habit. The hard shield-fern (*A. aculatum*) is a very beautiful, erect-growing species with ovate-lanceolate pinnate leaves several feet long including the stalk; pinnæ deeply cut or pinnatifid. Very hardy; fine for a rockery. The soft shield-fern (*A. angulare*) is an equally beautiful kind, with pinnate fronds of a softer texture. There are many varieties, some with crested fronds. *A. acrostichoides* is an evergreen species common in rocky woods. The leaves are pinnate, dark green, spreading, one or two feet long, forming low masses of foliage among stones and tree-roots. Beautiful for planting as an undergrowth in shrubberies.

Male-Fern, *Nephrodium Filix-mas*, resembles the lady-fern in habit, but has less finely divided leaves. Of this also there are many varieties.

Ostrich Fern, *Onoclea Germanica.*—Habit very regular, erect; fronds pinnate, broadly lanceolate, two or three feet high, of a tender green color in spring and early summer. A beautiful fern for half-shady positions in rich woods or shrubberies. The sensitive fern (*O. sensibilis*) is a very common species growing in moist open ground and spreading as a weed in moist pastures.

Dicksonia, *Dicksonia punctilobula.*— A very handsome fern with twice-pinnate leaves and finely cut leaflets. Height, one or two feet. Common by the side of woodland streams; very ornamental for a moist place in a rockery.

FIG. 172—FLOWERING FERN (OSMUNDA CINNAMOMEA).

406

Flowering Ferns, *Osmunda.*—These are generally found in very moist and rich ground, forming large imposing masses of pinnate or bi-pinnate leaves. The fertile fronds differ greatly from the sterile ones, and are generally crowded in the middle of the plant. *O. cinnamomea* grows three or four feet high; the fronds are long, pinnate, arching; fertile ones tall; all erect, with masses of yellow spore-cases. *O. Claytoniana* differs in having parts of the fertile fronds sterile, and developed like the rest of the sterile fronds. The royal fern (*O. regalis*) is more unique and characteristic. The leaves are twice pinnate, the leaflets being oblong and nearly entire. The spore-cases are borne at the apex of regularly developed fronds. Although flowering ferns prefer very moist positions in a wild state, they will grow well in any rich and moderately moist ground.

THE END.

INDEX OF COMMON NAMES.

INDEX OF BOTANICAL NAMES.